TRANSLATED
Translated Language Learning

Siddhartha
悉达多

An Indian Poem
印度诗歌

Hermann Hesse

赫尔曼·黑塞

English / 普通话

Copyright © 2024 Tranzlaty
All rights reserved
Published by Tranzlaty
Siddhartha – Eine Indische Dichtung
ISBN: 978-1-83566-676-0
Original text by Hermann Hesse
First published in German in 1922
www.tranzlaty.com

The Son of the Brahman
婆罗门之子

In the shade of the house
在房子的阴影里
in the sunshine of the riverbank
在河岸的阳光下
near the boats
靠近船只
in the shade of the Sal-wood forest
在娑罗树森林的树荫下
in the shade of the fig tree
在无花果树的树荫下
this is where Siddhartha grew up
这是悉达多长大的地方
he was the handsome son of a Brahman, the young falcon
他是一位婆罗门的英俊儿子,年轻的猎鹰
he grew up with his friend Govinda
他和他的朋友戈文达一起长大
Govinda was also the son of a Brahman
戈文达也是婆罗门的儿子
by the banks of the river the sun tanned his light shoulders
在河岸边,太阳晒黑了他白皙的肩膀
bathing, performing the sacred ablutions, making sacred offerings
沐浴、进行神圣沐浴、进行神圣供奉
In the mango garden, shade poured into his black eyes
在芒果园里,阴影涌进他的黑眼睛里
when playing as a boy, when his mother sang
当他还是个孩子时,当他妈妈唱歌时
when the sacred offerings were made
当神圣的祭品被奉献时
when his father, the scholar, taught him
当他的父亲,一位学者,教导他

when the wise men talked
当智者们谈话时
For a long time, Siddhartha had been partaking in the discussions of the wise men
很长一段时间以来,悉达多一直在参加智者的讨论
he practiced debating with Govinda
他和戈文达练习辩论
he practiced the art of reflection with Govinda
他和戈文达一起练习反思的艺术
and he practiced meditation
他练习冥想
He already knew how to speak the Om silently
他已经知道如何默念"Om"
he knew the word of words
他知道单词的意思
he spoke it silently into himself while inhaling
他一边吸气,一边默默地对自己说
he spoke it silently out of himself while exhaling
他一边呼气,一边默默地说出这句话
he did this with all the concentration of his soul
他全神贯注地做这件事
his forehead was surrounded by the glow of the clear-thinking spirit
他的额头被清晰思考的精神光芒所包围
He already knew how to feel Atman in the depths of his being
他已经知道如何在内心深处感受阿特曼
he could feel the indestructible
他能感受到坚不可摧
he knew what it was to be at one with the universe
他知道与宇宙合一是什么感觉
Joy leapt in his father's heart
父亲心里充满了喜悦
because his son was quick to learn

因为他的儿子学得很快
he was thirsty for knowledge
他渴望知识
his father could see him growing up to become a great wise man
他的父亲能看到他长大后成为一个伟大的智者
he could see him becoming a priest
他能看到他成为一名牧师
he could see him becoming a prince among the Brahmans
他能看到他成为婆罗门中的王子
Bliss leapt in his mother's breast when she saw him walking
母亲看见他走路,心里感到无比幸福
Bliss leapt in her heart when she saw him sit down and get up
当她看到他坐下又站起来时,她的心里充满了幸福
Siddhartha was strong and handsome
悉达多强壮英俊
he, who was walking on slender legs
他,迈着修长的双腿
he greeted her with perfect respect
他非常尊重地迎接她
Love touched the hearts of the Brahmans' young daughters
爱情触动了婆罗门年轻女儿的心
they were charmed when Siddhartha walked through the lanes of the town
当悉达多走过小镇的小巷时,他们被迷住了
his luminous forehead, his eyes of a king, his slim hips
他那闪亮的额头,他那国王般的眼睛,他那纤细的臀部
But most of all he was loved by Govinda
但他最受戈文达的喜爱
Govinda, his friend, the son of a Brahman
他的朋友戈文达,一位婆罗门的儿子
He loved Siddhartha's eye and sweet voice

他爱悉达多的眼睛和甜美的声音

he loved the way he walked
他喜欢他走路的样子

and he loved the perfect decency of his movements
他喜欢他动作的完美得体

he loved everything Siddhartha did and said
他热爱悉达多所做的一切和所说的一切

but what he loved most was his spirit
但他最爱的是他的精神

he loved his transcendent, fiery thoughts
他热爱他超然的、炽热的思想

he loved his ardent will and high calling
他热爱他的热忱和崇高的使命

Govinda knew he would not become a common Brahman
戈文达知道他不会成为一个普通的婆罗门

no, he would not become a lazy official
不，他不会成为一个懒惰的官员

no, he would not become a greedy merchant
不，他不会成为一个贪婪的商人

not a vain, vacuous speaker
不是一个空洞的演说家

nor a mean, deceitful priest
也不是卑鄙、欺骗的牧师

and he also would not become a decent, stupid sheep
也不会变成一只正经的、愚笨的绵羊

a sheep in the herd of the many
羊群中的一只羊

and he did not want to become one of those things
他不想成为其中的一员

he did not want to be one of those tens of thousands of Brahmans
他不想成为那成千上万的婆罗门之一

He wanted to follow Siddhartha; the beloved, the splendid
他想追随悉达多，那个深爱着的、辉煌的

in days to come, when Siddhartha would become a god, he would be there
将来悉达多成为神的时候,他就在那里
when he would join the glorious, he would be there
当他加入光荣时,他会在那里
Govinda wanted to follow him as his friend
戈文达想跟随他,作为他的朋友
he was his companion and his servant
他是他的同伴和他的仆人
he was his spear-carrier and his shadow
他是他的矛手,也是他的影子
Siddhartha was loved by everyone
悉达多深受人们爱戴
He was a source of joy for everybody
他是大家的快乐源泉
he was a delight for them all
他让大家都很高兴
But he, Siddhartha, was not a source of joy for himself
但他,悉达多,却没有为自己带来快乐。
he found no delight in himself
他发现自己并不快乐
he walked the rosy paths of the fig tree garden
他走在无花果园的玫瑰色小径上
he sat in the bluish shade in the garden of contemplation
他坐在沉思花园的蓝色树荫下
he washed his limbs daily in the bath of repentance
他每天在忏悔之浴中清洗四肢
he made sacrifices in the dim shade of the mango forest
他在芒果林的阴暗阴影下献祭
his gestures were of perfect decency
他的举止非常得体
he was everyone's love and joy
他是每个人的爱与欢乐
but he still lacked all joy in his heart

但他心里还是缺乏快乐
Dreams and restless thoughts came into his mind
梦想和不安的想法涌入他的脑海
his dreams flowed from the water of the river
他的梦想从河水中流出
his dreams sparked from the stars of the night
他的梦想因夜晚的星光而闪耀
his dreams melted from the beams of the sun
他的梦想在阳光下融化
dreams came to him, and a restlessness of the soul came to him
他开始做梦，心里也开始烦躁起来
his soul was fuming from the sacrifices
他的灵魂因献祭而怒火中烧
he breathed forth from the verses of the Rig-Veda
他从《梨俱吠陀》的诗句中呼吸而出
the verses were infused into him, drop by drop
诗句一点一滴地注入他的心中
the verses from the teachings of the old Brahmans
古代婆罗门教义中的诗句
Siddhartha had started to nurse discontent in himself
悉达多开始对自己心生不满
he had started to feel doubt about the love of his father
他开始怀疑父亲的爱
he doubted the love of his mother
他怀疑母亲的爱
and he doubted the love of his friend, Govinda
他怀疑他的朋友戈文达的爱
he doubted if their love could bring him joy forever and ever
他怀疑他们的爱情是否能给他带来永远的快乐
their love could not nurse him
他们的爱无法滋养他
their love could not feed him

their love could not satisfy him
他们的爱不能满足他
he had started to suspect his father's teachings
他开始怀疑父亲的教诲
perhaps he had shown him everything he knew
也许他已经向他展示了他所知道的一切
there were his other teachers, the wise Brahmans
还有他的其他老师,睿智的婆罗门
perhaps they had already revealed to him the best of their wisdom
也许他们已经向他透露了他们最好的智慧
he feared that they had already filled his expecting vessel
他担心他们已经填满了他期待的容器
despite the richness of their teachings, the vessel was not full
尽管他们的教义丰富,但容器却不够满
the spirit was not content
精神不满足
the soul was not calm
心灵并不平静
the heart was not satisfied
心里还没有满足
the ablutions were good, but they were water
沐浴很好,但都是水
the ablutions did not wash off the sin
洗礼并不能洗去罪孽
they did not heal the spirit's thirst
它们无法治愈心灵的饥渴
they did not relieve the fear in his heart
他们没有减轻他心中的恐惧
The sacrifices and the invocation of the gods were excellent
祭祀和祈求神灵的仪式非常出色
but was that all there was?

但这就是全部吗？
did the sacrifices give a happy fortune?
祭祀是否带来了好运？
and what about the gods?
那么神又如何呢？
Was it really Prajapati who had created the world?
真的是生主创造了世界吗？
Was it not the Atman who had created the world?
难道不是阿特曼创造了世界吗？
Atman, the only one, the singular one
阿特曼，唯一的，独一无二的
Were the gods not creations?
诸神不是被创造的吗？
were they not created like me and you?
难道它们不像我和你一样被创造出来吗？
were the Gods not subject to time?
难道神不受时间的束缚吗？
were the Gods mortal? Was it good?
神明都是凡人吗？这好吗？
was it right? was it meaningful?
这是正确的吗？这是有意义的吗？
was it the highest occupation to make offerings to the gods?
给神灵献祭是不是最高尚的职业？
For whom else were offerings to be made?
还要为谁献祭呢？
who else was to be worshipped?
还有谁值得崇拜？
who else was there, but Him?
除了他以外，还有谁在那里？
The only one, the Atman
唯一的，阿特曼
And where was Atman to be found?
那么阿特曼又在哪里呢？
where did He reside?

他住在哪里？
where did His eternal heart beat?
他的永恒之心在哪里跳动？
where else but in one's own self?
除了自身之外，还有哪里呢？
in its innermost indestructible part
在其最深处不可摧毁的部分
could he be that which everyone had in himself?
他能成为每个人都具有的那种人吗？
But where was this self?
但这个自我在哪里？
where was this innermost part?
这最深处在哪儿？
where was this ultimate part?
这最终部分在哪里？
It was not flesh and bone
它不是血肉之躯
it was neither thought nor consciousness
它既不是思想也不是意识
this is what the wisest ones taught
这是最聪明的人教的
So where was it?
那么它在哪儿？
the self, myself, the Atman
自我，我自己，阿特曼
To reach this place, there was another way
要到达这里，还有另一条路
was this other way worth looking for?
这条其他方法是否值得寻找？
Alas, nobody showed him this way
唉，没人教他这个方法
nobody knew this other way
没人知道这是其他方式
his father did not know it

他的父亲不知道

and the teachers and wise men did not know it
而教师和智者们却不知道

They knew everything, the Brahmans
婆罗门们无所不知

and their holy books knew everything
他们的圣书知道一切

they had taken care of everything
他们已经把一切都处理好了

they took care of the creation of the world
他们负责创造世界

they described origin of speech, food, inhaling, exhaling
他们描述了语言、食物、吸气、呼气的起源

they described the arrangement of the senses
他们描述了感官的排列

they described the acts of the gods
他们描述了众神的行为

their books knew infinitely much
他们的书知道无限多

but was it valuable to know all of this?
但了解这些有什么价值吗？

was there not only one thing to be known?
难道不只存在一件事需要了解吗？

was there still not the most important thing to know?
难道最重要的事情还不该知道吗？

many verses of the holy books spoke of this innermost, ultimate thing
圣书中的许多经文都谈到了这个最内在、最终极的东西

it was spoken of particularly in the Upanishades of Samaveda
《萨摩吠陀奥义书》中特别提到了这一点

they were wonderful verses
这些都是很棒的诗句

"Your soul is the whole world", this was written there
"你的灵魂就是整个世界"，上面写着

and it was written that man in deep sleep would meet with his innermost part
据记载，沉睡中的人类将与自己的内心深处相遇

and he would reside in the Atman
他将居住在阿特曼

Marvellous wisdom was in these verses
这些诗句蕴含着奇妙的智慧

all knowledge of the wisest ones had been collected here in magic words
所有最聪明的人的知识都以魔法词语的形式收集在这里

it was as pure as honey collected by bees
就像蜜蜂采集的蜂蜜一样纯净

No, the verses were not to be looked down upon
不，这些诗句不应该被轻视

they contained tremendous amounts of enlightenment
它们蕴含着巨大的启示

they contained wisdom which lay collected and preserved
它们蕴含着被收集和保存的智慧

wisdom collected by innumerable generations of wise Brahmans
无数代智慧婆罗门所收集的智慧

But where were the Brahmans?
但是婆罗门在哪里？

where were the priests?
牧师们在哪里？

where the wise men or penitents?
智者和忏悔者在哪里？

where were those that had succeeded?
那些成功的人在哪里？

where were those who knew more than deepest of all knowledge?

那些懂得比最深奥的知识还要多的人在哪里？

where were those that also lived out the enlightened wisdom?

那些也活出了开明智慧的人又在哪里呢？

Where was the knowledgeable one who brought Atman out of his sleep?

将阿特曼从睡梦中唤醒的那位博学之人在哪里？

who had brought this knowledge into the day?

谁将这些知识带到了今天？

who had taken this knowledge into their life?

谁将这些知识带入了他们的生活？

who carried this knowledge with every step they took?

谁每走一步都带着这些知识？

who had married their words with their deeds?

谁能言行一致？

Siddhartha knew many venerable Brahmans

悉达多认识许多尊贵的婆罗门

his father, the pure one

他的父亲，纯洁的人

the scholar, the most venerable one

学者，最受尊敬的人

His father was worthy of admiration

他的父亲值得敬佩

quiet and noble were his manners

他的举止安静而高贵

pure was his life, wise were his words

他的生活纯洁，他的话语睿智

delicate and noble thoughts lived behind his brow

他的额头上隐藏着精致而高尚的思想

but even though he knew so much, did he live in blissfulness?

但尽管他知道这么多，他生活得幸福吗？

despite all his knowledge, did he have peace?

尽管他知识渊博，但他心里感到平静吗？

was he not also just a searching man?
他不也只是一个搜寻的人吗？
was he still not a thirsty man?
他还不是一个口渴的人吗？
Did he not have to drink from holy sources again and again?
他不是必须一次又一次地饮圣水吗？
did he not drink from the offerings?
他没喝祭品里的水吗？
did he not drink from the books?
他不是从书上喝的吗？
did he not drink from the disputes of the Brahmans?
难道他没有参与婆罗门的争论吗？
Why did he have to wash off sins every day?
为什么他要每天洗去罪孽？
must he strive for a cleansing every day?
他必须每天努力清洁吗？
over and over again, every day
一遍又一遍，每天
Was Atman not in him?
难道阿特曼不在他心中吗？
did not the pristine source spring from his heart?
这纯净的源泉不是从他的心里涌出的吗？
the pristine source had to be found in one's own self
原始源头必须在一个人自己身上找到
the pristine source had to be possessed!
原始源头必须被拥有！
doing anything else else was searching
做其他任何事情都是在寻找
taking any other pass is a detour
走其他任何通道都是绕行
going any other way leads to getting lost
走其他路都会迷路
These were Siddhartha's thoughts
这是悉达多的想法

this was his thirst, and this was his suffering
这是他的渴望,这是他的痛苦
Often he spoke to himself from a Chandogya-Upanishad:
他常常自言自语,引用《唱赞奥义书》:
"Truly, the name of the Brahman is Satyam"
"确实,婆罗门的名字是萨蒂亚姆"
"he who knows such a thing, will enter the heavenly world every day"
"知道这些事的人,每天都会进入天国"
Often the heavenly world seemed near
天堂世界常常似乎近在咫尺
but he had never reached the heavenly world completely
但他从未完全到达天界
he had never quenched the ultimate thirst
他从来没有满足过终极的渴望
And among all the wise and wisest men, none had reached it
在所有聪明人和最聪明的人中,没有人达到这个境界
he received instructions from them
他收到了他们的指示
but they hadn't completely reached the heavenly world
但还没有完全到达天堂
they hadn't completely quenched their thirst
他们还没有完全解渴
because this thirst is an eternal thirst
因为这种渴望是永恒的渴望

"Govinda" Siddhartha spoke to his friend
"戈文达"悉达多对他的朋友说
"Govinda, my dear, come with me under the Banyan tree"
"戈文达,亲爱的,跟我到榕树下来吧。"
"let's practise meditation"
"让我们练习冥想"
They went to the Banyan tree
他们去了榕树

under the Banyan tree they sat down
他们坐在榕树下
Siddhartha was right here
悉达多就在这里
Govinda was twenty paces away
戈文达离我们二十步远
Siddhartha seated himself and he repeated murmuring the verse
悉达多坐下来，反复吟诵着这首诗
Om is the bow, the arrow is the soul
Om 是弓，箭是灵魂
The Brahman is the arrow's target
婆罗门是箭的目标
the target that one should incessantly hit
必须不断努力实现的目标
the usual time of the exercise in meditation had passed
平时的冥想时间已经过去了
Govinda got up, the evening had come
戈文达起床，夜幕降临
it was time to perform the evening's ablution
到了晚上沐浴的时间了
He called Siddhartha's name, but Siddhartha did not answer
他呼唤悉达多的名字，但悉达多没有回答
Siddhartha sat there, lost in thought
悉达多坐在那儿，陷入沉思
his eyes were rigidly focused towards a very distant target
他的眼睛紧紧盯着一个很远的目标
the tip of his tongue was protruding a little between the teeth
他的舌尖稍微突出在牙齿之间
he seemed not to breathe
他似乎没有呼吸
Thus sat he, wrapped up in contemplation
他就这样坐着，陷入沉思

he was deep in thought of the Om
他深思着 "Om"

his soul sent after the Brahman like an arrow
他的灵魂像箭一样追寻着婆罗门

Once, Samanas had travelled through Siddhartha's town
有一次,沙门经过悉达多的城镇

they were ascetics on a pilgrimage
他们是朝圣的苦行僧

three skinny, withered men, neither old nor young
三个瘦削枯瘦的男人,不老也不年轻

dusty and bloody were their shoulders
他们的肩膀上沾满尘土和血迹

almost naked, scorched by the sun, surrounded by loneliness
几乎赤身裸体,被太阳灼伤,周围充满孤独

strangers and enemies to the world
世界的陌生人和敌人

strangers and jackals in the realm of humans
人类世界中的陌生人和豺狼

Behind them blew a hot scent of quiet passion
他们身后飘来一股安静激情的热气

a scent of destructive service
破坏性服务的气味

a scent of merciless self-denial
一种无情的自我否定的气息

the evening had come
夜幕降临

after the hour of contemplation, Siddhartha spoke to Govinda
沉思了一小时后,悉达多对戈文达说

"Early tomorrow morning, my friend, Siddhartha will go to the Samanas"
"明天一早,我的朋友悉达多要去见沙门。"

"He will become a Samana"

"他将成为一名沙门"

Govinda turned pale when he heard these words
戈文达听了这些话,脸色苍白。

and he read the decision in the motionless face of his friend
他从朋友一动不动的脸上看出了他的决定

the determination was unstoppable, like the arrow shot from the bow
决心不可阻挡,就像离弓的箭一样

Govinda realized at first glance; now it is beginning
戈文达第一眼就意识到了;现在它开始了

now Siddhartha is taking his own way
现在悉达多正在走自己的路

now his fate is beginning to sprout
现在他的命运开始萌芽

and because of Siddhartha, Govinda's fate is sprouting too
而因为悉达多,戈文达的命运也开始萌芽

he turned pale like a dry banana-skin
他的脸色变得像干香蕉皮一样苍白

"Oh Siddhartha," he exclaimed
"噢,悉达多,"他惊呼道

"will your father permit you to do that?"
"你父亲会允许你这样做吗?"

Siddhartha looked over as if he was just waking up
悉达多望着他,仿佛他刚睡醒

like an Arrow he read Govinda's soul
像箭一样,他读懂了戈文达的灵魂

he could read the fear and the submission in him
他能读懂他内心的恐惧和屈服

"Oh Govinda," he spoke quietly, "let's not waste words"
"哦,戈文达,"他轻声说道,"我们就别多嘴了。"

"Tomorrow at daybreak I will begin the life of the Samanas"
"明天拂晓,我将开始沙门的生活。"

"let us speak no more of it"

"我们别再谈论这件事了"

Siddhartha entered the chamber where his father was sitting
悉达多走进父亲坐着的房间
his father was was on a mat of bast
他的父亲是在麻布垫上
Siddhartha stepped behind his father
悉达多站在父亲身后
and he remained standing behind him
他仍然站在他身后
he stood until his father felt that someone was standing behind him
他一直站着,直到他父亲感觉到有人站在他身后
Spoke the Brahman: "Is that you, Siddhartha?"
婆罗门问道:"是你吗,悉达多?"
"Then say what you came to say"
"那就直说吧"
Spoke Siddhartha: "With your permission, my father"
悉达多说道:"父亲,请您允许。"
"I came to tell you that it is my longing to leave your house tomorrow"
"我来告诉你,我渴望明天离开你的家"
"I wish to go to the ascetics"
"我希望去当苦行僧"
"My desire is to become a Samana"
"我的愿望是成为一名沙门"
"May my father not oppose this"
"愿我父亲不反对"
The Brahman fell silent, and he remained so for long
婆罗门沉默了很久,
the stars in the small window wandered
小窗里的星星在游荡
and they changed their relative positions
它们改变了相对位置

Silent and motionless stood the son with his arms folded
儿子双手抱胸，一动不动地站着，一言不发
silent and motionless sat the father on the mat
父亲一言不发，一动不动地坐在垫子上
and the stars traced their paths in the sky
星星在天空中划出它们的轨迹
Then spoke the father
然后父亲说
"it is not proper for a Brahman to speak harsh and angry words"
"婆罗门不宜说粗鲁和愤怒的话语"
"But indignation is in my heart"
"但我心里很愤慨"
"I wish not to hear this request for a second time"
"我不想再听到这个请求了"
Slowly, the Brahman rose
婆罗门慢慢地站了起来
Siddhartha stood silently, his arms folded
悉达多双手抱胸，静静地站着
"What are you waiting for?" asked the father
父亲问："你还在等什么？"
Spoke Siddhartha, "You know what I'm waiting for"
悉达多说道："你知道我在等什么。"
Indignant, the father left the chamber
父亲愤然离去
indignant, he went to his bed and lay down
他愤愤不平地走到床上躺下
an hour passed, but no sleep had come over his eyes
一个小时过去了，但他却毫无睡意。
the Brahman stood up and he paced to and fro
婆罗门站起来，走来走去
and he left the house in the night
他晚上就离开了家

Through the small window of the chamber he looked back inside
他透过房间的小窗户向里面望去
and there he saw Siddhartha standing
他看见悉达多站在那里
his arms were folded and he had not moved from his spot
他双臂交叉,没有从原地移动。
Pale shimmered his bright robe
他的长袍闪着淡淡的光芒
With anxiety in his heart, the father returned to his bed
父亲怀着焦虑的心情回到床上
another sleepless hour passed
又一个不眠之夜过去了
since no sleep had come over his eyes, the Brahman stood up again
由于毫无睡意,婆罗门又站了起来
he paced to and fro, and he walked out of the house
他走来走去,然后走出了房子
and he saw that the moon had risen
他看到月亮已经升起来
Through the window of the chamber he looked back inside
他透过房间的窗户向里面望去
there stood Siddhartha, unmoved from his spot
悉达多站在原地,一动不动。
his arms were folded, as they had been
他的双臂交叉,就像以前一样
moonlight was reflecting from his bare shins
月光映照在他裸露的小腿上
With worry in his heart, the father went back to bed
父亲心里担心极了,又回去睡觉了。
he came back after an hour
一小时后他回来了
and he came back again after two hours
两小时后他又回来了

he looked through the small window
他透过小窗户往外看
he saw Siddhartha standing in the moon light
他看见悉达多站在月光下
he stood by the light of the stars in the darkness
他站在黑暗中的星光旁
And he came back hour after hour
他一个小时又一个小时地回来
silently, he looked into the chamber
他默默地看着房间
he saw him standing in the same place
他看见他站在同一个地方
it filled his heart with anger
这让他心里充满了愤怒
it filled his heart with unrest
他的心里充满了不安
it filled his heart with anguish
这让他心里充满了痛苦
it filled his heart with sadness
他心里充满了悲伤
the night's last hour had come
夜晚的最后一刻已经到来
his father returned and stepped into the room
他的父亲回来了,走进了房间
he saw the young man standing there
他看见那个年轻人站在那里
he seemed tall and like a stranger to him
他看起来很高,对他来说就像一个陌生人
"Siddhartha," he spoke, "what are you waiting for?"
"悉达多,"他说道,"您还在等什么?"
"You know what I'm waiting for"
"你知道我在等什么"
"Will you always stand that way and wait?
"你就一直站在那里等待吗?

"I will always stand and wait"
　"我会一直站着等待"
"will you wait until it becomes morning, noon, and evening?"
　"你会等到早上、中午、晚上吗？"
"I will wait until it become morning, noon, and evening"
　"我会等到早晨、中午和晚上"
"You will become tired, Siddhartha"
　"你会累的，悉达多。"
"I will become tired"
　"我会累的"
"You will fall asleep, Siddhartha"
　"你会睡着的，悉达多。"
"I will not fall asleep"
　"我不会睡着的"
"You will die, Siddhartha"
　"你会死的，悉达多。"
"I will die," answered Siddhartha
　"我会死。"悉达多回答。
"And would you rather die, than obey your father?"
　"难道你宁愿死，也不愿听从你父亲的话吗？"
"Siddhartha has always obeyed his father"
　"悉达多一直很听父亲的话"
"So will you abandon your plan?"
　"那么你会放弃你的计划吗？"
"Siddhartha will do what his father will tell him to do"
　"悉达多会按照父亲的吩咐去做"

The first light of day shone into the room
第一缕阳光照进房间
The Brahman saw that Siddhartha knees were softly trembling
婆罗门看见悉达多的双膝在轻轻颤抖
In Siddhartha's face he saw no trembling
悉达多的脸上没有一丝颤抖

his eyes were fixed on a distant spot
他的目光注视着远处
This was when his father realized
这时他的父亲意识到
even now Siddhartha no longer dwelt with him in his home
即便如此，悉达多也不再和他住在一起
he saw that he had already left him
他发现他已经离开了他
The Father touched Siddhartha's shoulder
父亲摸了摸悉达多的肩膀
"You will," he spoke, "go into the forest and be a Samana"
"你将去森林里当沙门。" 他说。
"When you find blissfulness in the forest, come back"
"当你在森林中找到幸福时，就回来吧"
"come back and teach me to be blissful"
"回来教我如何幸福"
"If you find disappointment, then return"
"如果你感到失望，那就回来"
"return and let us make offerings to the gods together, again"
"回来吧，我们再一起祭拜神明吧"
"Go now and kiss your mother"
"现在去亲吻你的妈妈"
"tell her where you are going"
"告诉她你要去哪里"
"But for me it is time to go to the river"
"但对我来说，现在该去河边了"
"it is my time to perform the first ablution"
"现在是我进行第一次沐浴的时候了"
He took his hand from the shoulder of his son, and went outside
他把手从儿子的肩上拿开，走了出去
Siddhartha wavered to the side as he tried to walk
悉达多一边走，一边摇摇晃晃地往一边走。
He put his limbs back under control and bowed to his father

他恢复了四肢的控制，向父亲鞠躬致敬

he went to his mother to do as his father had said
他去找他母亲，按照他父亲说的去做

As he slowly left on stiff legs a shadow rose near the last hut
当他双腿僵硬地慢慢离开时，最后一间小屋附近出现了一个影子

who had crouched there, and joined the pilgrim?
谁蹲在那里并加入了朝圣者的行列？

"Govinda, you have come" said Siddhartha and smiled
"戈文达，你来了。"悉达多微笑着说道。

"I have come," said Govinda
"我来了。"戈文达说。

- 24 -

With the Samanas
与沙门

In the evening of this day they caught up with the ascetics
这天傍晚,他们追上了苦行僧
the ascetics; the skinny Samanas
苦行僧、瘦沙门
they offered them their companionship and obedience
他们给予他们陪伴和服从
Their companionship and obedience were accepted
他们的陪伴和服从被接受
Siddhartha gave his garments to a poor Brahman in the street
悉达多将自己的衣服送给街上的一位贫穷婆罗门
He wore nothing more than a loincloth and earth-coloured, unsown cloak
他只穿着一条缠腰布和一件土色的未缝制斗篷
He ate only once a day, and never anything cooked
他每天只吃一顿饭,而且从来不吃煮熟的东西
He fasted for fifteen days, he fasted for twenty-eight days
他禁食了十五天,他禁食了二十八天
The flesh waned from his thighs and cheeks
他的大腿和脸颊上的肉都消失了
Feverish dreams flickered from his enlarged eyes
狂热的梦想从他放大的眼睛里闪烁
long nails grew slowly on his parched fingers
他的干裂的手指上慢慢长出了长长的指甲
and a dry, shaggy beard grew on his chin
下巴上长着干枯、蓬乱的胡须
His glance turned to ice when he encountered women
当他遇到女人时,他的目光变得冷淡
he walked through a city of nicely dressed people
他穿过一座衣着讲究的城市
his mouth twitched with contempt for them

他嘴角抽搐,鄙视他们
He saw merchants trading and princes hunting
他看到商人在交易,看到王子在狩猎
he saw mourners wailing for their dead
他看到哀悼者为死者哀号
and he saw whores offering themselves
他看见妓女献出自己
physicians trying to help the sick
医生试图帮助病人
priests determining the most suitable day for seeding
祭司决定最适合播种的日子
lovers loving and mothers nursing their children
恋人相爱,母亲哺育孩子
and all of this was not worthy of one look from his eyes
而这一切都不值得他看一眼
it all lied, it all stank, it all stank of lies
一切都是谎言,一切都是恶臭,一切都是谎言的恶臭
it all pretended to be meaningful and joyful and beautiful
一切都假装有意义、快乐和美丽
and it all was just concealed putrefaction
而这一切都只是隐藏的腐烂
the world tasted bitter; life was torture
世界尝到了苦涩,生活就是折磨

A single goal stood before Siddhartha
悉达多面前只有一个目标
his goal was to become empty
他的目标是变得空虚
his goal was to be empty of thirst
他的目标是不渴
empty of wishing and empty of dreams
没有愿望,没有梦想
empty of joy and sorrow
无欢乐无悲伤

his goal was to be dead to himself
他的目标是忘掉自己
his goal was not to be a self any more
他的目标不再是成为自我
his goal was to find tranquillity with an emptied heart
他的目标是用一颗空虚的心寻找平静
his goal was to be open to miracles in unselfish thoughts
他的目标是以无私的思想接受奇迹
to achieve this was his goal
实现这一点就是他的目标
when all of his self was overcome and had died
当他所有的自我都被征服并死去时
when every desire and every urge was silent in the heart
当每一个愿望和冲动都在心里沉寂
then the ultimate part of him had to awake
那么他最终的部分就必须醒来
the innermost of his being, which is no longer his self
他内心深处不再是他自己
this was the great secret
这是最大的秘密

Silently, Siddhartha exposed himself to the burning rays of the sun
悉达多默默地将自己暴露在灼热的阳光下
he was glowing with pain and he was glowing with thirst
他因痛苦而脸红，也因口渴而脸红
and he stood there until he neither felt pain nor thirst
他站在那里，直到感觉不到疼痛和口渴
Silently, he stood there in the rainy season
他默默地站在雨季
from his hair the water was dripping over freezing shoulders
水从他的头发上滴落到冰冷的肩膀上
the water was dripping over his freezing hips and legs

水滴落在他冰冷的臀部和腿上
and the penitent stood there
忏悔者站在那里
he stood there until he could not feel the cold any more
他站在那里，直到感觉不到寒冷
he stood there until his body was silent
他站在那里直到身体沉寂
he stood there until his body was quiet
他站在那里直到身体安静下来
Silently, he cowered in the thorny bushes
他默默地躲在荆棘丛中
blood dripped from the burning skin
血从烧伤的皮肤上滴落下来
blood dripped from festering wounds
鲜血从溃烂的伤口滴落
and Siddhartha stayed rigid and motionless
悉达多依然僵硬地一动不动
he stood until no blood flowed any more
他站着直到不再流血
he stood until nothing stung any more
他站着直到不再刺痛
he stood until nothing burned any more
他站着直到一切都不再燃烧
Siddhartha sat upright and learned to breathe sparingly
悉达多端坐，学会节制呼吸
he learned to get along with few breaths
他学会了如何与少数人相处
he learned to stop breathing
他学会了停止呼吸
He learned, beginning with the breath, to calm the beating of his heart
他学会了从呼吸开始，平静心跳
he learned to reduce the beats of his heart
他学会了放慢心跳

he meditated until his heartbeats were only a few
他冥想到心跳只剩下几下
and then his heartbeats were almost none
然后他的心跳几乎停止了
Instructed by the oldest of the Samanas, Siddhartha practised self-denial
在最年长的沙门的指导下，悉达多修行克己
he practised meditation, according to the new Samana rules
他按照新的沙门规则进行冥想
A heron flew over the bamboo forest
一只苍鹭飞过竹林
Siddhartha accepted the heron into his soul
悉达多将苍鹭纳入他的灵魂
he flew over forest and mountains
他飞越森林和山脉
he was a heron, he ate fish
他是一只苍鹭，他吃鱼
he felt the pangs of a heron's hunger
他感受到苍鹭饥饿的痛苦
he spoke the heron's croak
他发出苍鹭的叫声
he died a heron's death
他死得像一只苍鹭
A dead jackal was lying on the sandy bank
一只死豺狼躺在沙滩上
Siddhartha's soul slipped inside the body of the dead jackal
悉达多的灵魂进入了死去豺狼的身体里
he was the dead jackal laying on the banks and bloated
他是躺在河岸上的死豺狼，肿胀着
he stank and decayed and was dismembered by hyenas
他发臭腐烂并被鬣狗肢解
he was skinned by vultures and turned into a skeleton
他被秃鹫剥皮，变成了一具骷髅
he was turned to dust and blown across the fields

他化为尘土,被吹过田野
And Siddhartha's soul returned
于是悉达多的灵魂又回来了
it had died, decayed, and was scattered as dust
它已死去,腐烂,散为尘土
it had tasted the gloomy intoxication of the cycle
它尝到了周期的阴郁醉意
it awaited with a new thirst, like a hunter in the gap
它怀着新的渴望等待着,就像一个在缝隙中的猎人
in the gap where he could escape from the cycle
在他可以逃离这个循环的地方
in the gap where an eternity without suffering began
在没有痛苦的永恒开始的地方
he killed his senses and his memory
他杀死了他的感官和记忆
he slipped out of his self into thousands of other forms
他脱离了自我,变成了成千上万种其他形态
he was an animal, a carrion, a stone
他是一只动物、一具腐尸、一块石头
he was wood and water
他是木也是水
and he awoke every time to find his old self again
每次他醒来都会发现自己又恢复了原来的样子
whether sun or moon, he was his self again
无论是太阳还是月亮,他都恢复了自我
he turned round in the cycle
他转了一圈
he felt thirst, overcame the thirst, felt new thirst
他感到口渴,克服了口渴,又感到了新的口渴

Siddhartha learned a lot when he was with the Samanas
悉达多在与沙门相处时学到了很多东西
he learned many ways leading away from the self
他学会了许多远离自我的方法

he learned how to let go
他学会了如何放手
He went the way of self-denial by means of pain
他通过痛苦走上了自我否定之路
he learned self-denial through voluntarily suffering and overcoming pain
他通过自愿忍受痛苦和克服痛苦学会了自我否定
he overcame hunger, thirst, and tiredness
他克服了饥饿、口渴和疲劳
He went the way of self-denial by means of meditation
他通过冥想走上了自我否定之路
he went the way of self-denial through imagining the mind to be void of all conceptions
他通过想象心灵没有任何概念，走上了自我否定的道路
with these and other ways he learned to let go
通过这些和其他方式他学会了放手
a thousand times he left his self
他千百遍地抛弃自我
for hours and days he remained in the non-self
数小时和数天他都处于无我状态
all these ways led away from the self
所有这些方式都远离了自我
but their path always led back to the self
但他们的道路总是回到自我
Siddhartha fled from the self a thousand times
悉达多千百次逃离自我
but the return to the self was inevitable
但回归自我是不可避免的
although he stayed in nothingness, coming back was inevitable
虽身处虚无，归来亦是必然
although he stayed in animals and stones, coming back was inevitable

尽管他留在动物和石头中,但回来是不可避免的。
he found himself in the sunshine or in the moonlight again
他发现自己又在阳光或月光下
he found himself in the shade or in the rain again
他发现自己又在树荫下或雨中
and he was once again his self; Siddhartha
他又恢复了自我;悉达多
and again he felt the agony of the cycle which had been forced upon him
他再次感受到了强加在他身上的循环的痛苦

by his side lived Govinda, his shadow
他的身边住着戈文达,他的影子
Govinda walked the same path and undertook the same efforts
Govinda 走了同样的路,做了同样的努力
they spoke to one another no more than the exercises required
他们彼此交谈的时间不超过练习所需的时间
occasionally the two of them went through the villages
偶尔他们俩会穿过村庄
they went to beg for food for themselves and their teachers
他们去为自己和老师乞讨食物
"How do you think we have progressed, Govinda" he asked
"你觉得我们进展如何,戈文达?"他问道
"Did we reach any goals?" Govinda answered
"我们达成目标了吗?"戈文达回答道
"We have learned, and we'll continue learning"
"我们已经学会了,并将继续学习"
"You'll be a great Samana, Siddhartha"
"你会成为一名伟大的沙门的,悉达多。"
"Quickly, you've learned every exercise"
"快点,你把所有练习都学会了"
"often, the old Samanas have admired you"

"老沙门们常常钦佩你"
"One day, you'll be a holy man, oh Siddhartha"
"有一天,你会成为一个圣人,悉达多。"
Spoke Siddhartha, "I can't help but feel that it is not like this, my friend"
悉达多说道:"我的朋友,我禁不住觉得事实并非如此。"
"What I've learned being among the Samanas could have been learned more quickly"
"我在沙门那里学到的东西本来可以学得更快"
"it could have been learned by simpler means"
"可以通过更简单的方法来学习"
"it could have been learned in any tavern"
"在任何酒馆里都可以学到"
"it could have been learned where the whorehouses are"
"人们可能会知道妓院在哪里"
"I could have learned it among carters and gamblers"
"我可能从车夫和赌徒那里学到了这一点"
Spoke Govinda, "Siddhartha is joking with me"
戈文达说:"悉达多在跟我开玩笑。"
"How could you have learned meditation among wretched people?"
"你怎么可能在那些可怜的人中间学习冥想呢?"
"how could whores have taught you about holding your breath?"
"妓女怎么能教你屏住呼吸呢?"
"how could gamblers have taught you insensitivity against pain?"
"赌徒怎么能教会你对痛苦麻木不仁呢?"
Siddhartha spoke quietly, as if he was talking to himself
悉达多轻声说道,仿佛在自言自语。
"What is meditation?"
"什么是冥想?"
"What is leaving one's body?"

"什么是离开人的身体？"

"What is fasting?"
"什么是斋戒？"

"What is holding one's breath?"
"什么是屏住呼吸？"

"It is fleeing from the self"
"这是在逃避自我"

"it is a short escape of the agony of being a self"
"这是逃离自我痛苦的短暂方式"

"it is a short numbing of the senses against the pain"
"这是一种短暂的麻痹感官以缓解疼痛"

"it is avoiding the pointlessness of life"
"这是在逃避生命的无意义"

"The same numbing is what the driver of an ox-cart finds in the inn"
"同样的麻木也是牛车夫在客栈里发现的"

"drinking a few bowls of rice-wine or fermented coconut-milk"
"喝几碗米酒或椰奶"

"Then he won't feel his self anymore"
"那么他就感觉不到自己了"

"then he won't feel the pains of life anymore"
"那么他就不会再感受到生活的痛苦了"

"then he finds a short numbing of the senses"
"然后他发现感觉短暂麻木"

"When he falls asleep over his bowl of rice-wine, he'll find the same what we find"
"当他喝着米酒睡着的时候，他会发现和我们一样的东西"

"he finds what we find when we escape our bodies through long exercises"
"他发现了我们通过长时间的锻炼逃离身体时发现的东西"

"all of us are staying in the non-self"

"我们每个人都处于无我之中"

"This is how it is, oh Govinda"
"事情就是这样的,哦,戈文达"

Spoke Govinda, "You say so, oh friend"
戈文达说:"你这么说,朋友。"

"and yet you know that Siddhartha is no driver of an ox-cart"
"但你知道悉达多不是牛车夫。"

"and you know a Samana is no drunkard"
"你知道,沙门不是酒鬼。"

"it's true that a drinker numbs his senses"
"喝酒确实会让人感觉麻木"

"it's true that he briefly escapes and rests"
"他确实短暂地逃脱并休息了"

"but he'll return from the delusion and finds everything to be unchanged"
"但他会从妄想中回来,发现一切都没有改变"

"he has not become wiser"
"他没有变得更聪明"

"he has gathered any enlightenment"
"他已经获得了任何启示"

"he has not risen several steps"
"他还没上几级台阶"

And Siddhartha spoke with a smile
悉达多微笑着说道

"I do not know, I've never been a drunkard"
"我不知道,我从来都不是一个酒鬼"

"I know that I find only a short numbing of the senses"
"我知道我发现的只是短暂的感官麻木"

"I find it in my exercises and meditations"
"我在锻炼和冥想中找到了它"

"and I find I am just as far removed from wisdom as a child in the mother's womb"
"我发现自己离智慧还很远,就像母亲子宫里的婴儿一样"

"this I know, oh Govinda"
"我知道,哦,戈文达"

And once again, another time, Siddhartha began to speak
又一次,悉达多开始说话
Siddhartha had left the forest, together with Govinda
悉达多和戈文达一起离开了森林
they left to beg for some food in the village
他们去村里乞讨食物
he said, "What now, oh Govinda?"
他说:"现在怎么办呢,戈文达?"
"are we on the right path?"
"我们走在正确的道路上吗?"
"are we getting closer to enlightenment?"
"我们是否越来越接近启蒙了?"
"are we getting closer to salvation?"
"我们离救赎更近了吗?"
"Or do we perhaps live in a circle?"
"或者我们生活在一个圈子里?"
"we, who have thought we were escaping the cycle"
"我们原本以为可以逃离这个循环"
Spoke Govinda, "We have learned a lot"
戈文达说:"我们学到了很多东西"
"Siddhartha, there is still much to learn"
"悉达多,还有很多东西要学"
"We are not going around in circles"
"我们不会绕圈子"
"we are moving up; the circle is a spiral"
"我们正在向上移动;圆圈是一个螺旋"
"we have already ascended many levels"
"我们已经上升了很多层"
Siddhartha answered, "How old would you think our oldest Samana is?"

悉达多问："你认为我们最年长的沙门有多大年纪了？"

"how old is our venerable teacher?"
"我们的师尊多少岁了？"

Spoke Govinda, "Our oldest one might be about sixty years of age"
戈文达说："我们最年长的一个大概六十岁了。"

Spoke Siddhartha, "He has lived for sixty years"
悉达多说："他已经活了六十年了。"

"and yet he has not reached the nirvana"
"但他还没有达到涅槃"

"He'll turn seventy and eighty"
"他已经七八十岁了"

"you and me, we will grow just as old as him"
"你和我，都会和他一样老"

"and we will do our exercises"
"我们会做练习"

"and we will fast, and we will meditate"
"我们将禁食，我们将冥想"

"But we will not reach the nirvana"
"但我们无法达到涅槃"

"he won't reach nirvana and we won't"
"他无法达到涅槃，我们也无法"

"there are uncountable Samanas out there"
"那里有无数的沙门"

"perhaps not a single one will reach the nirvana"
"也许没有人能达到涅槃"

"We find comfort, we find numbness, we learn feats"
"我们找到安慰，我们找到麻木，我们学习壮举"

"we learn these things to deceive others"
"我们学习这些东西是为了欺骗别人"

"But the most important thing, the path of paths, we will not find"
"但最重要的是，我们找不到那条路中的道路"

Spoke Govinda "If you only wouldn't speak such terrible words, Siddhartha!"
戈文达说道:"如果你不说出这么可怕的话就好了,悉达多!"

"there are so many learned men"
"有这么多的学者"

"how could not one of them not find the path of paths?"
"他们怎么可能找不到那条路呢?"

"how can so many Brahmans not find it?"
"那么多婆罗门怎么会找不到呢?"

"how can so many austere and venerable Samanas not find it?"
"为什么那么多苦行僧都找不到它呢?"

"how can all those who are searching not find it?"
"为什么所有寻找的人都找不到它呢?"

"how can the holy men not find it?"
"圣人怎么会找不到呢?"

But Siddhartha spoke with as much sadness as mockery
但悉达多说话时,既带着悲伤,又带着嘲讽。

he spoke with a quiet, a slightly sad, a slightly mocking voice
他说话的声音很平静,略带悲伤,略带嘲讽

"Soon, Govinda, your friend will leave the path of the Samanas"
"戈文达,你的朋友很快就会离开沙门之路了。"

"he has walked along your side for so long"
"他已经陪伴你很久了"

"I'm suffering of thirst"
"我口渴难耐"

"on this long path of a Samana, my thirst has remained as strong as ever"
"在这条漫长的沙门之路上,我的口渴感始终如一"

"I always thirsted for knowledge"
"我总是渴望知识"

"I have always been full of questions"
　"我一直有很多疑问"
"I have asked the Brahmans, year after year"
　"我年复一年地问婆罗门们"
"and I have asked the holy Vedas, year after year"
　"我年复一年地问询神圣的吠陀经"
"and I have asked the devoted Samanas, year after year"
　"我年复一年地向虔诚的沙门们询问"
"perhaps I could have learned it from the hornbill bird"
　"也许我可以从犀鸟那里学到这一点"
"perhaps I should have asked the chimpanzee"
　"也许我应该问问黑猩猩"
"It took me a long time"
　"我花了很长时间"
"and I am not finished learning this yet"
　"我还没学完呢"
"oh Govinda, I have learned that there is nothing to be learned!"
　"噢，戈文达，我明白了，没有什么可学的！"
"There is indeed no such thing as learning"
　"确实没有学习这回事"
"There is just one knowledge"
　"知识只有一个"
"this knowledge is everywhere, this is Atman"
　"这种知识无处不在，这就是阿特曼"
"this knowledge is within me and within you"
　"这些知识在我心中，也在你心中"
"and this knowledge is within every creature"
　"并且这种知识存在于每一个生物体内"
"this knowledge has no worse enemy than the desire to know it"
　"对于知识，最大的敌人就是对它的渴望"
"that is what I believe"
　"这就是我所相信的"

At this, Govinda stopped on the path
听到这里，戈文达在路上停了下来

he rose his hands, and spoke
他举起双手，说道

"If only you would not bother your friend with this kind of talk"
"如果你不拿这种话来打扰你的朋友就好了"

"Truly, your words stir up fear in my heart"
"确实，你的话让我心里很害怕"

"consider, what would become of the sanctity of prayer?"
"想想看，祈祷的神圣性会变成什么样？"

"what would become of the venerability of the Brahmans' caste?"
"婆罗门种姓的尊贵地位将会变成什么样子呢？"

"what would happen to the holiness of the Samanas?
"沙门的圣洁会怎样呢？

"What would then become of all of that is holy"
"那么，所有神圣的东西将会变成什么样子呢？"

"what would still be precious?"
"什么还会珍贵呢？"

And Govinda mumbled a verse from an Upanishad to himself
戈文达喃喃自语，念叨着《奥义书》中的一段话

"He who ponderingly, of a purified spirit, loses himself in the meditation of Atman"
"沉思的人，心灵净化，沉浸在对阿特曼的冥想中"

"inexpressible by words is the blissfulness of his heart"
"他内心的幸福无法用语言表达"

But Siddhartha remained silent
但悉达多保持沉默

He thought about the words which Govinda had said to him
他想起了戈文达对他说的话

and he thought the words through to their end
他把这些话想了个遍，直到最后

he thought about what would remain of all that which seemed holy
他思考着那些看似神圣的东西会剩下什么
What remains? What can stand the test?
还剩下什么？什么能经受住考验？
And he shook his head
他摇了摇头

the two young men had lived among the Samanas for about three years
这两个年轻人在沙门中生活了大约三年
some news, a rumour, a myth reached them
他们听到了一些消息、谣言、传言
the rumour had been retold many times
这个谣言已经被重复多次
A man had appeared, Gotama by name
出现了一个人，名叫乔达摩
the exalted one, the Buddha
佛陀
he had overcome the suffering of the world in himself
他已经战胜了世间的苦难
and he had halted the cycle of rebirths
他停止了轮回
He was said to wander through the land, teaching
据说他游历各地，教导
he was said to be surrounded by disciples
据说他周围都是门徒
he was said to be without possession, home, or wife
据说他没有财产、没有家、也没有妻子
he was said to be in just the yellow cloak of an ascetic
据说他只穿着苦行僧的黄色斗篷
but he was with a cheerful brow
但他却满脸笑容
and he was said to be a man of bliss

据说他是一个幸福的人
Brahmans and princes bowed down before him
婆罗门和王子们在他面前鞠躬下拜
and they became his students
他们成为了他的学生
This myth, this rumour, this legend resounded
这个神话,这个谣言,这个传说
its fragrance rose up, here and there, in the towns
它的香味飘散在城镇各处
the Brahmans spoke of this legend
婆罗门们流传着这个传说
and in the forest, the Samanas spoke of it
在森林里,沙门们谈到了这件事
again and again, the name of Gotama the Buddha reached the ears of the young men
佛陀的名字一次又一次地传到年轻人的耳中
there was good and bad talk of Gotama
关于乔达摩的传闻有好有坏
some praised Gotama, others defamed him
有人赞扬乔达摩,有人诽谤他
It was as if the plague had broken out in a country
就像一个国家爆发了瘟疫
news had been spreading around that in one or another place there was a man
有消息传开了,在某个地方,有一个男人
a wise man, a knowledgeable one
一个聪明的人,一个知识渊博的人
a man whose word and breath was enough to heal everyone
他的话语和气息足以治愈所有人
his presence could heal anyone who had been infected with the pestilence
他的存在可以治愈任何被瘟疫感染的人
such news went through the land, and everyone would talk about it

这样的消息传遍全国，每个人都会谈论它
many believed the rumours, many doubted them
许多人相信谣言，许多人怀疑谣言
but many got on their way as soon as possible
但许多人还是尽快上路
they went to seek the wise man, the helper
他们去寻找智者，帮助者
the wise man of the family of Sakya
萨迦派的智者
He possessed, so the believers said, the highest enlightenment
信徒们说，他拥有最高的启蒙
he remembered his previous lives; he had reached the nirvana
他记得前世，已经达到涅槃
and he never returned into the cycle
他再也没有回到这个循环
he was never again submerged in the murky river of physical forms
他再也没有被淹没在物质形态的浑浊河流中
Many wonderful and unbelievable things were reported of him
关于他的许多奇妙和令人难以置信的事情被报道出来
he had performed miracles
他创造了奇迹
he had overcome the devil
他战胜了魔鬼
he had spoken to the gods
他曾与诸神交谈
But his enemies and disbelievers said Gotama was a vain seducer
但他的敌人和不信者说乔达摩是一个虚荣的诱惑者
they said he spent his days in luxury
据说他过着奢侈的生活

they said he scorned the offerings
他们说他蔑视祭品
they said he was without learning
他们说他没有学识
they said he knew neither meditative exercises nor self-castigation
他们说他既不懂冥想练习,也不懂自我惩罚
The myth of Buddha sounded sweet
佛陀的神话听起来很甜蜜
The scent of magic flowed from these reports
这些报告中散发着魔法的气息
After all, the world was sick, and life was hard to bear
毕竟,世界病了,生活难以忍受
and behold, here a source of relief seemed to spring forth
看哪,这里似乎涌现出一股解脱的源泉
here a messenger seemed to call out
似乎有信使在这儿呼唤
comforting, mild, full of noble promises
令人欣慰、温和、充满崇高的承诺
Everywhere where the rumour of Buddha was heard, the young men listened up
无论何处,只要听到佛陀的传闻,年轻人就会侧耳倾听
everywhere in the lands of India they felt a longing
在印度各地,他们感受到一种渴望
everywhere where the people searched, they felt hope
无论人们在哪里寻找,他们都感到了希望
every pilgrim and stranger was welcome when he brought news of him
当他带来消息时,每个朝圣者和陌生人都会受到欢迎
the exalted one, the Sakyamuni
释迦牟尼
The myth had also reached the Samanas in the forest
这个神话也传到了森林里的沙门那里

and Siddhartha and Govinda heard the myth too
悉达多和戈文达也听到了神话
slowly, drop by drop, they heard the myth
慢慢地，一滴一滴，他们听到了神话
every drop was laden with hope
每一滴都充满希望
every drop was laden with doubt
每一滴都充满怀疑
They rarely talked about it
他们很少谈论它
because the oldest one of the Samanas did not like this myth
因为最年长的沙门不喜欢这个神话
he had heard that this alleged Buddha used to be an ascetic
他听说这个所谓的佛陀曾经是一个苦行僧
he heard he had lived in the forest
他听说他曾住在森林里
but he had turned back to luxury and worldly pleasures
但他又回归了奢侈和世俗的快乐
and he had no high opinion of this Gotama
他对乔达摩没什么好感

"Oh Siddhartha," Govinda spoke one day to his friend
"噢，悉达多。"戈文达有一天对他的朋友说道。
"Today, I was in the village"
"今天，我在村子里"
"and a Brahman invited me into his house"
"一位婆罗门邀请我去他家"
"and in his house, there was the son of a Brahman from Magadha"
"他的家里住着一位摩揭陀婆罗门的儿子"
"he has seen the Buddha with his own eyes"
"他亲眼见过佛陀"
"and he has heard him teach"
"他也听过他的教导"

"Verily, this made my chest ache when I breathed"
"说实话,这让我呼吸时胸口疼痛"

"and I thought this to myself:"
"我心里想着:"

"if only we heard the teachings from the mouth of this perfected man!"
"如果我们能听到这位完美之人的教诲就好了!"

"Speak, friend, wouldn't we want to go there too"
"说吧,朋友,我们也想去那里吗?"

"wouldn't it be good to listen to the teachings from the Buddha's mouth?"
"聆听佛陀的教诲不是很好吗?"

Spoke Siddhartha, "I had thought you would stay with the Samanas"
悉达多说道:"我原以为你会和沙门们待在一起。"

"I always had believed your goal was to live to be seventy"
"我一直相信你的目标是活到七十岁"

"I thought you would keep practising those feats and exercises"
"我以为你会继续练习那些技艺和功法"

"and I thought you would become a Samana"
"我还以为你会成为沙门呢。"

"But behold, I had not known Govinda well enough"
"但是,我对戈文达还不够了解。"

"I knew little of his heart"
"我对他的内心了解甚少"

"So now you want to take a new path"
"所以你现在想走一条新的路"

"and you want to go there where the Buddha spreads his teachings"
"你想去佛陀宣扬教义的地方"

Spoke Govinda, "You're mocking me"
戈文达说:"你在嘲笑我。"

"Mock me if you like, Siddhartha!"

"如果你想嘲笑我，就嘲笑我吧，悉达多！"

"But have you not also developed a desire to hear these teachings?"

"但你难道不也渴望听到这些教诲吗？"

"have you not said you would not walk the path of the Samanas for much longer?"

"你不是说过你不想再走沙门之路了吗？"

At this, Siddhartha laughed in his very own manner

听到这里，悉达多以他自己的方式笑了起来

the manner in which his voice assumed a touch of sadness

他的声音中带着一丝悲伤

but it still had that touch of mockery

但仍然带有一丝嘲讽意味

Spoke Siddhartha, "Govinda, you've spoken well"

悉达多说道："戈文达，你说得真好。"

"you've remembered correctly what I said"

"你记得没错我说的话"

"If only you remembered the other thing you've heard from me"

"如果你还记得我告诉你的另一件事就好了"

"I have grown distrustful and tired against teachings and learning"

"我对教诲和学习变得不信任和厌倦"

"my faith in words, which are brought to us by teachers, is small"

"我对老师传授的语言的信任度很低"

"But let's do it, my dear"

"但我们还是行动吧，亲爱的"

"I am willing to listen to these teachings"

"我愿意聆听这些教诲"

"though in my heart I do not have hope"

"尽管我心里不抱有任何希望"

"I believe that we've already tasted the best fruit of these teachings"

"我相信我们已经尝到了这些教义的最好果实"
Spoke Govinda, "Your willingness delights my heart"
戈文达说道，"您的乐意令我心旷神怡"
"But tell me, how should this be possible?"
"但是告诉我，这怎么可能呢？"
"How can the Gotama's teachings have already revealed their best fruit to us?"
"乔达摩的教诲怎么已经向我们展现其最好的成果了呢？"
"we have not heard his words yet"
"我们还没有听到他的话"
Spoke Siddhartha, "Let us eat this fruit"
悉达多说："我们吃这颗果子吧。"
"and let us wait for the rest, oh Govinda!"
"让我们等待剩下的事吧，哦，戈文达！"
"But this fruit consists in him calling us away from the Samanas"
"但这种成果在于他让我们远离了沙门"
"and we have already received it thanks to the Gotama!"
"我们已经从乔达摩那儿得到了它！"
"Whether he has more, let us await with calm hearts"
"无论他是否还有更多，让我们平静地等待"

On this very same day Siddhartha spoke to the oldest Samana
就在这一天，悉达多对最年长的沙门说
he told him of his decision to leaves the Samanas
他告诉他他决定离开沙门
he informed the oldest one with courtesy and modesty
他礼貌而谦虚地告诉最年长的人
but the Samana became angry that the two young men wanted to leave him
但沙门却因为这两个年轻人要离开他而生气
and he talked loudly and used crude words

他大声说话，说粗话
Govinda was startled and became embarrassed
戈文达吓了一跳，感到很尴尬
But Siddhartha put his mouth close to Govinda's ear
但悉达多却把嘴凑到戈文达耳边
"Now, I want to show the old man what I've learned from him"
"现在，我想让老人看看我从他身上学到的东西"
Siddhartha positioned himself closely in front of the Samana
悉达多站在沙门面前
with a concentrated soul, he captured the old man's glance
他全神贯注地捕捉老人的目光
he deprived him of his power and made him mute
他剥夺了他的权力，让他哑口无言
he took away his free will
他剥夺了他的自由意志
he subdued him under his own will, and commanded him
他使他屈服于自己的意志，并命令他
his eyes became motionless, and his will was paralysed
他的眼睛一动不动，他的意志也麻痹了
his arms were hanging down without power
他的手臂无力地垂下
he had fallen victim to Siddhartha's spell
他成了悉达多咒语的受害者
Siddhartha's thoughts brought the Samana under their control
悉达多的思想控制了沙门
he had to carry out what they commanded
他必须执行他们的命令
And thus, the old man made several bows
于是，老人鞠躬行礼
he performed gestures of blessing
他做了祝福的手势

he spoke stammeringly a godly wish for a good journey
他结结巴巴地祝愿旅途愉快
the young men returned the good wishes with thanks
年轻人用感谢回应了他们的祝福
they went on their way with salutations
他们带着问候离开了
On the way, Govinda spoke again
路上,戈文达又说话了
"Oh Siddhartha, you have learned more from the Samanas than I knew"
"悉达多啊,你从沙门那里学到的东西比我学到的还多。"
"It is very hard to cast a spell on an old Samana"
"对一个老沙门施咒是很难的"
"Truly, if you had stayed there, you would soon have learned to walk on water"
"真的,如果你留在那里,你很快就会学会在水上行走"
"I do not seek to walk on water" said Siddhartha
悉达多说:"我不想在水上行走。"
"Let old Samanas be content with such feats!"
"让老沙门们满足于这样的壮举吧!"

Gotama
乔达摩

In Savathi, every child knew the name of the exalted Buddha
在舍卫城,每个孩子都知道佛陀的名字
every house was prepared for his coming
每家每户都为他的到来做好了准备
each house filled the alms-dishes of Gotama's disciples
每家每户都盛满了乔达摩弟子的供品
Gotama's disciples were the silently begging ones
乔达摩的弟子们都是默默乞讨的人
Near the town was Gotama's favourite place to stay
乔达摩最喜欢住在镇子附近
he stayed in the garden of Jetavana
他住在祇园祇园
the rich merchant Anathapindika had given the garden to Gotama
富商阿那塔品第卡把花园送给了乔达摩
he had given it to him as a gift
他把它作为礼物送给了他
he was an obedient worshipper of the exalted one
他是至高者的顺从崇拜者
the two young ascetics had received tales and answers
两位年轻的苦行僧得到了故事和答案
all these tales and answers pointed them to Gotama's abode
所有这些故事和答案都指向了乔达摩的住所
they arrived in the town of Savathi
他们到达了萨瓦蒂镇
they went to the very first door of the town
他们来到小镇的第一道门前
and they begged for food at the door
他们在门口乞讨食物
a woman offered them food

一名妇女给他们提供食物
and they accepted the food
他们接受了食物
Siddhartha asked the woman
悉达多问女人
"oh charitable one, where does the Buddha dwell?"
"世尊,佛住何处?"
"we are two Samanas from the forest"
"我们是两个来自森林的沙门"
"we have come to see the perfected one"
"我们来见完美者"
"we have come to hear the teachings from his mouth"
"我们来聆听他的教诲"
Spoke the woman, "you Samanas from the forest"
女人说道,"你们这些来自森林的沙门"
"you have truly come to the right place"
"你确实来对地方了"
"you should know, in Jetavana, there is the garden of Anathapindika"
"你应该知道,在Jetavana,有一个Anathapindika的花园"
"that is where the exalted one dwells"
"那是至尊者居住的地方"
"there you pilgrims shall spend the night"
"你们朝圣者将在那里过夜"
"there is enough space for the innumerable, who flock here"
"这里有足够的空间容纳无数人聚集在这里"
"they too come to hear the teachings from his mouth"
"他们也来听他口中的教诲"
This made Govinda happy, and full of joy
戈文达听了很高兴,心里充满了喜悦
he exclaimed, "we have reached our destination"
他大叫道:"我们到达目的地了"
"our path has come to an end!"

"我们的道路,已经走到尽头了!"
"But tell us, oh mother of the pilgrims"
"但是请告诉我们,朝圣者的母亲啊"
"do you know him, the Buddha?"
"你认识他吗,佛陀?"
"have you seen him with your own eyes?"
"你亲眼见过他吗?"
Spoke the woman, "Many times I have seen him, the exalted one"
女人说道:"我多次见过他,尊贵的他。"
"On many days I have seen him"
"我经常见到他"
"I have seen him walking through the alleys in silence"
"我看见他默默地走过小巷"
"I have seen him wearing his yellow cloak"
"我看见他穿着黄色斗篷"
"I have seen him presenting his alms-dish in silence"
"我看见他默默地奉献着施舍的盘子"
"I have seen him at the doors of the houses"
"我曾在家门口见过他"
"and I have seen him leaving with a filled dish"
"我看到他端着盛满食物的盘子离开"
Delightedly, Govinda listened to the woman
戈文达很高兴地听着女人的话
and he wanted to ask and hear much more
他想问更多,听更多
But Siddhartha urged him to walk on
但悉达多鼓励他继续前行
They thanked the woman and left
他们向那位女士道谢后就离开了
they hardly had to ask for directions
他们几乎不需要问路
many pilgrims and monks were on their way to the Jetavana
许多朝圣者和僧侣正在前往祇园精舍

they reached it at night, so there were constant arrivals
他们晚上才到达,所以不断有人来
and those who sought shelter got it
那些寻求庇护的人得到了庇护
The two Samanas were accustomed to life in the forest
两位沙门已经习惯了森林生活
so without making any noise they quickly found a place to stay
所以他们很快就安静地找到了住处
and they rested there until the morning
他们就在那里休息,直到早晨

At sunrise, they saw with astonishment the size of the crowd
日出时,他们惊讶地看到人群的规模
a great many number of believers had come
很多信徒来了
and a great number of curious people had spent the night here
许多好奇的人在这里过夜
On all paths of the marvellous garden, monks walked in yellow robes
在这片奇妙的花园里,每条小路上都行走着身穿黄色僧袍的僧侣
under the trees they sat here and there, in deep contemplation
他们坐在树下,陷入沉思
or they were in a conversation about spiritual matters
或者他们正在谈论精神问题
the shady gardens looked like a city
阴凉的花园看起来像一座城市
a city full of people, bustling like bees
一座人山人海、熙熙攘攘的城市
The majority of the monks went out with their alms-dish
大多数僧侣都带着钵盂出去了

they went out to collect food for their lunch
他们出去收集午餐食物
this would be their only meal of the day
这将是他们一天中唯一的一顿饭
The Buddha himself, the enlightened one, also begged in the mornings
佛陀本人，开悟者，也在早晨乞讨
Siddhartha saw him, and he instantly recognised him
悉达多看见了他，立刻认出了他
he recognised him as if a God had pointed him out
他认出了他，就像上帝指出了他一样
He saw him, a simple man in a yellow robe
他看见了他，一个穿着黄色长袍的朴素男子
he was bearing the alms-dish in his hand, walking silently
他手捧钵盂，默默地走着
"Look here!" Siddhartha said quietly to Govinda
"看这儿！"悉达多轻声对戈文达说。
"This one is the Buddha"
"此人是佛陀"
Attentively, Govinda looked at the monk in the yellow robe
戈文达仔细地看着身穿黄色僧袍的僧人
this monk seemed to be in no way different from any of the others
这个和尚看起来和其他的和尚没什么不同
but soon, Govinda also realized that this is the one
但很快，戈文达也意识到，这就是
And they followed him and observed him
他们跟随他，观察他
The Buddha went on his way, modestly and deep in his thoughts
佛陀继续前行，谦虚而深思
his calm face was neither happy nor sad
他平静的脸上没有快乐也没有悲伤
his face seemed to smile quietly and inwardly

他的脸上似乎在悄悄地、内心地微笑

his smile was hidden, quiet and calm
他的笑容隐藏起来,安静而平静

the way the Buddha walked somewhat resembled a healthy child
佛陀的走路方式有点像一个健康的孩子

he walked just as all of his monks did
他像他的僧侣一样行走

he placed his feet according to a precise rule
他按照精确的规则放置双脚

his face and his walk, his quietly lowered glance
他的脸、他的步态、他悄悄低垂的目光

his quietly dangling hand, every finger of it
他静静地垂下的手,每一根手指

all these things expressed peace
所有这些都表达了和平

all these things expressed perfection
所有这些都体现了完美

he did not search, nor did he imitate
他没有寻找,也没有模仿

he softly breathed inwardly an unwhithering calm
他轻轻地呼吸着内心无尽的平静

he shone outwardly an unwhithering light
他向外散发着不凋零的光芒

he had about him an untouchable peace
他周围有一种不可触及的平静。

the two Samanas recognised him solely by the perfection of his calm
两位沙门仅凭他那完美的镇定就认出了他

they recognized him by the quietness of his appearance
他们从他平静的外表认出了他

the quietness in his appearance in which there was no searching
他外表平静,毫无探寻之意

there was no desire, nor imitation
没有欲望，也没有模仿
there was no effort to be seen
看不到任何努力
only light and peace was to be seen in his appearance
他的外表只能看到光明与和平
"Today, we'll hear the teachings from his mouth" said Govinda
"今天，我们将聆听他的教诲。"戈文达说
Siddhartha did not answer
悉达多没有回答。
He felt little curiosity for the teachings
他对教义没什么好奇心
he did not believe that they would teach him anything new
他不相信他们会教他任何新东西
he had heard the contents of this Buddha's teachings again and again
他曾一遍又一遍地听过佛陀的教诲
but these reports only represented second hand information
但这些报道仅代表二手信息
But attentively he looked at Gotama's head
但他仔细地看着乔达摩的头
his shoulders, his feet, his quietly dangling hand
他的肩膀、他的脚、他静静地垂下的手
it was as if every finger of this hand was of these teachings
仿佛这只手的每一个手指都蕴含着这些教诲
his fingers spoke of truth
他的手指诉说着真相
his fingers breathed and exhaled the fragrance of truth
他的手指呼吸着并散发着真理的芬芳
his fingers glistened with truth
他的手指闪烁着真理的光芒
this Buddha was truthful down to the gesture of his last finger

佛陀的最后一根手指都是真实的
Siddhartha could see that this man was holy
悉达多看得出这个人很神圣
Never before, Siddhartha had venerated a person so much
悉达多从来没有如此崇敬过一个人
he had never before loved a person as much as this one
他从来没有像现在这样爱过一个人
They both followed the Buddha until they reached the town
他们俩跟着佛陀,直到到达城镇
and then they returned to their silence
然后他们又恢复了沉默
they themselves intended to abstain on this day
他们自己打算在这一天弃权
They saw Gotama returning the food that had been given to him
他们看到乔达摩把给他的食物还给他
what he ate could not even have satisfied a bird's appetite
他吃的东西甚至不能满足一只鸟的胃口
and they saw him retiring into the shade of the mango-trees
他们看见他退到芒果树的树荫里

in the evening the heat had cooled down
晚上天气变凉了
everyone in the camp started to bustle about and gathered around
营地里的每个人都开始忙碌起来,聚集在一起
they heard the Buddha teaching, and his voice
他们听到佛陀的教导,他的声音
and his voice was also perfected
他的声音也变得完美
his voice was of perfect calmness
他的声音非常平静
his voice was full of peace
他的声音充满平静

Gotama taught the teachings of suffering
乔达摩教导苦难的教义

he taught of the origin of suffering
他教导苦难的起源

he taught of the way to relieve suffering
他教导如何减轻痛苦

Calmly and clearly his quiet speech flowed on
平静而清晰地,他的平静的演讲继续进行

Suffering was life, and full of suffering was the world
人生充满苦难,世界充满苦难

but salvation from suffering had been found
但痛苦的救赎已经找到

salvation was obtained by him who would walk the path of the Buddha
行佛道的人,得救了

With a soft, yet firm voice the exalted one spoke
尊者用柔和而坚定的声音说道

he taught the four main doctrines
他教导了四个主要教义

he taught the eight-fold path
他教导八正道

patiently he went the usual path of the teachings
他耐心地走着通常的教学路线

his teachings contained the examples
他的教导包含例子

his teaching made use of the repetitions
他的教学利用了重复

brightly and quietly his voice hovered over the listeners
他的声音明亮而安静地萦绕在听众的耳边

his voice was like a light
他的声音就像一道光

his voice was like a starry sky
他的声音就像星空

When the Buddha ended his speech, many pilgrims stepped forward
佛陀讲完后,许多朝圣者走上前来
they asked to be accepted into the community
他们要求被社区接纳
they sought refuge in the teachings
他们寻求教义的庇护
And Gotama accepted them by speaking
乔达摩接受了他们的请求,说道
"You have heard the teachings well"
"你们已经听闻了这些教诲"
"join us and walk in holiness"
"加入我们,走向圣洁"
"put an end to all suffering"
"结束一切苦难"
Behold, then Govinda, the shy one, also stepped forward and spoke
瞧,害羞的戈文达也走上前来,说道
"I also take my refuge in the exalted one and his teachings"
"我也皈依至尊者和他的教诲"
and he asked to be accepted into the community of his disciples
他请求加入他的门徒团体
and he was accepted into the community of Gotama's disciples
他被接纳为乔达摩弟子团体的一员

the Buddha had retired for the night
佛陀已休息了
Govinda turned to Siddhartha and spoke eagerly
戈文达转向悉达多,急切地说道
"Siddhartha, it is not my place to scold you"
"悉达多,我没有资格责骂你。"
"We have both heard the exalted one"

"我们都听见了至高者的话"
"we have both perceived the teachings"
"我们都领悟了教诲"
"Govinda has heard the teachings"
"戈文达已经听完了教诲"
"he has taken refuge in the teachings"
"他皈依了佛法"
"But, my honoured friend, I must ask you"
"但是，我尊敬的朋友，我必须问你"
"don't you also want to walk the path of salvation?"
"你不也想走救赎之路吗？"
"Would you want to hesitate?"
"你还想犹豫吗？"
"do you want to wait any longer?"
"你还要等吗？"
Siddhartha awakened as if he had been asleep
悉达多醒来，仿佛刚刚睡着
For a long time, he looked into Govinda's face
他久久地注视着戈文达的脸
Then he spoke quietly, in a voice without mockery
然后他平静地开口，语气中没有嘲讽
"Govinda, my friend, now you have taken this step"
"戈文达，我的朋友，现在你已经迈出了这一步"
"now you have chosen this path"
"现在你已经选择了这条路"
"Always, oh Govinda, you've been my friend"
"噢，戈文达，你永远是我的朋友。"
"you've always walked one step behind me"
"你总是落后我一步"
"Often I have thought about you"
"我经常想起你"
"'Won't Govinda for once also take a step by himself'"
" '戈文达难道不愿意自己迈出一步吗？' "
"'won't Govinda take a step without me?'"

- 61 -

"'没有我，戈文达不会迈出一步吗？'"
"'won't he take a step driven by his own soul?'"
"'他不会迈出由自己的灵魂驱动的一步吗？'"

"Behold, now you've turned into a man"
"看哪，现在你已经变成一个男人了"

"you are choosing your path for yourself"
"你正在为自己选择道路"

"I wish that you would go it up to its end"
"我希望你能坚持到底"

"oh my friend, I hope that you shall find salvation!"
"噢，我的朋友，我希望你能得到救赎！"

Govinda, did not completely understand it yet
Govinda，还没有完全明白

he repeated his question in an impatient tone
他不耐烦地重复了他的问题

"Speak up, I beg you, my dear!"
"讲点儿话吧，亲爱的！"

"Tell me, since it could not be any other way"
"告诉我，因为没有别的办法"

"won't you also take your refuge with the exalted Buddha?"
"你不也皈依世尊佛陀吗？"

Siddhartha placed his hand on Govinda's shoulder
悉达多把手放在戈文达的肩膀上

"You failed to hear my good wish for you"
"你没听到我对你的祝福"

"I'm repeating my wish for you"
"我重复我对你的愿望"

"I wish that you would go this path"
"我希望你走这条路"

"I wish that you would go up to this path's end"
"我希望你能走到这条路的尽头"

"I wish that you shall find salvation!"
"我希望你能得到救赎！"

In this moment, Govinda realized that his friend had left him
此刻,戈文达意识到他的朋友已经离开了他

when he realized this he started to weep
当他意识到这一点时,他开始哭泣

"Siddhartha!" he exclaimed lamentingly
"悉达多!"他悲叹道。

Siddhartha kindly spoke to him
悉达多和蔼地跟他说话

"don't forget, Govinda, who you are"
"别忘了,戈文达,你是谁"

"you are now one of the Samanas of the Buddha"
"你现在是佛陀的沙门之一了"

"You have renounced your home and your parents"
"你已经抛弃了你的家和你的父母"

"you have renounced your birth and possessions"
"你已经放弃了你的出生和财产"

"you have renounced your free will"
"你已经放弃了你的自由意志"

"you have renounced all friendship"
"你已经放弃了所有的友谊"

"This is what the teachings require"
"这就是教义所要求的"

"this is what the exalted one wants"
"这就是尊者所希望的"

"This is what you wanted for yourself"
"这就是你想要的"

"Tomorrow, oh Govinda, I will leave you"
"明天,哦,戈文达,我将离开你"

For a long time, the friends continued walking in the garden
朋友们在花园里走了好久

for a long time, they lay there and found no sleep
他们躺在那里很久都没睡着

And over and over again, Govinda urged his friend

戈文达一次又一次地鼓励他的朋友

"why would you not want to seek refuge in Gotama's teachings?"
"为什么你不想皈依乔达摩的教义呢?"

"what fault could you find in these teachings?"
"你能在这些教义中发现什么错误吗?"

But Siddhartha turned away from his friend
但悉达多却抛弃了他的朋友

every time he said, "Be content, Govinda!"
每次他都说:"知足吧,戈文达!"

"Very good are the teachings of the exalted one"
"世尊的教诲非常好"

"how could I find a fault in his teachings?"
"我怎么能挑出他的教诲中的毛病呢?"

it was very early in the morning
当时是清晨

one of the oldest monks went through the garden
一位最年长的僧人穿过花园

he called to those who had taken their refuge in the teachings
他呼吁那些皈依教义的人

he called them to dress them up in the yellow robe
他叫他们穿上黄色长袍

and he instruct them in the first teachings and duties of their position
他教导他们最初的教义和职责

Govinda once again embraced his childhood friend
Govinda 再次拥抱了他的童年好友

and then he left with the novices
然后他和新手们一起离开了

But Siddhartha walked through the garden, lost in thought
但悉达多在花园里漫步,陷入沉思

Then he happened to meet Gotama, the exalted one

然后他偶然遇见了世尊乔达摩
he greeted him with respect
他很尊重地迎接他
the Buddha's glance was full of kindness and calm
佛陀的目光充满慈悲和平静
the young man summoned his courage
年轻人鼓起勇气
he asked the venerable one for the permission to talk to him
他请求尊者允许他和他谈话
Silently, the exalted one nodded his approval
尊者默默地点头表示同意
Spoke Siddhartha, "Yesterday, oh exalted one"
悉达多说道："昨天，世人啊。"
"I had been privileged to hear your wondrous teachings"
"我很荣幸能聆听您的精彩教诲"
"Together with my friend, I had come from afar, to hear your teachings"
"我和我的朋友从远方而来，聆听您的教诲"
"And now my friend is going to stay with your people"
"现在我的朋友要和你们的人在一起了"
"he has taken his refuge with you"
"他已经向你寻求庇护了"
"But I will again start on my pilgrimage"
"但我将再次踏上朝圣之旅"
"As you please," the venerable one spoke politely
"随你便吧，"尊者礼貌地说道
"Too bold is my speech," Siddhartha continued
"我的言论太大胆了，"悉达多继续说道
"but I do not want to leave the exalted on this note"
"但我不想就此放弃崇高的地位"
"I want to share with the most venerable one my honest thoughts"
"我想与最尊贵的人分享我的真实想法"

- 65 -

"Does it please the venerable one to listen for one moment longer?"
"尊者能否再听我一会儿？"
Silently, the Buddha nodded his approval
佛陀默默地点头表示同意
Spoke Siddhartha, "oh most venerable one"
悉达多说道，"尊者啊"
"there is one thing I have admired in your teachings most of all"
"在您的教诲中，有一件事是我最敬佩的"
"Everything in your teachings is perfectly clear"
"您的教诲非常清晰"
"what you speak of is proven"
"你所说的已经得到证实"
"you are presenting the world as a perfect chain"
"你把世界呈现为一个完美的链条"
"a chain which is never and nowhere broken"
"一条永远不会断的锁链"
"an eternal chain the links of which are causes and effects"
"一条永恒的链条，其环节是原因和结果"
"Never before, has this been seen so clearly"
"以前从未如此清晰地看到过这一点"
"never before, has this been presented so irrefutably"
"以前从来没有如此无可辩驳地提出这一点"
"truly, the heart of every Brahman has to beat stronger with love"
"确实，每个婆罗门的心都必须因爱而跳动得更强烈"
"he has seen the world through your perfectly connected teachings"
"他通过你完美相连的教导看到了世界"
"without gaps, clear as a crystal"
"毫无缝隙，晶莹剔透"
"not depending on chance, not depending on Gods"

"不依靠机会,不依靠神灵"
"he has to accept it whether it may be good or bad"
"无论好坏,他都必须接受"
"he has to live by it whether it would be suffering or joy"
"他必须靠它生存,无论是痛苦还是快乐"
"but I do not wish to discuss the uniformity of the world"
"但我不想讨论世界的统一性"
"it is possible that this is not essential"
"这可能不是必需的"
"everything which happens is connected"
"发生的一切都是相互关联的"
"the great and the small things are all encompassed"
"大事小事都包括在内"
"they are connected by the same forces of time"
"它们被相同的时间力量联系在一起"
"they are connected by the same law of causes"
"它们是由同一因果律联系在一起的"
"the causes of coming into being and of dying"
"存在和死亡的原因"
"this is what shines brightly out of your exalted teachings"
"这就是你崇高教义的闪光之处"
"But, according to your very own teachings, there is a small gap"
"但是,按照你的教导,还是有一点差距的。"
"this unity and necessary sequence of all things is broken in one place"
"万物的统一性和必然性顺序在一处被打破"
"this world of unity is invaded by something alien"
"这个团结的世界被某种外星生物入侵了"
"there is something new, which had not been there before"
"有一些新的东西,以前没有过"
"there is something which cannot be demonstrated"
"有些事情无法证明"
"there is something which cannot be proven"

"有些事情无法证明"
"these are your teachings of overcoming the world"
"这就是你战胜世界的教诲"
"these are your teachings of salvation"
"这些是你的救赎教义"
"But with this small gap, the eternal breaks apart again"
"但随着这小小的差距,永恒再次崩塌"
"with this small breach, the law of the world becomes void"
"只要有一点小小的违反,世界的法律就会失效"
"Please forgive me for expressing this objection"
"请原谅我表达这一反对意见"
Quietly, Gotama had listened to him, unmoved
乔达摩静静地听着他说,无动于衷
Now he spoke, the perfected one, with his kind and polite clear voice
现在他开口说话了,他是一个完美的人,用他亲切、礼貌、清晰的声音
"You've heard the teachings, oh son of a Brahman"
"婆罗门之子啊,你已经听到教诲了。"
"and good for you that you've thought about it this deeply"
"你能如此深入地思考这个问题真是太好了"
"You've found a gap in my teachings, an error"
"你发现了我的教导中的一个漏洞,一个错误"
"You should think about this further"
"你应该再考虑一下"
"But be warned, oh seeker of knowledge, of the thicket of opinions"
"但是,求知者啊,要警惕纷繁复杂的意见。"
"be warned of arguing about words"
"小心不要为言语争吵"
"There is nothing to opinions"
"没什么可发表意见的"
"they may be beautiful or ugly"
"它们可能美丽或丑陋"

"opinions may be smart or foolish"
"意见可能是聪明的,也可能是愚蠢的"
"everyone can support opinions, or discard them"
"每个人都可以支持观点,也可以抛弃它"
"But the teachings, you've heard from me, are no opinion"
"但你从我这里听到的教诲并不是意见。"
"their goal is not to explain the world to those who seek knowledge"
"他们的目标不是向那些寻求知识的人解释世界"
"They have a different goal"
"他们有不同的目标"
"their goal is salvation from suffering"
"他们的目标是从苦难中解脱出来"
"This is what Gotama teaches, nothing else"
"这就是乔达摩所教的,没有别的。"
"I wish that you, oh exalted one, would not be angry with me" said the young man
"我希望你,哦,尊贵的,不要对我生气。"年轻人说。
"I have not spoken to you like this to argue with you"
"我跟你这样说话,不是为了跟你争论"
"I do not wish to argue about words"
"我不想争论词语"
"You are truly right, there is little to opinions"
"你说得对,没什么可说的"
"But let me say one more thing"
"但是我再说一件事"
"I have not doubted in you for a single moment"
"我一刻也没有怀疑过你"
"I have not doubted for a single moment that you are Buddha"
"我一刻也没有怀疑过你是佛。"
"I have not doubted that you have reached the highest goal"
"我毫不怀疑你已经达到了最高目标"

"the highest goal towards which so many Brahmans are on their way"
"许多婆罗门追寻的最高目标"

"You have found salvation from death"
"你已经从死亡中找到了救赎"

"It has come to you in the course of your own search"
"它已经在你自己的探索过程中来到你身边了"

"it has come to you on your own path"
"它已经沿着你自己的道路来到你身边"

"it has come to you through thoughts and meditation"
"它通过思想和冥想来到你身边"

"it has come to you through realizations and enlightenment"
"它通过领悟和启蒙来到你身边"

"but it has not come to you by means of teachings!"
"但它不是通过教导来到你们这里的!"

"And this is my thought"
"这是我的想法"

"nobody will obtain salvation by means of teachings!"
"没有人能通过教义获得救赎!"

"You will not be able to convey your hour of enlightenment"
"你将无法传达你的顿悟时刻"

"words of what has happened to you won't convey the moment!"
"语言无法表达你所经历的那一刻!"

"The teachings of the enlightened Buddha contain much"
"佛陀的教诲包含很多内容"

"it teaches many to live righteously"
"它教导很多人过正义的生活"

"it teaches many to avoid evil"
"它教导很多人远离邪恶"

"But there is one thing which these teachings do not contain"
"但这些教义没有提到一件事"

"they are clear and venerable, but the teachings miss something"

"这些教诲清晰而庄严,但教义缺少了一些东西"
"the teachings do not contain the mystery"
"教义并不包含奥秘"
"the mystery of what the exalted one has experienced for himself"
"至高者亲身经历的奥秘"
"among hundreds of thousands, only he experienced it"
"千万人之中,只有他经历过"
"This is what I have thought and realized, when I heard the teachings"
"当我听到这些教诲时,我是这样想的,并且领悟到了这一点"
"This is why I am continuing my travels"
"这就是我继续旅行的原因"
"this is why I do not to seek other, better teachings"
"这就是为什么我不去寻求其他更好的教导"
"I know there are no better teachings"
"我知道没有比这更好的教导了"
"I leave to depart from all teachings and all teachers"
"我将离开一切教诲和一切老师"
"I leave to reach my goal by myself, or to die"
"我离开是为了自己达到目标,或者去死"
"But often, I'll think of this day, oh exalted one"
"但我时常会想起这一天,哦,尊贵的上帝。"
"and I'll think of this hour, when my eyes beheld a holy man"
"我会想起此刻,我的眼睛看见一位圣人"
The Buddha's eyes quietly looked to the ground
佛陀的眼睛静静地看着地面
quietly, in perfect equanimity, his inscrutable face was smiling
他那神秘莫测的脸上,静静地、镇定地微笑着
the venerable one spoke slowly
尊者慢慢地说道

"I wish that your thoughts shall not be in error"
"我希望你的想法不会有错误"
"I wish that you shall reach the goal!"
"祝你能够达成目标！"
"But there is something I ask you to tell me"
"但是我请你告诉我一件事"
"Have you seen the multitude of my Samanas?"
"您看见我的沙门这么多吗？"
"they have taken refuge in the teachings"
"他们皈依了教义"
"do you believe it would be better for them to abandon the teachings?"
"您认为他们放弃这些教义会更好吗？"
"should they to return into the world of desires?"
"难道他们还要回到欲望的世界吗？"
"Far is such a thought from my mind" exclaimed Siddhartha
"我根本没想过这个，"悉达多惊呼道
"I wish that they shall all stay with the teachings"
"我希望他们都能坚守教诲"
"I wish that they shall reach their goal!"
"祝愿他们能够达成目标！"
"It is not my place to judge another person's life"
"我没有资格评判别人的生活"
"I can only judge my own life "
"我只能评判我自己的人生"
"I must decide, I must chose, I must refuse"
"我必须决定，我必须选择，我必须拒绝"
"Salvation from the self is what we Samanas search for"
"我们沙门所追求的，就是摆脱自我"
"oh exalted one, if only I were one of your disciples"
"噢，世人，如果我是你的门徒之一就好了"
"I'd fear that it might happen to me"
"我担心这种事也会发生在我身上"
"only seemingly, would my self be calm and be redeemed"

"只有表面上，我才能平静下来，才能得到救赎"
"but in truth it would live on and grow"
"但事实上它会继续生存和成长"
"because then I would replace my self with the teachings"
"因为那样我就会用教义取代我自己"
"my self would be my duty to follow you"
"我的责任就是追随你"
"my self would be my love for you"
"我的自我就是我对你的爱"
"and my self would be the community of the monks!"
"而我自己将成为僧侣团体！"
With half of a smile Gotama looked into the stranger's eyes
乔达摩微笑着看着陌生人的眼睛
his eyes were unwaveringly open and kind
他的眼睛始终睁开，充满善意
he bid him to leave with a hardly noticeable gesture
他用一个几乎不引人注意的手势叫他离开
"You are wise, oh Samana" the venerable one spoke
"你真聪明，沙门。"尊者说道
"You know how to talk wisely, my friend"
"你知道如何明智地说话，我的朋友"
"Be aware of too much wisdom!"
"要警惕过多的智慧！"
The Buddha turned away
佛陀转身离去
Siddhartha would never forget his glance
悉达多永远不会忘记他的目光
his half smile remained forever etched in Siddhartha's memory
他的微笑永远铭刻在悉达多的记忆中
Siddhartha thought to himself
悉达多心里想着
"I have never before seen a person glance and smile this way"

"我从未见过有人能如此凝视和微笑"
"no one else sits and walks like he does"
"没有人像他那样坐着、走路"
"truly, I wish to be able to glance and smile this way"
"真的,我希望能够这样一瞥和微笑"
"I wish to be able to sit and walk this way, too"
"我也希望能够这样坐着、这样走路"
"liberated, venerable, concealed, open, childlike and mysterious"
"解放、庄严、隐秘、开放、童真、神秘"
"he must have succeeded in reaching the innermost part of his self"
"他一定已经成功触及到了他内心的最深处"
"only then can someone glance and walk this way"
"只有这样,才会有人瞥一眼并走这边"
"I will also seek to reach the innermost part of my self"
"我也会努力触及自我的最深处"
"I saw a man" Siddhartha thought
"我看到了一个人"悉达多想道
"a single man, before whom I would have to lower my glance"
"一个让我不得不低下头的男人"
"I do not want to lower my glance before anyone else"
"我不想在别人面前低下头来"
"No teachings will entice me more anymore"
"没有什么教义能比这更吸引我了"
"because this man's teachings have not enticed me"
"因为这个人的教导没有吸引我"
"I am deprived by the Buddha" thought Siddhartha
悉达多想:"佛陀剥夺了我一切。"
"I am deprived, although he has given so much"
"尽管他给了我很多,但我还是感到失落"
"he has deprived me of my friend"
"他夺走了我的朋友"

"my friend who had believed in me"
"我的朋友一直相信我"

"my friend who now believes in him"
"我的朋友现在相信他了"

"my friend who had been my shadow"
"我的朋友曾是我的影子"

"and now he is Gotama's shadow"
"现在他是乔达摩的影子"

"but he has given me Siddhartha"
"但他给了我悉达多"

"he has given me myself"
"他把自己给了我"

Awakening
唤醒

Siddhartha left the mango grove behind him
悉达多离开了芒果园
but he felt his past life also stayed behind
但他感觉自己过去的生活也留在了后面
the Buddha, the perfected one, stayed behind
佛陀，圆满者，留下来
and Govinda stayed behind too
戈文达也留下来了
and his past life had parted from him
过去的生活也离他而去
he pondered as he was walking slowly
他一边慢慢走着，一边思考着
he pondered about this sensation, which filled him completely
他沉思着这种感觉，它充满了他的内心
He pondered deeply, like diving into a deep water
他陷入沉思，就像潜入深水一样
he let himself sink down to the ground of the sensation
他让自己沉入感觉的地面
he let himself sink down to the place where the causes lie
他让自己沉沦到原因所在的地方
to identify the causes is the very essence of thinking
寻找原因是思考的本质
this was how it seemed to him
他觉得是这样
and by this alone, sensations turn into realizations
仅凭这一点，感觉就变成了认识
and these sensations are not lost
这些感觉并没有消失
but the sensations become entities
但感觉变成了实体

and the sensations start to emit what is inside of them
感觉开始释放出它们内部的东西
they show their truths like rays of light
它们像光线一样展现真理
Slowly walking along, Siddhartha pondered
悉达多一边慢慢地走着,一边沉思着
He realized that he was no youth any more
他意识到自己不再是年轻人了
he realized that he had turned into a man
他意识到自己已经变成了一个男人
He realized that something had left him
他意识到有什么东西离开了他
the same way a snake is left by its old skin
就像蛇会留下旧皮一样
what he had throughout his youth no longer existed in him
他年轻时拥有的一切在他身上已不复存在
it used to be a part of him; the wish to have teachers
这曾经是他的一部分;希望有老师
the wish to listen to teachings
听闻教诲的愿望
He had also left the last teacher who had appeared on his path
他也离开了出现在他人生道路上的最后一位老师
he had even left the highest and wisest teacher
他甚至离开了最高尚、最有智慧的老师
he had left the most holy one, Buddha
他离开了最神圣的佛陀
he had to part with him, unable to accept his teachings
他不得不与他分开,无法接受他的教导
Slower, he walked along in his thoughts
他放慢脚步,在思绪中前行
and he asked himself, "But what is this?"
他问自己:"但是这是什么?"

"what have you sought to learn from teachings and from teachers?"
"你想从教义和老师那里学到什么？"

"and what were they, who have taught you so much?"
"他们是谁，教会了你这么多东西？"

"what are they if they have been unable to teach you?"
"如果他们无法教你，那他们是什么呢？"

And he found, "It was the self"
他发现，"这就是自我"

"it was the purpose and essence of which I sought to learn"
"这就是我所寻求学习的目的和本质"

"It was the self I wanted to free myself from"
"我想要摆脱的是自我"

"the self which I sought to overcome"
"我试图克服的自我"

"But I was not able to overcome it"
"但我没能克服它"

"I could only deceive it"
"我只能欺骗它"

"I could only flee from it"
"我只能逃离它"

"I could only hide from it"
"我只能躲避它"

"Truly, no thing in this world has kept my thoughts so busy"
"真的，世界上没有什么事情能让我的思绪如此忙碌"

"I have been kept busy by the mystery of me being alive"
"我一直忙于寻找我活着的秘密"

"the mystery of me being one"
"我成为其中一员的奥秘"

"the mystery if being separated and isolated from all others"
"与其他人分离和孤立的奥秘"

"the mystery of me being Siddhartha!"
"我就是悉达多的秘密！"

"And there is no thing in this world I know less about"
"世界上没有比我更不了解的事情了"
he had been pondering while slowly walking along
他一边慢慢走着,一边思考着
he stopped as these thoughts caught hold of him
他停了下来,因为这些想法占据了他
and right away another thought sprang forth from these thoughts
另一个想法立刻从这些想法中冒了出来
"there's one reason why I know nothing about myself"
"我对自己一无所知,原因只有一个"
"there's one reason why Siddhartha has remained alien to me"
"席特哈尔塔对我来说始终很陌生,原因就在于此"
"all of this stems from one cause"
"这一切都源于一个原因"
"I was afraid of myself, and I was fleeing"
"我害怕自己,所以我在逃避"
"I have searched for both Atman and Brahman"
"我寻找的是阿特曼和梵天"
"for this I was willing to dissect my self"
"为此我愿意剖析自己"
"and I was willing to peel off all of its layers"
"我愿意剥去它所有的外皮"
"I wanted to find the core of all peels in its unknown interior"
"我想在一切果皮未知的内部找到其核心"
"the Atman, life, the divine part, the ultimate part"
"阿特曼,生命,神圣的部分,终极的部分"
"But I have lost myself in the process"
"但我在这个过程中迷失了自己"
Siddhartha opened his eyes and looked around
悉达多睁开双眼,环顾四周
looking around, a smile filled his face

环顾四周,他的脸上洋溢着微笑

a feeling of awakening from long dreams flowed through him

一种从长梦中醒来的感觉涌上心头

the feeling flowed from his head down to his toes

这种感觉从他的头流到脚趾

And it was not long before he walked again

不久他又能走路了

he walked quickly, like a man who knows what he has got to do

他走得很快,就像一个知道自己该做什么的人

"now I will not let Siddhartha escape from me again!"

"现在我不会再让悉达多从我身边逃走!"

"I no longer want to begin my thoughts and my life with Atman"

"我不再想以阿特曼开始我的思想和我的生活"

"nor do I want to begin my thoughts with the suffering of the world"

"我也不想从世界的苦难开始我的思考"

"I do not want to kill and dissect myself any longer"

"我不想再杀戮和解剖自己了"

"Yoga-Veda shall not teach me anymore"

"瑜伽吠陀不会再教我了"

"nor Atharva-Veda, nor the ascetics"

"阿闼婆吠陀,苦行僧"

"there will not be any kind of teachings"

"不会有任何形式的教导"

"I want to learn from myself and be my student"

"我想向自己学习并成为我的学生"

"I want to get to know myself; the secret of Siddhartha"

"我想要了解我自己;悉达多的秘密"

He looked around, as if he was seeing the world for the first time

他环顾四周，仿佛第一次看到这个世界
Beautiful and colourful was the world
世界是美丽而多彩的
strange and mysterious was the world
世界是陌生而神秘的
Here was blue, there was yellow, here was green
这里是蓝色，那里是黄色，这里是绿色
the sky and the river flowed
天空和河流流淌
the forest and the mountains were rigid
森林和山脉都很坚硬
all of the world was beautiful
整个世界都很美丽
all of it was mysterious and magical
这一切都是神秘而神奇的
and in its midst was he, Siddhartha, the awakening one
而他，悉达多，就是那位觉醒者
and he was on the path to himself
他走在自我的道路上
all this yellow and blue and river and forest entered Siddhartha
这一切黄色、蓝色、河流和森林都进入了悉达多的心中
for the first time it entered through the eyes
第一次通过眼睛进入
it was no longer a spell of Mara
这不再是玛拉的咒语
it was no longer the veil of Maya
它不再是玛雅的面纱
it was no longer a pointless and coincidental
这不再是一个毫无意义的巧合
things were not just a diversity of mere appearances
事物不仅仅是外表的多样性
appearances despicable to the deeply thinking Brahman

对于深思熟虑的婆罗门来说,这些外表是卑鄙的
the thinking Brahman scorns diversity, and seeks unity
有思想的婆罗门蔑视多样性,寻求统一

Blue was blue and river was river
蓝色是蓝色,河流是河流

the singular and divine lived hidden in Siddhartha
独特而神圣的存在隐藏在悉达多身上

divinity's way and purpose was to be yellow here, and blue there
神的方式和目的是这里是黄色,那里是蓝色

there sky, there forest, and here Siddhartha
那里有天空,那里有森林,这里还有悉达多

The purpose and essential properties was not somewhere behind the things
目的和本质属性并不隐藏在事物的背后

the purpose and essential properties was inside of everything
目的和本质属性存在于万物之中

"How deaf and stupid have I been!" he thought
"我真是又聋又蠢!"他想。

and he walked swiftly along
他快步走过去

"When someone reads a text he will not scorn the symbols and letters"
"当人们阅读文本时,他不会轻视其中的符号和字母"

"he will not call the symbols deceptions or coincidences"
"他不会称这些符号为欺骗或巧合"

"but he will read them as they were written"
"但他会按照所写的读出来"

"he will study and love them, letter by letter"
"他将逐字逐句地研究并喜爱这些信件"

"I wanted to read the book of the world and scorned the letters"

"我想读世界之书，蔑视文字"
"I wanted to read the book of myself and scorned the symbols"
"我想读我自己的书并蔑视其中的符号"
"I called my eyes and my tongue coincidental"
"我称我的眼睛和我的舌头是巧合"
"I said they were worthless forms without substance"
"我说它们只是毫无意义的形式，没有实质内容"
"No, this is over, I have awakened"
"不，这已经结束了，我已经醒了"
"I have indeed awakened"
"我确实醒了"
"I had not been born before this very day"
"今天之前我还没出生"
In thinking these thoughts, Siddhartha suddenly stopped once again
正想着这些事情的时候，悉达多突然又停了下来。
he stopped as if there was a snake lying in front of him
他停了下来，就像有一条蛇躺在他面前一样
suddenly, he had also become aware of something else
突然，他还意识到了其他的事情
He was indeed like someone who had just woken up
他确实像刚睡醒的人
he was like a new-born baby starting life anew
他就像一个新生的婴儿开始新的生活
and he had to start again at the very beginning
他必须从头开始
in the morning he had had very different intentions
早上他有完全不同的意图
he had thought to return to his home and his father
他本想回家，回到父亲身边
But now he stopped as if a snake was lying on his path
但现在他停了下来，就像一条蛇躺在他的路上一样。
he made a realization of where he was

他意识到自己身在何处

"I am no longer the one I was"
"我不再是原来的我了"

"I am no ascetic anymore"
"我不再是苦行僧了"

"I am not a priest anymore"
"我不再是一名牧师了"

"I am no Brahman anymore"
"我不再是婆罗门了"

"Whatever should I do at my father's place?"
"我到我爸爸那儿去干什么好呢?"

"Study? Make offerings? Practise meditation?"
"学习?供养?修行?"

"But all this is over for me"
"但对我来说这一切都结束了"

"all of this is no longer on my path"
"这一切都不再在我的道路上"

Motionless, Siddhartha remained standing there
悉达多一动不动地站在那里

and for the time of one moment and breath, his heart felt cold
一瞬间,他的心感觉冰冷

he felt a coldness in his chest
他感觉胸口一阵冰冷

the same feeling a small animal feels when it sees how alone it is
就像小动物看到自己有多孤独时的感觉一样

For many years, he had been without home and had felt nothing
多年来,他一直无家可归,什么感觉也没有。

Now, he felt he had been without a home
现在他感觉自己无家可归

Still, even in the deepest meditation, he had been his father's son

然而，即使在最深沉的冥想中，他仍然是他父亲的儿子

he had been a Brahman, of a high caste
他是一个婆罗门，属于高种姓

he had been a cleric
他曾是一名牧师

Now, he was nothing but Siddhartha, the awoken one
现在，他只是悉达多，一个觉醒者

nothing else was left of him
他什么也没剩下

Deeply, he inhaled and felt cold
他深吸一口气，感觉一阵寒冷

a shiver ran through his body
他浑身发抖

Nobody was as alone as he was
没有人像他一样孤独

There was no nobleman who did not belong to the noblemen
没有一个贵族不属于贵族

there was no worker that did not belong to the workers
没有一个工人不属于工人

they had all found refuge among themselves
他们都找到了自己的避难所

they shared their lives and spoke their languages
他们分享生活、讲语言

there are no Brahman who would not be regarded as Brahmans
不存在不被视为婆罗门的婆罗门

and there are no Brahmans that didn't live as Brahmans
不存在不以婆罗门身份生活的婆罗门

there are no ascetic who could not find refuge with the Samanas
没有一个苦行者不能得到沙门的庇护

and even the most forlorn hermit in the forest was not alone

即使是森林中最孤独的隐士也不是孤独的
he was also surrounded by a place he belonged to
他周围也有他所属的地方
he also belonged to a caste in which he was at home
他也属于一个他熟悉的种姓
Govinda had left him and became a monk
戈文达离开了他，成为一名僧人
and a thousand monks were his brothers
他的兄弟有一千名僧侣
they wore the same robe as him
他们穿着和他一样的长袍
they believed in his faith and spoke his language
他们相信他的信仰，说他的语言
But he, Siddhartha, where did he belong to?
但他，悉达多，他属于哪里？
With whom would he share his life?
他会与谁分享他的生活？
Whose language would he speak?
他会说谁的语言？
the world melted away all around him
他周围的世界都消失了
he stood alone like a star in the sky
他孤独地矗立着，就像天空中的一颗星星
cold and despair surrounded him
寒冷和绝望包围了他
but Siddhartha emerged out of this moment
但悉达多却在此刻出现了
Siddhartha emerged more his true self than before
悉达多比以前更加真实地展现了自我
he was more firmly concentrated than he had ever been
他比以前更加集中注意力
He felt; "this had been the last tremor of the awakening"
他感到，"这是觉醒的最后一次震动"
"the last struggle of this birth"

"此次诞生的最后一次挣扎"
And it was not long until he walked again in long strides
不久之后,他又迈开大步走了。
he started to proceed swiftly and impatiently
他开始急躁地快速前进
he was no longer going home
他不再回家了
he was no longer going to his father
他不再去找他父亲了

Part Two
第二部分

***

Kamala
卡马拉

Siddhartha learned something new on every step of his path
悉达多在他的人生道路上每走一步都会学到新的东西
because the world was transformed and his heart was enchanted
因为世界被改变了，他的心被迷住了
He saw the sun rising over the mountains
他看到太阳从山上升起
and he saw the sun setting over the distant beach
他看到太阳在远处的海滩上落下
At night, he saw the stars in the sky in their fixed positions
晚上，他看到天空中的星星在固定的位置
and he saw the crescent of the moon floating like a boat in the blue
他看见一弯新月像一艘小船一样漂浮在蔚蓝的天空中
He saw trees, stars, animals, and clouds
他看到了树木、星星、动物和云朵
rainbows, rocks, herbs, flowers, streams and rivers
彩虹、岩石、草本植物、花朵、溪流和河流
he saw the glistening dew in the bushes in the morning
清晨，他看见灌木丛中闪闪发光的露珠
he saw distant high mountains which were blue
他看见远处的高山是蓝色的
wind blew through the rice-field
风吹过稻田
all of this, a thousand-fold and colourful, had always been there

这一切千姿百态、色彩斑斓，一直都在那里
the sun and the moon had always shone
太阳和月亮一直闪耀
rivers had always roared and bees had always buzzed
河流总是咆哮，蜜蜂总是嗡嗡叫
but in former times all of this had been a deceptive veil
但在过去，这一切都是一层欺骗性的面纱
to him it had been nothing more than fleeting
对他来说，这不过是转瞬即逝的
it was supposed to be looked upon in distrust
人们本应以不信任的态度看待它
it was destined to be penetrated and destroyed by thought
它注定要被思想渗透和摧毁
since it was not the essence of existence
因为它不是存在的本质
since this essence lay beyond, on the other side of, the visible
因为这个本质存在于可见事物的另一边
But now, his liberated eyes stayed on this side
但现在，他解放出来的目光却停留在这边
he saw and became aware of the visible
他看到并意识到可见的
he sought to be at home in this world
他想在这个世界上找到归属感
he did not search for the true essence
他没有寻找真正的本质
he did not aim at a world beyond
他的目标并不是超越世界
this world was beautiful enough for him
这个世界对他来说已经足够美丽
looking at it like this made everything childlike
这样看着，一切都变得童真起来
Beautiful were the moon and the stars
月亮和星星很美丽

beautiful was the stream and the banks
溪流和河岸很美

the forest and the rocks, the goat and the gold-beetle
森林和岩石、山羊和金甲虫

the flower and the butterfly; beautiful and lovely it was
花和蝴蝶,美丽又可爱

to walk through the world was childlike again
走遍世界又恢复了童真

this way he was awoken
这样他就被唤醒了

this way he was open to what is near
这样他就能对即将发生的事情持开放态度

this way he was without distrust
这样他就不再怀疑了

differently the sun burnt the head
不同的是太阳灼伤了头部

differently the shade of the forest cooled him down
不同的是,森林的树荫让他凉爽下来

differently the pumpkin and the banana tasted
南瓜和香蕉的味道不同

Short were the days, short were the nights
白天短暂,夜晚短暂

every hour sped swiftly away like a sail on the sea
每一个小时都像海上的船帆一样飞快地流逝

and under the sail was a ship full of treasures, full of joy
船帆下是一艘满载宝藏的船,满载欢乐

Siddhartha saw a group of apes moving through the high canopy
悉达多看见一群猿猴在高高的树冠间穿梭

they were high in the branches of the trees
它们在树枝上

and he heard their savage, greedy song
他听到了他们野蛮贪婪的歌声

Siddhartha saw a male sheep following a female one and mating with her
悉达多看见一只公羊跟着一只母羊,并和母羊交配
In a lake of reeds, he saw the pike hungrily hunting for its dinner
在一片芦苇湖里,他看到一条梭子鱼正在饥饿地寻找晚餐
young fish were propelling themselves away from the pike
小鱼正在远离梭子鱼
they were scared, wiggling and sparkling
它们很害怕,扭动着,闪闪发光
the young fish jumped in droves out of the water
小鱼成群结队地跳出水面
the scent of strength and passion came forcefully out of the water
力量和激情的气息从水中强烈地散发出来
and the pike stirred up the scent
梭子鱼激起了气味
All of this had always existed
这一切一直存在
and he had not seen it, nor had he been with it
他既没有看见它,也没有和它在一起
Now he was with it and he was part of it
现在他已融入其中并成为其中的一部分
Light and shadow ran through his eyes
光与影在他眼中穿梭
stars and moon ran through his heart
星星和月亮穿过他的心

Siddhartha remembered everything he had experienced in the Garden Jetavana
悉达多记得他在祇园所经历的一切
he remembered the teaching he had heard there from the divine Buddha

他记得在那里听到的佛陀的教诲
he remembered the farewell from Govinda
他记得戈文达的告别
he remembered the conversation with the exalted one
他想起了与尊贵者的对话
Again he remembered his own words that he had spoken to the exalted one
他又想起自己对至高者说过的话
he remembered every word
他记得每一个字
he realized he had said things which he had not really known
他意识到自己说了一些他并不知道的事情
he astonished himself with what he had said to Gotama
他对乔达摩说的话令他自己都感到惊讶
the Buddha's treasure and secret was not the teachings
佛陀的宝藏和秘密不是教诲
but the secret was the inexpressible and not teachable
但这个秘密是无法表达和无法传授的
the secret which he had experienced in the hour of his enlightenment
他在开悟的时刻所经历的秘密
the secret was nothing but this very thing which he had now gone to experience
秘密就是他现在要去体验的这件事
the secret was what he now began to experience
秘密在于他现在开始经历
Now he had to experience his self
现在他必须体验自我
he had already known for a long time that his self was Atman
他早就知道他自己就是阿特曼
he knew Atman bore the same eternal characteristics as Brahman

他知道阿特曼具有与梵天相同的永恒特征
But he had never really found this self
但他从未真正找到过这个自我
because he had wanted to capture the self in the net of thought
因为他想把自我困在思想之网里
but the body was not part of the self
但身体不是自我的一部分
it was not the spectacle of the senses
这不是感官的奇观
so it also was not the thought, nor the rational mind
所以这也不是思想，也不是理性的
it was not the learned wisdom, nor the learned ability
这不是后天习得的智慧，也不是后天习得的能力
from these things no conclusions could be drawn
从这些事情无法得出结论
No, the world of thought was also still on this side
不，思想的世界也还在这边
Both, the thoughts as well as the senses, were pretty things
思想和感觉都是美好的事物
but the ultimate meaning was hidden behind both of them
但两者背后都隐藏着最终的意义
both had to be listened to and played with
两者都需要被倾听和玩弄
neither had to be scorned nor overestimated
既不值得蔑视，也不值得高估
there were secret voices of the innermost truth
有内心深处的秘密声音
these voices had to be attentively perceived
这些声音必须被仔细聆听
He wanted to strive for nothing else
他不想为其他事情奋斗
he would do what the voice commanded him to do
他会按照声音的命令去做

he would dwell where the voices advised him to
他会住在声音建议他住的地方
Why had Gotama sat down under the Bodhi tree?
乔达摩为何坐在菩提树下？
He had heard a voice in his own heart
他听到了自己内心的一个声音
a voice which had commanded him to seek rest under this tree
一个声音命令他在这棵树下休息
he could have gone on to make offerings
他本可以继续奉献
he could have performed his ablutions
他本可以进行沐浴
he could have spent that moment in prayer
他本可以用那一刻来祈祷
he had chosen not to eat or drink
他选择不吃不喝
he had chosen not to sleep or dream
他选择不睡觉，不做梦
instead, he had obeyed the voice
相反，他听从了声音
To obey like this was good
如此顺服是好的
it was good not to obey to an external command
不服从外部命令是件好事
it was good to obey only the voice
只听从声音就好了
to be ready like this was good and necessary
做好这样的准备是好的而且是必要的
there was nothing else that was necessary
没有其他必要的事情

in the night Siddhartha got to a river
夜里，悉达多来到一条河边

he slept in the straw hut of a ferryman
他睡在船夫的草屋里
this night Siddhartha had a dream
这天晚上,悉达多做了一个梦
Govinda was standing in front of him
戈文达站在他面前
he was dressed in the yellow robe of an ascetic
他穿着苦行僧的黄色长袍
Sad was how Govinda looked
Govinda 看起来很悲伤
sadly he asked, "Why have you forsaken me?"
他悲伤地问道:"你为什么抛弃我?"
Siddhartha embraced Govinda, and wrapped his arms around him
悉达多拥抱了戈文达,用双臂紧紧地抱住了他
he pulled him close to his chest and kissed him
他把他拉到胸前并亲吻他
but it was not Govinda anymore, but a woman
但那不再是戈文达,而是一个女人
a full breast popped out of the woman's dress
一个丰满的乳房从女人的衣服里凸出来
Siddhartha lay and drank from the breast
悉达多躺下,喝着奶水
sweetly and strongly tasted the milk from this breast
尝起来甜甜的,浓浓的,来自这乳房的乳汁
It tasted of woman and man
它有男人和女人的味道
it tasted of sun and forest
它有阳光和森林的味道
it tasted of animal and flower
它有动物和花的味道
it tasted of every fruit and every joyful desire
它尝到了每一种水果和每一种快乐的愿望
It intoxicated him and rendered him unconscious

它使他陶醉并失去意识
Siddhartha woke up from the dream
悉达多从梦中醒来
the pale river shimmered through the door of the hut
苍白的河水透过小屋的门闪闪发光
a dark call of an owl resounded deeply through the forest
猫头鹰的阴沉叫声响彻森林
Siddhartha asked the ferryman to get him across the river
悉达多请求船夫送他过河
The ferryman got him across the river on his bamboo-raft
船夫用竹筏把他送过河
the water shimmered reddish in the light of the morning
晨曦中，水面泛着微红的光芒
"This is a beautiful river," he said to his companion
他对同伴说："这是一条美丽的河流。"
"Yes," said the ferryman, "a very beautiful river"
"是的，"船夫说，"一条非常美丽的河流。"
"I love it more than anything"
"我比任何人都更爱它"
"Often I have listened to it"
"我经常听它"
"often I have looked into its eyes"
"我经常看着它的眼睛"
"and I have always learned from it"
"我一直从中吸取教训"
"Much can be learned from a river"
"从河流中可以学到很多东西"
"I thank you, my benefactor" spoke Siddhartha
"谢谢你，我的恩人。"悉达多说道。
he disembarked on the other side of the river
他在河对岸下船
"I have no gift I could give you for your hospitality, my dear"
"亲爱的，我没有礼物可以回报你的热情款待。"

"and I also have no payment for your work"
"而且我也没有得到你的报酬"

"I am a man without a home"
"我是一个没有家的人"

"I am the son of a Brahman and a Samana"
"我是婆罗门与沙门的儿子"

"I did see it," spoke the ferryman
"我确实看见了，"船夫说。

"I did not expect any payment from you"
"我没指望你付钱"

"it is custom for guests to bear a gift"
"按照习俗，客人要带礼物"

"but I did not expect this from you either"
"但我也没有想到你会这么做"

"You will give me the gift another time"
"你下次再给我礼物吧"

"Do you think so?" asked Siddhartha, bemusedly
"你这样认为吗？"悉达多困惑地问道。

"I am sure of it," replied the ferryman
船夫回答说："我确信如此。"

"This too, I have learned from the river"
"这也是我从河流中学到的"

"everything that goes comes back!"
"逝去的一切都将重来！"

"You too, Samana, will come back"
"沙门，你也会回来的。"

"Now farewell! Let your friendship be my reward"
"现在再见！愿你的友谊成为我的奖赏"

"Commemorate me, when you make offerings to the gods"
"当你向神灵献祭时，请纪念我"

Smiling, they parted from each other
他们微笑着分开

Smiling, Siddhartha was happy about the friendship
悉达多微笑着，对友谊感到高兴

and he was happy about the kindness of the ferryman
他对渡船夫的好意感到高兴

"He is like Govinda," he thought with a smile
"他就像戈文达，" 他笑着想道。

"all I meet on my path are like Govinda"
"我一路上遇见的所有人都像戈文达一样"

"All are thankful for what they have"
"每个人都对自己拥有的一切心存感激"

"but they are the ones who would have a right to receive thanks"
"但他们才是有权获得感谢的人"

"all are submissive and would like to be friends"
"所有人都很顺从，愿意成为朋友"

"all like to obey and think little"
"大家都喜欢服从，很少思考"

"all people are like children"
"所有人都像孩子一样"

At about noon, he came through a village
中午时分，他经过一个村庄，

In front of the mud cottages, children were rolling about in the street
在泥屋前，孩子们在街上打滚

they were playing with pumpkin-seeds and sea-shells
他们正在玩南瓜籽和贝壳

they screamed and wrestled with each other
他们尖叫着，互相扭打

but they all timidly fled from the unknown Samana
但他们都胆怯地逃离了这位不知名的沙门

In the end of the village, the path led through a stream
村子尽头有一条小路穿过一条小溪

by the side of the stream, a young woman was kneeling
小溪边，一名年轻女子跪着

she was washing clothes in the stream

她正在溪里洗衣服
When Siddhartha greeted her, she lifted her head
当悉达多向她打招呼时,她抬起了头
and she looked up to him with a smile
她抬头微笑地看着他
he could see the white in her eyes glistening
他看到她眼白闪闪发光
He called out a blessing to her
他向她祈福
this was the custom among travellers
这是旅行者的习俗
and he asked how far it was to the large city
他问到大城市有多远
Then she got up and came to him
然后她站起来走向他
beautifully her wet mouth was shimmering in her young face
她湿润的嘴唇在年轻的脸上闪闪发光
She exchanged humorous banter with him
她和他开玩笑
she asked whether he had eaten already
她问他是否已经吃饭了
and she asked curious questions
她问了一些好奇的问题
"is it true that the Samanas slept alone in the forest at night?"
"沙门们晚上真的独自在森林里睡觉吗?"
"is it true Samanas are not allowed to have women with them"
"沙门真的不允许带女人吗?"
While talking, she put her left foot on his right one
说话的时候,她把左脚放在他的右脚上
the movement of a woman who would want to initiate sexual pleasure
想要引发性快感的女性的动作

- 99 -

the textbooks call this "climbing a tree"
教科书称之为"爬树"
Siddhartha felt his blood heating up
悉达多感觉血液在沸腾
he had to think of his dream again
他不得不再次回想他的梦想
he bend slightly down to the woman
他向女人微微弯下腰
and he kissed with his lips the brown nipple of her breast
他用嘴唇亲吻她棕色的乳头
Looking up, he saw her face smiling
抬头看见她脸上带着微笑
and her eyes were full of lust
她的眼睛里充满了欲望
Siddhartha also felt desire for her
悉达多也对她心生渴望
he felt the source of his sexuality moving
他感觉到他的性欲源头在移动
but he had never touched a woman before
但他从未碰过女人
so he hesitated for a moment
所以他犹豫了一下
his hands were already prepared to reach out for her
他的双手已经准备好向她伸出
but then he heard the voice of his innermost self
但随后他听到了内心深处的声音
he shuddered with awe at his voice
他听到他的声音,不禁颤抖起来
and this voice told him no
这个声音告诉他不
all charms disappeared from the young woman's smiling face
年轻女子的笑脸不再迷人
he no longer saw anything else but a damp glance

他再也看不到别的，只有一双湿漉漉的眼睛
all he could see was female animal in heat
他所看到的只是发情的雌性动物
Politely, he petted her cheek
他礼貌地抚摸着她的脸颊
he turned away from her and disappeared away
他转身离开了她
he left from the disappointed woman with light steps
他轻盈地从失望的女人身边离开
and he disappeared into the bamboo-wood
然后他消失在竹林里

he reached the large city before the evening
傍晚之前他到达了这座大城市
and he was happy to have reached the city
他很高兴到达了这座城市
because he felt the need to be among people
因为他觉得需要和人们在一起
or a long time, he had lived in the forests
或者很长一段时间，他一直住在森林里
for first time in a long time he slept under a roof
这是他很长时间以来第一次在屋檐下睡觉
Before the city was a beautifully fenced garden
在城市成为一座美丽的围栏花园之前
the traveller came across a small group of servants
旅行者遇到了一小群仆人
the servants were carrying baskets of fruit
仆人们提着一篮篮水果
four servants were carrying an ornamental sedan-chair
四个仆人抬着一顶花轿
on this chair sat a woman, the mistress
椅子上坐着一位女人，是女主人
she was on red pillows under a colourful canopy
她躺在五彩缤纷的华盖下的红色枕头上

Siddhartha stopped at the entrance to the pleasure-garden
悉达多在花园门口停了下来
and he watched the parade go by
他看着游行队伍经过
he saw saw the servants and the maids
他看见了仆人和女仆
he saw the baskets and the sedan-chair
他看见了篮子和轿子
and he saw the lady on the chair
他看见椅子上的那位女士
Under her black hair he saw a very delicate face
在她黑色的头发下,他看见一张非常精致的脸
a bright red mouth, like a freshly cracked fig
鲜红的嘴巴,像一颗刚裂开的无花果
eyebrows which were well tended and painted in a high arch
眉毛修得非常好,而且画得很高
they were smart and watchful dark eyes
那是一双聪明而警觉的黑眼睛
a clear, tall neck rose from a green and golden garment
一条清晰而高大的脖子从绿色和金色的衣服中升起。
her hands were resting, long and thin
她的手又长又细
she had wide golden bracelets over her wrists
她的手腕上戴着宽大的金手镯
Siddhartha saw how beautiful she was, and his heart rejoiced
悉达多看到她如此美丽,心里很高兴
He bowed deeply, when the sedan-chair came closer
当轿子靠近时,他深深地鞠了一躬
straightening up again, he looked at the fair, charming face
他重新直起身子,看着那张白净迷人的脸
he read her smart eyes with the high arcs
他读懂了她那双高挑的漂亮眼睛

he breathed in a fragrance of something he did not know
他呼吸着一种他不知道的香味
With a smile, the beautiful woman nodded for a moment
美女微笑着点了点头
then she disappeared into the garden
然后她消失在花园里
and then the servants disappeared as well
然后仆人们也消失了
"I am entering this city with a charming omen" Siddhartha thought
"我带着一个迷人的预兆进入这座城市" 悉达多想道
He instantly felt drawn into the garden
他立刻被花园吸引住了
but he thought about his situation
但他考虑了自己的处境
he became aware of how the servants and maids had looked at him
他意识到仆人和女仆们是如何看着他的
they thought him despicable, distrustful, and rejected him
他们认为他卑鄙无耻，不信任他，并拒绝了他
"I am still a Samana" he thought
"我还是个沙门。"他想。
"I am still an ascetic and beggar"
"我仍然是一个苦行僧和乞丐"
"I must not remain like this"
"我不能再这样下去了"
"I will not be able to enter the garden like this," he laughed
他笑着说："这样我就进不了花园了。"
he asked the next person who came along the path about the garden
他向下一个走过来的人询问花园的情况
and he asked for the name of the woman
他问那女人的名字

he was told that this was the garden of Kamala, the famous courtesan
有人告诉他,这是著名妓女卡玛拉的花园
and he was told that she also owned a house in the city
并被告知她在城里也有一所房子
Then, he entered the city with a goal
然后他带着目标进入这座城市
Pursuing his goal, he allowed the city to suck him in
为了追求自己的目标,他让这座城市将他吞没
he drifted through the flow of the streets
他穿梭在街道人流中
he stood still on the squares in the city
他静静地站在城市的广场上
he rested on the stairs of stone by the river
他在河边的石阶上休息
When the evening came, he made friends with a barber's assistant
到了晚上,他和一位理发师助理交上了朋友
he had seen him working in the shade of an arch
他看见他在拱门的阴影下工作
and he found him again praying in a temple of Vishnu
他又发现他在毗湿奴神庙里祈祷
he told about stories of Vishnu and the Lakshmi
他讲述了毗湿奴和拉克希米的故事
Among the boats by the river, he slept this night
在河边的船只中,他睡了一夜
Siddhartha came to him before the first customers came into his shop
在第一批顾客进入他的商店之前,悉达多就来找他
he had the barber's assistant shave his beard and cut his hair
他让理发师的助手刮掉胡子并剪掉头发
he combed his hair and anointed it with fine oil
他梳理头发,涂上上好的油
Then he went to take his bath in the river

然后他去河里洗澡

late in the afternoon, beautiful Kamala approached her garden
下午晚些时候,美丽的卡马拉来到她的花园
Siddhartha was standing at the entrance again
悉达多又站在门口
he made a bow and received the courtesan's greeting
他鞠躬接受妓女的问候
he got the attention of one of the servant
他引起了一个仆人的注意
he asked him to inform his mistress
他要求他通知他的情妇
"a young Brahman wishes to talk to her"
"一位年轻的婆罗门想和她谈谈"
After a while, the servant returned
过了一会儿,仆人回来了
the servant asked Siddhartha to follow him
仆人叫悉达多跟着他
Siddhartha followed the servant into a pavilion
悉达多跟着仆人走进了一座亭子。
here Kamala was lying on a couch
卡马拉正躺在沙发上
and the servant left him alone with her
仆人就留下他和她单独在一起
"Weren't you also standing out there yesterday, greeting me?" asked Kamala
"你昨天不是也站在那里跟我打招呼吗?"卡玛拉问道
"It's true that I've already seen and greeted you yesterday"
"确实,我昨天已经见过你,还跟你打过招呼了。"
"But didn't you yesterday wear a beard, and long hair?"
"但是你昨天不是留着胡子和长发吗?"
"and was there not dust in your hair?"

"你的头发里没有灰尘吗？"

"You have observed well, you have seen everything"
"你观察得很好，你看到了一切"

"You have seen Siddhartha, the son of a Brahman"
"你见到的是婆罗门之子悉达多。"

"the Brahman who has left his home to become a Samana"
"出家为沙门的婆罗门"

"the Brahman who has been a Samana for three years"
"当了三年沙门的婆罗门"

"But now, I have left that path and came into this city"
"但现在，我离开了那条路，来到了这座城市。"

"and the first one I met, even before I had entered the city, was you"
"而我还没进城，第一个遇见的人就是你"

"To say this, I have come to you, oh Kamala!"
"我来找你就是想告诉你这些，卡玛拉！"

"before, Siddhartha addressed all woman with his eyes to the ground"
"此前，悉达多一直低着头对所有的女人说话。"

"You are the first woman whom I address otherwise"
"你是第一个我用不同方式对待的女人"

"Never again do I want to turn my eyes to the ground"
"我再也不想低头看地了"

"I won't turn when I'm coming across a beautiful woman"
"当我遇到美女时我不会转身"

Kamala smiled and played with her fan of peacocks' feathers

卡玛拉微笑着，玩弄着她的孔雀羽毛扇子

"And only to tell me this, Siddhartha has come to me?"
"悉达多来找我，只是为了告诉我这件事吗？"

"To tell you this and to thank you for being so beautiful"
"告诉你这些并感谢你如此美丽"

"I would like to ask you to be my friend and teacher"
"我想请你做我的朋友和老师"

"for I know nothing yet of that art which you have mastered"
"因为我还不知道你所掌握的艺术"

At this, Kamala laughed aloud
听到这里,卡玛拉哈哈大笑起来

"Never before this has happened to me, my friend"
"我的朋友,这种事从来没有发生在我身上"

"a Samana from the forest came to me and wanted to learn from me!"
"一位来自森林的沙门来到我面前,想向我学习!"

"Never before this has happened to me"
"我以前从来没有遇到过这种事"

"a Samana came to me with long hair and an old, torn loincloth!"
"一位沙门向我走来,他留着长发,身上缠着一条破旧的缠腰布!"

"Many young men come to me"
"很多年轻人来找我"

"and there are also sons of Brahmans among them"
"其中也有婆罗门之子"

"but they come in beautiful clothes"
"但他们穿着漂亮的衣服"

"they come in fine shoes"
"他们穿着精致的鞋子"

"they have perfume in their hair
"她们的头发上都有香水

"and they have money in their pouches"
"他们的口袋里有钱"

"This is how the young men are like, who come to me"
"来找我的年轻人都是这样的"

Spoke Siddhartha, "Already I am starting to learn from you"
悉达多说道:"我已经开始向你学习了。"

"Even yesterday, I was already learning"
"昨天我就已经开始学习了"

"I have already taken off my beard"

"我已经把胡子剃掉了"

"I have combed the hair"
"我梳理过头发了"

"and I have oil in my hair"
"而且我的头发上有油"

"There is little which is still missing in me"
"我身上几乎还缺少什么"

"oh excellent one, fine clothes, fine shoes, money in my pouch"
"哦,太棒了,漂亮的衣服,漂亮的鞋子,我的袋子里还有钱"

"You shall know Siddhartha has set harder goals for himself"
"你应该知道悉达多为自己设定了更艰巨的目标"

"and he has reached these goals"
"他已经实现了这些目标"

"How shouldn't I reach that goal?"
"我怎么就达不到那个目标呢?"

"the goal which I have set for myself yesterday"
"我昨天为自己设定的目标"

"to be your friend and to learn the joys of love from you"
"成为你的朋友,从你身上学习爱的乐趣"

"You'll see that I'll learn quickly, Kamala"
"你会发现我学得很快,卡玛拉"

"I have already learned harder things than what you're supposed to teach me"
"我已经学到了比你教给我的更难的东西"

"And now let's get to it"
"现在我们开始吧"

"You aren't satisfied with Siddhartha as he is?"
"您对悉达多现在的样子不满意吗?"

"with oil in his hair, but without clothes"
"头发上抹着油,却没有穿衣服"

"Siddhartha without shoes, without money"

"悉达多没有鞋子,没有钱"

Laughing, Kamala exclaimed, "No, my dear"
卡玛拉大笑着说:"不,亲爱的。"

"he doesn't satisfy me, yet"
"他还不能让我满意"

"Clothes are what he must have"
"衣服是他必须拥有的东西"

"pretty clothes, and shoes is what he needs"
"他需要漂亮的衣服和鞋子"

"pretty shoes, and lots of money in his pouch"
"漂亮的鞋子,口袋里有很多钱"

"and he must have gifts for Kamala"
"他一定给卡玛拉准备了礼物"

"Do you know it now, Samana from the forest?"
"现在你知道了吗,森林里的沙门?"

"Did you mark my words?"
"你记住我的话了吗?"

"Yes, I have marked your words," Siddhartha exclaimed
"是的,我记住了你的话。" 悉达多大声说道。

"How should I not mark words which are coming from such a mouth!"
"我怎么能不记住从这样的嘴里说出的话呢!"

"Your mouth is like a freshly cracked fig, Kamala"
"你的嘴就像一颗刚裂开的无花果,卡玛拉"

"My mouth is red and fresh as well"
"我的嘴巴也变得红润清新了"

"it will be a suitable match for yours, you'll see"
"这将是一场适合你的比赛,你会看到的"

"But tell me, beautiful Kamala"
"但是告诉我吧,美丽的卡玛拉"

"aren't you at all afraid of the Samana from the forest""
"难道你一点也不害怕森林里的沙门吗?"

"the Samana who has come to learn how to make love"
"来学习做爱的沙门"

"Whatever for should I be afraid of a Samana?"
　"我为何怕沙门？"

"a stupid Samana from the forest"
　"来自森林的愚蠢沙门"

"a Samana who is coming from the jackals"
　"从豺狼群中走出来的沙门"

"a Samana who doesn't even know yet what women are?"
　"一个连女人是什么都不知道的沙门？"

"Oh, he's strong, the Samana"
　"噢，他很强大，沙门。"

"and he isn't afraid of anything"
　"他什么都不怕"

"He could force you, beautiful girl"
　"他可以强迫你，美丽的女孩"

"He could kidnap you and hurt you"
　"他可能会绑架你并伤害你"

"No, Samana, I am not afraid of this"
　"不，沙门，我不怕这个。"

"Did any Samana or Brahman ever fear someone might come and grab him?"
　"沙门或婆罗门有没有担心过有人会来抓他？"

"could he fear someone steals his learning?
　"他会担心有人窃取他的学习成果吗？

"could anyone take his religious devotion"
　"有人能夺走他的宗教信仰吗"

"is it possible to take his depth of thought?
　"有可能夺走他的思想深度吗？

"No, because these things are his very own"
　"不，因为这些东西都是他自己的。"

"he would only give away the knowledge he is willing to give"
　"他只会分享他愿意分享的知识"

"he would only give to those he is willing to give to"
　"他只会给予那些他愿意给予的人"

"precisely like this it is also with Kamala"
"Kamala 也同样如此"
"and it is the same way with the pleasures of love"
"爱情的快乐也一样"
"Beautiful and red is Kamala's mouth," answered Siddhartha
"卡玛拉的嘴又红又美。"悉达多回答道。
"but don't try to kiss it against Kamala's will"
"但不要违背卡玛拉的意愿去亲吻它"
"because you will not obtain a single drop of sweetness from it"
"因为你得不到一滴甜蜜"
"You are learning easily, Siddhartha"
"你学得真容易，悉达多。"
"you should also learn this"
"你也应该学这个"
"love can be obtained by begging, buying"
"爱情可以通过乞讨、购买获得"
"you can receive it as a gift"
"你可以将其作为礼物收到"
"or you can find it in the street"
"或者你也可以在街上找到它"
"but love cannot be stolen"
"但爱情是不能被偷走的"
"In this, you have come up with the wrong path"
"从这个意义上来说，你们走错了路"
"it would be a pity if you would want to tackle love in such a wrong manner"
"如果你想用这种错误的方式来对待爱情，那真是太可惜了"
Siddhartha bowed with a smile
悉达多微笑着鞠躬
"It would be a pity, Kamala, you are so right"
"那太可惜了，卡玛拉，你说得太对了"
"It would be such a great pity"

"这真是太可惜了"

"No, I shall not lose a single drop of sweetness from your mouth"

"不,我不会失去你嘴里哪怕一滴甜蜜"

"nor shall you lose sweetness from my mouth"

"你也不会失去我嘴里的甜蜜"

"So it is agreed. Siddhartha will return"

"就这么说定了。悉达多会回来的。"

"Siddhartha will return once he has what he still lacks"

"悉达多一旦得到他所缺少的东西就会回来"

"he will come back with clothes, shoes, and money"

"他会带着衣服、鞋子和钱回来"

"But speak, lovely Kamala, couldn't you still give me one small advice?"

"但是说吧,可爱的卡玛拉,你难道不能给我一个小建议吗?"

"Give you an advice? Why not?"

"给你一个建议?为什么不呢?"

"Who wouldn't like to give advice to a poor, ignorant Samana?"

"谁不愿意给一个贫穷、无知的沙门提些建议呢?"

"Dear Kamala, where I should go to find these three things most quickly?"

"亲爱的卡玛拉,我应该去哪里才能最快找到这三件东西?"

"Friend, many would like to know this"

"朋友,很多人都想知道这个"

"You must do what you've learned and ask for money"

"你必须做你所学的并要求金钱"

"There is no other way for a poor man to obtain money"

"穷人没有其他方法来获得金钱"

"What might you be able to do?"

"你能做什么呢?"

"I can think. I can wait. I can fast" said Siddhartha

悉达多说："我可以思考，我可以等待，我可以禁食。"

"Nothing else?" asked Kamala
"没别的事了？"卡玛拉问

"yes, I can also write poetry"
"是的，我也会写诗"

"Would you like to give me a kiss for a poem?"
"你愿意为了一首诗而吻我一下吗？"

"I would like to, if I like your poem"
"如果我喜欢你的诗，我愿意"

"What would be its title?"
"它的名字是什么？"

Siddhartha spoke, after he had thought about it for a moment
悉达多想了一会儿，说道

"Into her shady garden stepped the pretty Kamala"
"美丽的卡玛拉走进了她那阴凉的花园"

"At the garden's entrance stood the brown Samana"
"棕色的萨马纳站在花园的入口处"

"Deeply, seeing the lotus's blossom, Bowed that man"
"看到莲花盛开，那人深深鞠躬致敬"

"and smiling, Kamala thanked him"
"卡玛拉微笑着向他道谢"

"More lovely, thought the young man, than offerings for gods"
"比献给神的祭品更可爱，"年轻人想道。

Kamala clapped her hands so loud that the golden bracelets clanged
卡玛拉拍手声如此之大，以至于金手镯叮当作响

"Beautiful are your verses, oh brown Samana"
"你的诗句很美，棕色的沙门啊"

"and truly, I'm losing nothing when I'm giving you a kiss for them"
"说实话，当我为你亲吻时，我并没有失去什么"

She beckoned him with her eyes
她用眼神向他招手

he tilted his head so that his face touched hers
他歪着头,脸贴着她的脸

and he placed his mouth on her mouth
然后他把他的嘴贴在她的嘴上

the mouth which was like a freshly cracked fig
嘴巴就像刚裂开的无花果

For a long time, Kamala kissed him
卡玛拉吻了他很久

and with a deep astonishment Siddhartha felt how she taught him
悉达多惊讶地发现,她教他

he felt how wise she was
他觉得她很聪明

he felt how she controlled him
他感受到了她如何控制着他

he felt how she rejected him
他感受到了她对他的拒绝

he felt how she lured him
他感觉到她是如何引诱他的

and he felt how there were to be more kisses
他觉得还有更多的吻

every kiss was different from the others
每一个吻都与众不同

he was still, when he received the kisses
当他收到吻时,他一动不动

Breathing deeply, he remained standing where he was
他深吸了一口气,仍然站在原地

he was astonished like a child about the things worth learning
他像孩子一样对值得学习的东西感到惊讶

the knowledge revealed itself before his eyes
知识展现在他眼前

"Very beautiful are your verses" exclaimed Kamala
卡玛拉赞叹道："你的诗句非常优美。"

"if I were rich, I would give you pieces of gold for them"
"如果我很富有，我会给你几块金子"

"But it will be difficult for you to earn enough money with verses"
"但你很难靠写诗赚到足够的钱。"

"because you need a lot of money, if you want to be Kamala's friend"
"因为如果你想成为 Kamala 的朋友，你需要很多钱"

"The way you're able to kiss, Kamala!" stammered Siddhartha
"你居然能接吻，卡玛拉！"悉达多结结巴巴地说。

"Yes, this I am able to do"
"是的，我能做到"

"therefore I do not lack clothes, shoes, bracelets"
"因此我不缺衣服，鞋子，手镯"

"I have all the beautiful things"
"我拥有一切美好的东西"

"But what will become of you?"
"但是你会变成什么样子呢？"

"Aren't you able to do anything else?"
"你就不能做点别的事吗？"

"can you do more than think, fast, and make poetry?"
"除了思考、快速和创作诗歌，你还能做更多的事情吗？"

"I also know the sacrificial songs" said Siddhartha
悉达多说："我也知道祭祀的歌曲。"

"but I do not want to sing those songs anymore"
"但我不想再唱那些歌了"

"I also know how to make magic spells"
"我还知道如何施展魔法"

"but I do not want to speak them anymore"

"但我不想再说这些话了"

"I have read the scriptures"
"我读过经文"

"Stop!" Kamala interrupted him
"停!"卡玛拉打断了他

"You're able to read and write?"
"你会读写吗?"

"Certainly, I can do this, many people can"
"当然,我能做到,很多人都能做到"

"Most people can't," Kamala replied
"大多数人都做不到,"卡马拉回答道

"I am also one of those who can't do it"
"我也是做不到的人之一"

"It is very good that you're able to read and write"
"你能读写真是太好了"

"you will also find use for the magic spells"
"你也会发现魔法咒语的用处"

In this moment, a maid came running in
这时,一个女仆跑了进来

she whispered a message into her mistress's ear
她悄悄地在女主人耳边说了一句话

"There's a visitor for me" exclaimed Kamala
卡玛拉惊呼:"有客人来找我。"

"Hurry and get yourself away, Siddhartha"
"赶紧走吧,悉达多。"

"nobody may see you in here, remember this!"
"没有人会看到你在这里,记住这一点!"

"Tomorrow, I'll see you again"
"明天,再来看你"

Kamala ordered her maid to give Siddhartha white garments
卡玛拉命令女仆给悉达多穿上白色的衣服

and then Siddhartha found himself being dragged away by the maid
然后悉达多发现自己被女仆拖走了

he was brought into a garden-house out of sight of any paths
他被带进了一座看不到任何小路的花园房子
then he was led into the bushes of the garden
然后他被带到了花园的灌木丛里
he was urged to get himself out of the garden as soon as possible
他被敦促尽快离开花园
and he was told he must not be seen
并告诉他不能被人看见
he did as he had been told
他按吩咐做了
he was accustomed to the forest
他已经习惯了森林
so he managed to get out without making a sound
所以他设法悄无声息地逃了出来

he returned to the city carrying the rolled up garments under his arm
他把卷起的衣服夹在腋下，回到城里
At the inn, where travellers stay, he positioned himself by the door
在旅客下榻的客栈里，他站在门口
without words he asked for food
他默默地要食物
without a word he accepted a piece of rice-cake
他二话不说就接过一块年糕
he thought about how he had always begged
他想起自己总是乞讨
"Perhaps as soon as tomorrow I will ask no one for food anymore"
"也许明天我就不会再向任何人要食物了"
Suddenly, pride flared up in him
突然，他心中燃起骄傲之情
He was no Samana any more

他不再是沙门了
it was no longer appropriate for him to beg for food
他不再适合乞讨食物
he gave the rice-cake to a dog
他把年糕给了一只狗
and that night he remained without food
那天晚上他没有吃东西
Siddhartha thought to himself about the city
悉达多心里想着这座城市
"Simple is the life which people lead in this world"
"简单是人们在这个世界上所过的生活"
"this life presents no difficulties"
"此生无难事"
"Everything was difficult and toilsome when I was a Samana"
"当我做沙门的时候,一切都很艰难,很辛苦"
"as a Samana everything was hopeless"
"作为沙门,一切都毫无希望"
"but now everything is easy"
"但现在一切都变得简单了"
"it is easy like the lesson in kissing from Kamala"
"这就像卡玛拉的接吻课一样简单"
"I need clothes and money, nothing else"
"我需要衣服和钱,不需要其他东西"
"these goals are small and achievable"
"这些目标很小而且可以实现"
"such goals won't make a person lose any sleep"
"这样的目标不会让人失眠"

the next day he returned to Kamala's house
第二天他回到了卡玛拉的家
"Things are working out well" she called out to him
"事情进展顺利," 她对他喊道
"They are expecting you at Kamaswami's"

"他们在卡马斯瓦米那儿等你"
"he is the richest merchant of the city"
"他是这个城市最富有的商人"
"If he likes you, he'll accept you into his service"
"如果他喜欢你,他就会接受你为他服务"
"but you must be smart, brown Samana"
"但你一定很聪明,棕色的萨玛纳"
"I had others tell him about you"
"我让别人告诉他你的事情"
"Be polite towards him, he is very powerful"
"对他要有礼貌,他很厉害"
"But I warn you, don't be too modest!"
"不过我警告你,别太谦虚了!"
"I do not want you to become his servant"
"我不想让你成为他的仆人"
"you shall become his equal"
"你将与他平等"
"or else I won't be satisfied with you"
"否则我不会对你满意"
"Kamaswami is starting to get old and lazy"
"卡马斯瓦米开始变得又老又懒了"
"If he likes you, he'll entrust you with a lot"
"如果他喜欢你,他会托付很多事情给你"
Siddhartha thanked her and laughed
悉达多向她道谢,并大笑起来
she found out that he had not eaten
她发现他还没吃饭
so she sent him bread and fruits
所以她给他送了面包和水果
"You've been lucky" she said when they parted
"你真幸运",他们分手时她说
"I'm opening one door after another for you"
"我为你打开一扇又一扇门"
"How come? Do you have a spell?"

"怎么会？你有咒语吗？"

"I told you I knew how to think, to wait, and to fast"
"我告诉过你我知道如何思考、如何等待、如何禁食"

"but you thought this was of no use"
"但你认为这没用"

"But it is useful for many things"
"但它对很多事情都很有用"

"Kamala, you'll see that the stupid Samanas are good at learning"
"卡玛拉，你会发现，那些愚蠢的沙门们也善于学习。"

"you'll see they are able to do many pretty things in the forest"
"你会发现它们能在森林里做很多美丽的事情"

"things which the likes of you aren't capable of"
"像你这样的人做不到的事情"

"The day before yesterday, I was still a shaggy beggar"
"前天我还是个毛茸茸的乞丐"

"as recently as yesterday I have kissed Kamala"
"就在昨天，我还亲吻了卡玛拉"

"and soon I'll be a merchant and have money"
"很快我就会成为一名商人并拥有金钱"

"and I'll have all those things you insist upon"
"我会得到你所坚持的一切"

"Well yes," she admitted, "but where would you be without me?"
"嗯，是的，"她承认道，"但是没有我你会在哪里呢？"

"What would you be, if Kamala wasn't helping you?"
"如果卡玛拉不帮助你，你会怎么样？"

"Dear Kamala" said Siddhartha
悉达多说："亲爱的卡玛拉。"

and he straightened up to his full height

他挺直身子

"when I came to you into your garden, I did the first step"
"当我来到你的花园时,我迈出了第一步"

"It was my resolution to learn love from this most beautiful woman"
"我决心向这位最美丽的女人学习爱"

"that moment I had made this resolution"
"那一刻我就下定了这个决心"

"and I knew I would carry it out"
"我知道我会实现它"

"I knew that you would help me"
"我知道你会帮助我"

"at your first glance at the entrance of the garden I already knew it"
"当你在花园入口的第一眼,我就已经知道了"

"But what if I hadn't been willing?" asked Kamala
"但如果我不愿意呢?"卡玛拉问

"You were willing" replied Siddhartha
悉达多回答:"你愿意。"

"When you throw a rock into water, it takes the fastest course to the bottom"
"当你把一块石头扔进水里时,它会以最快的速度沉到水底"

"This is how it is when Siddhartha has a goal"
"当悉达多有目标的时候,就会这样"

"Siddhartha does nothing; he waits, he thinks, he fasts"
"悉达多什么也不做;他等待,他思考,他禁食"

"but he passes through the things of the world like a rock through water"
"但他穿过世间的万物,就像岩石穿过水一样"

"he passed through the water without doing anything"
"他什么也没做就穿过了水"

"he is drawn to the bottom of the water"
"他被沉到了水底"

"he lets himself fall to the bottom of the water"
"他让自己沉入水底"
"His goal attracts him towards it"
"他的目标吸引着他向其靠近"
"he doesn't let anything enter his soul which might oppose the goal"
"他不允许任何可能阻碍他实现目标的东西进入他的灵魂"
"This is what Siddhartha has learned among the Samanas"
"这是悉达多在沙门那里学到的东西"
"This is what fools call magic"
"这就是傻子们所谓的魔法"
"they think it is done by daemons"
"他们认为这是由守护进程完成的"
"but nothing is done by daemons"
"但守护进程什么也没做"
"there are no daemons in this world"
"这个世界上没有恶魔"
"Everyone can perform magic, should they choose to"
"每个人都可以施展魔法,只要他们愿意"
"everyone can reach his goals if he is able to think"
"只要有思考能力,每个人都能实现自己的目标"
"everyone can reach his goals if he is able to wait"
"只要愿意等待,每个人都可以实现自己的目标"
"everyone can reach his goals if he is able to fast"
"如果能够禁食,每个人都可以实现自己的目标"
Kamala listened to him; she loved his voice
卡玛拉听了他的歌,她喜欢他的声音
she loved the look from his eyes
她喜欢他看她的眼神
"Perhaps it is as you say, friend"
"也许正如你所说,朋友。"
"But perhaps there is another explanation"
"但也许还有其他解释"

"Siddhartha is a handsome man"
　"悉达多是一个英俊的男人"
"his glance pleases the women"
　"他的目光让女人心生愉悦"
"good fortune comes towards him because of this"
　"因此,好运会降临到他头上"
With one kiss, Siddhartha bid his farewell
悉达多用一个吻告别
"I wish that it should be this way, my teacher"
　"我希望事情能这样,我的老师。"
"I wish that my glance shall please you"
　"我希望我的目光能让你愉悦"
"I wish that that you always bring me good fortune"
　"我希望你总是给我带来好运"

With the Childlike People
和童心未泯的人在一起

Siddhartha went to Kamaswami the merchant
悉达多去见商人卡玛斯瓦米
he was directed into a rich house
他被领进一户富裕的家庭
servants led him between precious carpets into a chamber
仆人们领着他穿过珍贵的地毯,走进一个房间
in the chamber was where he awaited the master of the house
他在房间里等候主人
Kamaswami entered swiftly into the room
卡马斯瓦米迅速走进房间
he was a smoothly moving man
他是一个行动流畅的人
he had very gray hair and very intelligent, cautious eyes
他有一头灰白的头发和一双聪明谨慎的眼睛。
and he had a greedy mouth
他有一张贪婪的嘴
Politely, the host and the guest greeted one another
主人和客人礼貌地互相问候
"I have been told that you were a Brahman" the merchant began
"我听说你是一个婆罗门。"商人说道。
"I have been told that you are a learned man"
"我听说你是一位博学之人"
"and I have also been told something else"
"我还被告知了其他一些事情"
"you seek to be in the service of a merchant"
"你想为商人服务"
"Might you have become destitute, Brahman, so that you seek to serve?"

"婆罗门，你是否已经变得一贫如洗，所以才寻求服务？"

"No," said Siddhartha, "I have not become destitute"
"不，"悉达多说，"我并没有变得一贫如洗。"

"nor have I ever been destitute" added Siddhartha
悉达多补充道："我也从来没有穷过。"

"You should know that I'm coming from the Samanas"
"你应该知道我来自沙门。"

"I have lived with them for a long time"
"我和他们一起生活了很长时间"

"you are coming from the Samanas"
"你来自沙门"

"how could you be anything but destitute?"
"你怎么可能不穷困潦倒呢？"

"Aren't the Samanas entirely without possessions?"
"沙门不是完全没有任何财产的吗？"

"I am without possessions, if that is what you mean" said Siddhartha
"如果你指的是这个，我就是一无所有。"悉达多说。

"But I am without possessions voluntarily"
"但我自愿不拥有任何财产"

"and therefore I am not destitute"
"因此我并不贫困"

"But what are you planning to live from, being without possessions?"
"但是，如果你没有财产，你打算靠什么生活呢？"

"I haven't thought of this yet, sir"
"我还没想过这个，先生"

"For more than three years, I have been without possessions"
"三年多来，我一无所有"

"and I have never thought about of what I should live"
"我从来没有想过我应该怎样生活"

"So you've lived of the possessions of others"

"原来你靠别人的财物生活啊"

"Presumable, this is how it is?"
"想必,是这样的吧?"

"Well, merchants also live of what other people own"
"商人也是靠别人的财产过活的。"

"Well said," granted the merchant
"说得好。"商人答应道。

"But he wouldn't take anything from another person for nothing"
"但他不会无缘无故地从别人那里拿走任何东西"

"he would give his merchandise in return" said Kamaswami
卡马斯瓦米说:"他会用他的商品作为回报。"

"So it seems to be indeed"
"看来确实如此。"

"Everyone takes, everyone gives, such is life"
"每个人都索取,每个人都付出,这就是生活"

"But if you don't mind me asking, I have a question"
"但如果你不介意的话,我有一个问题"

"being without possessions, what would you like to give?"
"如果你一无所有,你愿意给予什么?"

"Everyone gives what he has"
"每个人都贡献出自己所拥有的"

"The warrior gives strength"
"战士给予力量"

"the merchant gives merchandise"
"商人提供商品"

"the teacher gives teachings"
"老师传授教义"

"the farmer gives rice"
"农夫送稻米"

"the fisher gives fish"
"渔夫送鱼"

"Yes indeed. And what is it that you've got to give?"
"是的。你能给我什么呢?"

"What is it that you've learned?"
"你学到了什么？"

"what you're able to do?"
"你能做什么？"

"I can think. I can wait. I can fast"
"我可以思考。我可以等待。我可以禁食"

"That's everything?" asked Kamaswami
"就这些了？"卡马斯瓦米问

"I believe that is everything there is!"
"我相信这就是一切！"

"And what's the use of that?"
"那有什么用呢？"

"For example; fasting. What is it good for?"
"例如禁食。这有什么好处呢？"

"It is very good, sir"
"非常好，先生。"

"there are times a person has nothing to eat"
"有时一个人没有东西吃"

"then fasting is the smartest thing he can do"
"那么禁食就是他能做的最聪明的事情"

"there was a time where Siddhartha hadn't learned to fast"
"曾经有一段时间悉达多还没有学会斋戒"

"in this time he had to accept any kind of service"
"在这段时间里他必须接受任何形式的服务"

"because hunger would force him to accept the service"
"因为饥饿会迫使他接受这项服务"

"But like this, Siddhartha can wait calmly"
"但这样，悉达多就可以平静地等待了。"

"he knows no impatience, he knows no emergency"
"他不知道不耐烦，他不知道紧急情况"

"for a long time he can allow hunger to besiege him"
"他可以长期忍受饥饿的折磨"

"and he can laugh about the hunger"
"他可以笑着面对饥饿"

"This, sir, is what fasting is good for"
"先生，这就是斋戒的好处"

"You're right, Samana" acknowledged Kamaswami
"你说得对，沙门。"卡玛斯瓦米承认道

"Wait for a moment" he asked of his guest
"等一下。"他问客人

Kamaswami left the room and returned with a scroll
卡马斯瓦米离开房间，带着一卷卷轴回来

he handed Siddhartha the scroll and asked him to read it
他把卷轴递给悉达多，请他读一读

Siddhartha looked at the scroll handed to him
悉达多看着递给他的卷轴

on the scroll a sales-contract had been written
卷轴上写着一份销售合同

he began to read out the scroll's contents
他开始读卷轴上的内容

Kamaswami was very pleased with Siddhartha
迦摩斯华密对悉达多非常满意

"would you write something for me on this piece of paper?"
"你能在这张纸上为我写点什么吗？"

He handed him a piece of paper and a pen
他递给他一张纸和一支笔

Siddhartha wrote, and returned the paper
悉达多写了，然后把纸还给了

Kamaswami read, "Writing is good, thinking is better"
卡马斯瓦米读道："写作很好，思考更好"

"Being smart is good, being patient is better"
"聪明是好事，耐心更好"

"It is excellent how you're able to write" the merchant praised him
"你写得真好。"商人称赞他

"Many a thing we will still have to discuss with one another"
"我们还有很多事情需要彼此讨论"

"For today, I'm asking you to be my guest"

"今天，我请你做我的客人"
"please come to live in this house"
"请来这所房子里居住"

Siddhartha thanked Kamaswami and accepted his offer
悉达多感谢卡玛斯瓦米并接受了他的提议

he lived in the dealer's house from now on
从此他就住在毒贩的家里

Clothes were brought to him, and shoes
有人给他送来了衣服和鞋子

and every day, a servant prepared a bath for him
每天，都有仆人为他准备沐浴露

Twice a day, a plentiful meal was served
每天两次提供丰盛的餐食

but Siddhartha only ate once a day
但悉达多每天只吃一顿饭

and he ate neither meat, nor did he drink wine
他既不吃肉，也不喝酒

Kamaswami told him about his trade
卡马斯瓦米向他讲述了他的职业

he showed him the merchandise and storage-rooms
他向他展示了货物和储藏室

he showed him how the calculations were done
他向他展示了如何进行计算

Siddhartha got to know many new things
悉达多学到了很多新东西

he heard a lot and spoke little
他听得多，说得少

but he did not forget Kamala's words
但他没有忘记卡玛拉的话

so he was never subservient to the merchant
所以他从不屈从于商人

he forced him to treat him as an equal
他强迫他平等对待他

perhaps he forced him to treat him as even more than an equal
也许他强迫他以平等的身份对待他
Kamaswami conducted his business with care
卡马斯瓦米（Kamaswami）谨慎地经营生意
and he was very passionate about his business
他对自己的事业充满热情
but Siddhartha looked upon all of this as if it was a game
但悉达多却把这一切看作一场游戏
he tried hard to learn the rules of the game precisely
他努力学习游戏规则
but the contents of the game did not touch his heart
但游戏的内容并没有触动他的心
He had not been in Kamaswami's house for long
他刚到卡马斯瓦米家不久
but soon he took part in his landlord's business
但很快他就参与了房东的生意

every day he visited beautiful Kamala
他每天都会去美丽的卡马拉
Kamala had an hour appointed for their meetings
卡马拉与她们的会面时间已约定了一个小时
she was wearing pretty clothes and fine shoes
她穿着漂亮的衣服和精致的鞋子
and soon he brought her gifts as well
很快他也给她带来了礼物
Much he learned from her red, smart mouth
他从她那张红红的、聪明的嘴里学到了很多东西
Much he learned from her tender, supple hand
他从她那温柔、柔韧的手中学到了很多东西
regarding love, Siddhartha was still a boy
对于爱情，悉达多还是个孩子
and he had a tendency to plunge into love blindly
他有盲目投入爱情的倾向

he fell into lust like into a bottomless pit
他陷入了欲望之中，就像陷入了无底深渊
she taught him thoroughly, starting with the basics
她从最基础的开始，彻底地教他
pleasure cannot be taken without giving pleasure
享受快乐不能不给予快乐
every gesture, every caress, every touch, every look
每一个动作、每一次爱抚、每一次触碰、每一个眼神
every spot of the body, however small it was, had its secret
身体的每一个部位，无论多小，都有它的秘密
the secrets would bring happiness to those who know them
这些秘密会给那些知道的人带来幸福
lovers must not part from one another after celebrating love
恋人们在庆祝爱情后不应该分开
they must not part without one admiring the other
他们必须彼此欣赏，才能分开
they must be as defeated as they have been victorious
他们必须像胜利一样失败
neither lover should start feeling fed up or bored
双方都不应该开始感到厌烦或无聊
they should not get the evil feeling of having been abusive
他们不应该有被虐待的邪恶感觉
and they should not feel like they have been abused
他们不应该觉得自己受到了虐待
Wonderful hours he spent with the beautiful and smart artist
他与这位美丽而聪明的艺术家度过了美好的时光
he became her student, her lover, her friend
他成为她的学生，她的爱人，她的朋友
Here with Kamala was the worth and purpose of his present life
和卡玛拉在一起，就是他现在生活的价值和目的
his purpose was not with the business of Kamaswami
他的目的不是为卡马斯瓦米做事

Siddhartha received important letters and contracts
悉达多收到了重要的信件和合同
Kamaswami began discussing all important affairs with him
卡马斯瓦米开始和他讨论所有重要的事情
He soon saw that Siddhartha knew little about rice and wool
他很快就发现悉达多对大米和羊毛知之甚少
but he saw that he acted in a fortunate manner
但他觉得自己做得很幸运
and Siddhartha surpassed him in calmness and equanimity
悉达多在平静与镇定方面胜过他
he surpassed him in the art of understanding previously unknown people
他在理解陌生人方面比他更胜一筹
Kamaswami spoke about Siddhartha to a friend
卡马斯瓦米（Kamaswami）和朋友谈论悉达多（Siddhartha）
"**This Brahman is no proper merchant**"
"这个婆罗门不是一个正派的商人"
"**he will never be a merchant**"
"他永远不会成为一名商人"
"**for business there is never any passion in his soul**"
"他的心里从来没有对商业有任何热情"
"**But he has a mysterious quality about him**"
"但他身上有一种神秘的气质"
"**this quality brings success about all by itself**"
"这种品质本身就带来了成功"
"**it could be from a good Star of his birth**"
"这可能是来自他出生时的一颗好星"
"**or it could be something he has learned among Samanas**"
"或者这可能是他在沙门那里学到的东西"
"**He always seems to be merely playing with our business-affairs**"
"他似乎总是在玩弄我们的生意"

"his business never fully becomes a part of him"
"他的生意从未完全成为他的一部分"
"his business never rules over him"
"他的生意从来不会管他"
"he is never afraid of failure"
"他从不害怕失败"
"he is never upset by a loss"
"他从不因损失而沮丧"
The friend advised the merchant
朋友建议商家
"Give him a third of the profits he makes for you"
"把他为你创造的利润的三分之一给他"
"but let him also be liable when there are losses"
"但如果发生损失,他也应承担责任"
"Then, he'll become more zealous"
"那么,他会变得更加热心"
Kamaswami was curious, and followed the advice
卡马斯瓦米很好奇,于是就听从了建议
But Siddhartha cared little about loses or profits
但悉达多并不在乎亏损或盈利
When he made a profit, he accepted it with equanimity
当他获利时,他平静地接受
when he made losses, he laughed it off
当他亏损时,他一笑置之
It seemed indeed, as if he did not care about the business
看起来他确实不关心生意
At one time, he travelled to a village
有一次,他去了一个村庄
he went there to buy a large harvest of rice
他去那里买了大批稻米
But when he got there, the rice had already been sold
但当他到达那里时,大米已经卖完了
another merchant had gotten to the village before him
另一个商人比他先到达了村庄

Nevertheless, Siddhartha stayed for several days in that village
尽管如此,悉达多还是在那个村子里住了几天。
he treated the farmers for a drink
他请农民喝了一杯
he gave copper-coins to their children
他给他们的孩子铜币
he joined in the celebration of a wedding
他参加了一场婚礼的庆祝活动
and he returned extremely satisfied from his trip
他旅行归来,十分满意
Kamaswami was angry that Siddhartha had wasted time and money
卡马斯瓦米对悉达多浪费时间和金钱感到愤怒
Siddhartha answered "Stop scolding, dear friend!"
悉达多回答道:"别再责骂了,亲爱的朋友!"
"Nothing was ever achieved by scolding"
"责骂不会有任何效果"
"If a loss has occurred, let me bear that loss"
"如果有损失,就让我来承担"
"I am very satisfied with this trip"
"我对这次旅行非常满意"
"I have gotten to know many kinds of people"
"我认识了各种各样的人"
"a Brahman has become my friend"
"一位婆罗门成为了我的朋友"
"children have sat on my knees"
"孩子们坐在我的膝盖上"
"farmers have shown me their fields"
"农民向我展示了他们的田地"
"nobody knew that I was a merchant"
"没有人知道我是个商人"
"That's all very nice," exclaimed Kamaswami indignantly
"那太好了,"卡马斯瓦米愤慨地说道

"but in fact, you are a merchant after all"
"但事实上你毕竟是个商人"
"Or did you have only travel for your amusement?"
"或者你旅行只是为了消遣？"
"of course I have travelled for my amusement" Siddhartha laughed
"当然，我旅行是为了娱乐。"悉达多笑着说。
"For what else would I have travelled?"
"我还要为了什么而旅行呢？"
"I have gotten to know people and places"
"我认识了人们和地方"
"I have received kindness and trust"
"我得到了善意和信任"
"I have found friendships in this village"
"我在这个村子里找到了友谊"
"if I had been Kamaswami, I would have travelled back annoyed"
"如果我是卡马斯瓦米，我就会心烦意乱地回去"
"I would have been in hurry as soon as my purchase failed"
"一旦购买失败，我就会很着急"
"and time and money would indeed have been lost"
"确实会浪费时间和金钱"
"But like this, I've had a few good days"
"不过就这样，我也度过了几天好日子"
"I've learned from my time there"
"我在那里学到了很多东西"
"and I have had joy from the experience"
"我从这段经历中得到了快乐"
"I've neither harmed myself nor others by annoyance and hastiness"
"我没有因为烦恼和急躁而伤害自己或他人"
"if I ever return friendly people will welcome me"
"如果我回来，友好的人们会欢迎我"

"if I return to do business friendly people will welcome me too"
"如果我回来做生意，友好的人们也会欢迎我"

"I praise myself for not showing any hurry or displeasure"
"我赞扬自己没有表现出任何着急或不快"

"So, leave it as it is, my friend"
"所以，就让它这样吧，我的朋友"

"and don't harm yourself by scolding"
"不要因为责骂而伤害自己"

"If you see Siddhartha harming himself, then speak with me"
"如果你看到悉达多伤害自己，就跟我说。"

"and Siddhartha will go on his own path"
"而悉达多则会走他自己的路"

"But until then, let's be satisfied with one another"
"但在那之前，让我们彼此满足吧"

the merchant's attempts to convince Siddhartha were futile
商人试图说服悉达多，但没有成功

he could not make Siddhartha eat his bread
他不能让悉达多吃他的面包

Siddhartha ate his own bread
悉达多吃自己的面包

or rather, they both ate other people's bread
或者说，他们都吃别人的面包

Siddhartha never listened to Kamaswami's worries
悉达多从不听卡玛斯瓦米的担忧

and Kamaswami had many worries he wanted to share
卡马斯瓦米有很多忧虑想要分享

there were business-deals going on in danger of failing
正在进行的商业交易面临失败的危险

shipments of merchandise seemed to have been lost
货物似乎已经丢失

debtors seemed to be unable to pay
债务人似乎无力偿还

Kamaswami could never convince Siddhartha to utter words of worry
卡马斯瓦米永远无法说服悉达多说出担忧的话
Kamaswami could not make Siddhartha feel anger towards business
卡马斯瓦米无法让悉达多对生意感到愤怒
he could not get him to to have wrinkles on the forehead
他没法让他额头上长皱纹
he could not make Siddhartha sleep badly
他不能让悉达多睡不好

one day, Kamaswami tried to speak with Siddhartha
有一天,卡马斯瓦米试图和悉达多交谈
"Siddhartha, you have failed to learn anything new"
"悉达多,你还没学到任何新东西"
but again, Siddhartha laughed at this
但悉达多又笑了起来
"Would you please not kid me with such jokes"
"你能不能别跟我开这种玩笑"
"What I've learned from you is how much a basket of fish costs"
"我从你那里了解到一筐鱼要多少钱"
"and I learned how much interest may be charged on loaned money"
"我了解到借钱要收多少利息"
"These are your areas of expertise"
"这些是你的专业领域"
"I haven't learned to think from you, my dear Kamaswami"
"我还没有从你那里学会思考,亲爱的卡玛斯瓦米"
"you ought to be the one seeking to learn from me"
"你应该向我学习"
Indeed his soul was not with the trade
事实上,他的灵魂并不属于这个行业

The business was good enough to provide him with money for Kamala
生意很好，足以让他有钱为卡马拉

and it earned him much more than he needed
他因此赚得比需要的还多

Besides Kamala, Siddhartha's curiosity was with the people
除了卡玛拉，悉达多的好奇心还在于人们

their businesses, crafts, worries, and pleasures
他们的生意、手艺、烦恼和快乐

all these things used to be alien to him
所有这些事情对他来说都是陌生的

their acts of foolishness used to be as distant as the moon
他们的愚蠢行为曾经像月球一样遥远

he easily succeeded in talking to all of them
他很容易就和他们所有人交谈了

he could live with all of them
他可以忍受所有这些

and he could continue to learn from all of them
他可以继续向他们学习

but there was something which separated him from them
但有些东西把他和他们分开了

he could feel a divide between him and the people
他能感觉到他和人民之间的隔阂

this separating factor was him being a Samana
这个分离因素就是他是一个沙门

He saw mankind going through life in a childlike manner
他看到人类以孩子般的方式度过一生

in many ways they were living the way animals live
在很多方面，他们的生活方式和动物一样

he loved and also despised their way of life
他既爱他们的生活方式，又鄙视他们的生活方式

He saw them toiling and suffering
他看到他们辛苦劳作、饱受苦难

they were becoming gray for things unworthy of this price

对于不值这个价钱的东西，它们已经变成灰色

they did things for money and little pleasures
他们做事是为了钱和一些小乐趣

they did things for being slightly honoured
他们做事是为了获得一点荣誉

he saw them scolding and insulting each other
他看到他们互相责骂和侮辱

he saw them complaining about pain
他看到他们抱怨疼痛

pains at which a Samana would only smile
苦行僧对此只会微笑

and he saw them suffering from deprivations
他看到他们饱受贫困之苦

deprivations which a Samana would not feel
沙门不会感受到的剥夺

He was open to everything these people brought his way
他乐于接受这些人向他提出的一切要求

welcome was the merchant who offered him linen for sale
欢迎向他出售亚麻布的商人

welcome was the debtor who sought another loan
欢迎债务人寻求另一笔贷款

welcome was the beggar who told him the story of his poverty
欢迎乞丐向他讲述他的贫穷故事

the beggar who was not half as poor as any Samana
乞丐并不比沙门穷一半

He did not treat the rich merchant and his servant different
他并没有区别对待富商和他的仆人

he let street-vendor cheat him when buying bananas
他买香蕉时被街头小贩欺骗了

Kamaswami would often complain to him about his worries
卡马斯瓦米经常向他抱怨他的烦恼

or he would reproach him about his business
或者他会责备他的生意

he listened curiously and happily
他好奇又高兴地听着
but he was puzzled by his friend
但他对他的朋友感到困惑
he tried to understand him
他试图理解他
and he admitted he was right, up to a certain point
他承认在一定程度上他是对的
there were many who asked for Siddhartha
许多人都来求见悉达多
many wanted to do business with him
很多人想和他做生意
there were many who wanted to cheat him
有很多人想欺骗他
many wanted to draw some secret out of him
许多人想从他身上套出一些秘密
many wanted to appeal to his sympathy
许多人想引起他的同情
many wanted to get his advice
许多人想听听他的建议
He gave advice to those who wanted it
他给那些需要帮助的人提供建议
he pitied those who needed pity
他怜悯那些需要怜悯的人
he made gifts to those who liked presents
他为那些喜欢礼物的人做礼物
he let some cheat him a bit
他让一些人欺骗了他
this game which all people played occupied his thoughts
所有人都在玩的这个游戏占据了他的思想
he thought about this game just as much as he had about the Gods
他对这个游戏的思考，就如同他对诸神的思考一样
deep in his chest he felt a dying voice

他感觉到胸腔深处传来一个垂死的声音
this voice admonished him quietly
这个声音悄悄地告诫他
and he hardly perceived the voice inside of himself
他几乎听不到自己内心的声音
And then, for an hour, he became aware of something
然后,一个小时后,他意识到了一些事情
he became aware of the strange life he was leading
他意识到自己过着奇怪的生活
he realized this life was only a game
他意识到人生不过是一场游戏
at times he would feel happiness and joy
有时他会感到幸福和快乐
but real life was still passing him by
但现实生活仍然在他身边
and it was passing by without touching him
它从他身边经过,却没有碰到他
Siddhartha played with his business-deals
悉达多玩弄他的商业交易
Siddhartha found amusement in the people around him
悉达多从周围的人身上找到了乐趣
but regarding his heart, he was not with them
但他的心却不与他们同在,
The source ran somewhere, far away from him
来源已经逃到离他很远的地方
it ran and ran invisibly
它无形地跑了又跑
it had nothing to do with his life any more
这已经和他的生活无关了
at several times he became scared on account of such thoughts
有好几次他因为这样的想法而感到害怕
he wished he could participate in all of these childlike games

- 141 -

他希望自己能参加所有这些儿童游戏
he wanted to really live
他想真正地活下去
he wanted to really act in their theatre
他想真正地在他们的剧院里表演
he wanted to really enjoy their pleasures
他想真正享受他们的快乐
and he wanted to live, instead of just standing by as a spectator
他想活下去,而不是只是站在一旁看

But again and again, he came back to beautiful Kamala
但他一次又一次回到美丽的卡玛拉身边
he learned the art of love
他学会了爱的艺术
and he practised the cult of lust
他热衷于淫欲崇拜
lust, in which giving and taking becomes one
欲望,给予和索取合二为一
he chatted with her and learned from her
他和她聊天并向她学习
he gave her advice, and he received her advice
他给了她建议,他也接受了她的建议
She understood him better than Govinda used to understand him
她比戈文达更了解他
she was more similar to him than Govinda had been
她比戈文达更像他
"You are like me," he said to her
他对她说:"你和我一样。"
"you are different from most people"
"你和大多数人都不一样"
"You are Kamala, nothing else"
"你就是卡玛拉,仅此而已"

"and inside of you, there is a peace and refuge"
"而你的内心则充满着平静与庇护"

"a refuge to which you can go at every hour of the day"
"一天中任何时候都可以去的避难所"

"you can be at home with yourself"
"你可以待在家里，和自己相处"

"I can do this too"
"我也能做到"

"Few people have this place"
"很少有人拥有这个地方"

"and yet all of them could have it"
"但所有人都可以拥有它"

"Not all people are smart" said Kamala
Kamala 说："不是所有人都很聪明"

"No," said Siddhartha, "that's not the reason why"
"不，"悉达多说，"原因并非如此。"

"Kamaswami is just as smart as I am"
"卡马斯瓦米和我一样聪明"

"but he has no refuge in himself"
"但他自己却无处可躲"

"Others have it, although they have the minds of children"
"其他人也有这种能力，尽管他们的心智还像孩子一样"

"Most people, Kamala, are like a falling leaf"
"卡玛拉，大多数人都像一片落叶"

"a leaf which is blown and is turning around through the air"
"一片被吹动并在空中旋转的叶子"

"a leaf which wavers, and tumbles to the ground"
"一片摇曳并落到地上的叶子"

"But others, a few, are like stars"
"但其他人，少数人，就像星星一样"

"they go on a fixed course"
"他们沿着固定的路线前进"

"no wind reaches them"
"没有风吹到他们那里"

"in themselves they have their law and their course"
"他们有自己的法则和路线"

"Among all the learned men I have met, there was one of this kind"
"在我见过的所有博学之人中,有一个是这样的"

"he was a truly perfected one"
"他是一个真正完美的人"

"I'll never be able to forget him"
"我永远都忘不了他"

"It is that Gotama, the exalted one"
"是那位乔达摩,世尊。"

"Thousands of followers are listening to his teachings every day"
"每天有成千上万的追随者聆听他的教诲"

"they follow his instructions every hour"
"他们每小时都遵循他的指示"

"but they are all falling leaves"
"但它们都是落叶"

"not in themselves they have teachings and a law"
"他们自己没有教义和法律"

Kamala looked at him with a smile
卡玛拉微笑着看着他

"Again, you're talking about him," she said
温情道:"你又在说他了。"

"again, you're having a Samana's thoughts"
"你又有了沙门的想法"

Siddhartha said nothing, and they played the game of love
悉达多什么也没说,他们玩起了爱情游戏

one of the thirty or forty different games Kamala knew
卡马拉知道的三四十种游戏之一

Her body was flexible like that of a jaguar
她的身体像美洲虎一样灵活

flexible like the bow of a hunter
像猎人的弓一样灵活
he who had learned from her how to make love
他从她那里学会了如何做爱
he was knowledgeable of many forms of lust
他了解多种形式的欲望
he that learned from her knew many secrets
从她那里学到了很多秘密
For a long time, she played with Siddhartha
她和悉达多一起玩了很长时间
she enticed him and rejected him
她引诱他又拒绝了他
she forced him and embraced him
她强迫他并拥抱他
she enjoyed his masterful skills
她欣赏他精湛的技艺
until he was defeated and rested exhausted by her side
直到他被打败,精疲力竭地躺在她身边
The courtesan bent over him
妓女俯身向他
she took a long look at his face
她久久地注视着他的脸
she looked at his eyes, which had grown tired
她看着他的眼睛,已经疲惫不堪
"You are the best lover I have ever seen" she said thoughtfully
她若有所思地说:"你是我见过的最好的情人。"
"You're stronger than others, more supple, more willing"
"你比其他人更强大、更灵活、更愿意"
"You've learned my art well, Siddhartha"
"悉达多,你已将我的艺术学得很好了。"
"At some time, when I'll be older, I'd want to bear your child"
"等我长大了,我想为你生个孩子"

"And yet, my dear, you've remained a Samana"
"然而，亲爱的，你仍是一个沙门。"

"and despite this, you do not love me"
"但尽管如此，你还是不爱我"

"there is nobody that you love"
"你没有爱过任何人"

"Isn't it so?" asked Kamala
"不是这样吗？"卡玛拉问。

"It might very well be so," Siddhartha said tiredly
"很有可能，"悉达多疲惫地说道。

"I am like you, because you also do not love"
"我和你们一样，因为你们也不爱"

"how else could you practise love as a craft?"
"否则你怎么能把爱情当成一门手艺来实践呢？"

"Perhaps, people of our kind can't love"
"或许，我们这种人，无法去爱"

"The childlike people can love, that's their secret"
"童心未泯的人能够爱，这是他们的秘密"

Sansara
轮回

For a long time, Siddhartha had lived in the world and lust
长期以来，悉达多一直生活在世俗和欲望之中
he lived this way though, without being a part of it
他虽然过着这样的生活，却没有参与其中
he had killed this off when he had been a Samana
他在做沙门的时候就把这东西杀了
but now they had awoken again
但现在他们又醒了
he had tasted riches, lust, and power
他尝到了财富、欲望和权力的滋味
for a long time he had remained a Samana in his heart
长期以来，他内心一直是一个沙门
Kamala, being smart, had realized this quite right
聪明的卡玛拉已经意识到了这一点
thinking, waiting, and fasting still guided his life
思考、等待和禁食仍然指导着他的生活
the childlike people remained alien to him
他仍然觉得那些孩子气的人很陌生
and he remained alien to the childlike people
他仍然对孩子气的人们感到陌生
Years passed by; surrounded by the good life
岁月流逝，被美好的生活包围
Siddhartha hardly felt the years fading away
悉达多几乎感觉不到岁月的流逝
He had become rich and possessed a house of his own
他变得富有，拥有了自己的房子
he even had his own servants
他甚至有自己的仆人
he had a garden before the city, by the river
他在城前有一座花园，在河边
The people liked him and came to him for money or advice

人们喜欢他,向他寻求金钱或建议
but there was nobody close to him, except Kamala
但他身边没有人,除了卡玛拉
the bright state of being awake
清醒的明亮状态
the feeling which he had experienced at the height of his youth
他年轻时所经历的感觉
in those days after Gotama's sermon
在乔达摩布道之后的那些日子里
after the separation from Govinda
与戈文达分开后
the tense expectation of life
紧张的生活预期
the proud state of standing alone
孤独的骄傲
being without teachings or teachers
无教无师
the supple willingness to listen to the divine voice in his own heart
愿意聆听自己内心深处的神圣声音
all these things had slowly become a memory
这些都慢慢变成了记忆
the memory had been fleeting, distant, and quiet
记忆转瞬即逝,遥远而安静
the holy source, which used to be near, now only murmured
曾经近在咫尺的圣源,如今只发出低语
the holy source, which used to murmur within himself
圣源,曾经在他内心低语
Nevertheless, many things he had learned from the Samanas
尽管如此,他从沙门那里学到了很多东西
he had learned from Gotama
他从乔达摩那里学到
he had learned from his father the Brahman

他从他的父亲婆罗门那里学到

his father had remained within his being for a long time
他的父亲已经在他的心中存在了很长时间

moderate living, the joy of thinking, hours of meditation
适度的生活,思考的乐趣,冥想的时间

the secret knowledge of the self; his eternal entity
自我的秘密知识;他的永恒实体

the self which is neither body nor consciousness
既不是身体也不是意识的自我

Many a part of this he still had
他仍然拥有很多

but one part after another had been submerged
但一部分又一部分被淹没

and eventually each part gathered dust
最后每个部分都积满灰尘

a potter's wheel, once in motion, will turn for a long time
陶轮一旦转动,就会转动很长时间

it loses its vigour only slowly
它只是慢慢地失去活力

and it comes to a stop only after time
经过一段时间后它才会停止

Siddhartha's soul had kept on turning the wheel of asceticism
悉达多的灵魂一直在苦行修行

the wheel of thinking had kept turning for a long time
思维之轮已经转动了很久

the wheel of differentiation had still turned for a long time
分化之轮仍旧转动了很长时间

but it turned slowly and hesitantly
但它转得很慢,很犹豫

and it was close to coming to a standstill
几乎陷入停滞

Slowly, like humidity entering the dying stem of a tree
慢慢地,就像湿气进入枯树的树干

filling the stem slowly and making it rot
慢慢地填满茎并使其腐烂
the world and sloth had entered Siddhartha's soul
世俗和懒惰已经进入了悉达多的灵魂
slowly it filled his soul and made it heavy
慢慢地，它充满了他的灵魂，使它变得沉重
it made his soul tired and put it to sleep
它使他的灵魂疲惫并沉睡
On the other hand, his senses had become alive
另一方面，他的感官变得活跃起来
there was much his senses had learned
他的感官已经学到了很多东西
there was much his senses had experienced
他的感官经历了很多
Siddhartha had learned to trade
悉达多学会了做生意
he had learned how to use his power over people
他已经学会了如何利用自己的权力来控制别人
he had learned how to enjoy himself with a woman
他学会了如何与女人一起享乐
he had learned how to wear beautiful clothes
他学会了如何穿漂亮的衣服
he had learned how to give orders to servants
他学会了如何向仆人发号施令
he had learned how to bathe in perfumed waters
他学会了如何在香水水中沐浴
He had learned how to eat tenderly and carefully prepared food
他学会了如何温柔地吃精心准备的食物
he even ate fish, meat, and poultry
他甚至吃鱼、肉和家禽
spices and sweets and wine, which causes sloth and forgetfulness
香料、糖果和酒，导致懒惰和健忘

He had learned to play with dice and on a chess-board
他学会了玩骰子和棋盘
he had learned to watch dancing girls
他学会了观看跳舞的女孩
he learned to have himself carried about in a sedan-chair
他学会了坐轿子
he learned to sleep on a soft bed
他学会了在柔软的床上睡觉
But still he felt different from others
但他仍觉得自己与别人不同
he still felt superior to the others
他仍然觉得自己比别人优越
he always watched them with some mockery
他总是用嘲讽的眼光看着他们
there was always some mocking disdain to how he felt about them
他对他们总是带着一种嘲讽和蔑视
the same disdain a Samana feels for the people of the world
沙门对世人的蔑视也是一样的

Kamaswami was ailing and felt annoyed
卡马斯瓦米病了,感到很恼火
he felt insulted by Siddhartha
他觉得悉达多侮辱了他
and he was vexed by his worries as a merchant
他为自己作为商人的烦恼而烦恼
Siddhartha had always watched these things with mockery
悉达多总是以嘲讽的眼光看待这些事情
but his mockery had become more tired
但他的嘲讽已变得更加疲倦
his superiority had become more quiet
他的优越感变得更加安静
as slowly imperceptible as the rainy season passing by
就像雨季悄悄流逝一样

slowly, Siddhartha had assumed something of the childlike people's ways
慢慢地，悉达多也养成了孩子般的习惯
he had gained some of their childishness
他继承了他们的一些孩子气
and he had gained some of their fearfulness
他也变得有些畏惧了。
And yet, the more be become like them the more he envied them
然而，他越像他们，他就越羡慕他们
He envied them for the one thing that was missing from him
他羡慕他们，因为他身上缺少一样东西
the importance they were able to attach to their lives
他们能够重视自己的生活
the amount of passion in their joys and fears
他们的欢乐和恐惧中充满激情
the fearful but sweet happiness of being constantly in love
一直处于爱情之中的恐惧但甜蜜的幸福
These people were in love with themselves all of the time
这些人总是爱自己
women loved their children, with honours or money
女人爱自己的孩子，不管是用荣誉还是金钱
the men loved themselves with plans or hopes
男人爱自己，有计划或有希望
But he did not learn this from them
但他并没有从他们那里学到这一点
he did not learn the joy of children
他没有学会孩子们的快乐
and he did not learn their foolishness
他没有学会他们的愚昧
what he mostly learned were their unpleasant things
他学到的大多是他们的不愉快的事情
and he despised these things
他鄙视这些东西

in the morning, after having had company
早上，在有客人之后
more and more he stayed in bed for a long time
他越来越长时间地躺在床上
he felt unable to think, and was tired
他感觉无法思考，而且很累
he became angry and impatient when Kamaswami bored him with his worries
当卡马斯瓦米对他的担忧感到厌烦时，他变得愤怒和不耐烦
he laughed just too loud when he lost a game of dice
当他输掉一局骰子时，他笑得太大声了
His face was still smarter and more spiritual than others
他的面容依然比别人更加聪明、更加有灵气
but his face rarely laughed anymore
但他的脸上却很少再笑了
slowly, his face assumed other features
慢慢地，他的脸上出现了其他特征
the features often found in the faces of rich people
富人脸上常见的特征
features of discontent, of sickliness, of ill-humour
不满、病态、坏心情的特征
features of sloth, and of a lack of love
懒惰和缺乏爱的特征
the disease of the soul which rich people have
富人所患的心灵疾病
Slowly, this disease grabbed hold of him
慢慢地，这种疾病控制了他
like a thin mist, tiredness came over Siddhartha
疲倦像薄雾一样笼罩着悉达多
slowly, this mist got a bit denser every day
慢慢地，雾气一天比一天浓了一点
it got a bit murkier every month
每个月都变得更加模糊

and every year it got a bit heavier
每年都会变得更重一些
dresses become old with time
衣服会随着时间而变旧
clothes lose their beautiful colour over time
衣服会随着时间的推移而失去美丽的颜色
they get stains, wrinkles, worn off at the seams
它们有污渍、皱纹、接缝处磨损
they start to show threadbare spots here and there
它们开始到处出现破损的斑点
this is how Siddhartha's new life was
这就是悉达多的新生活
the life which he had started after his separation from Govinda
他与戈文达分开后开始的生活
his life had grown old and lost colour
他的生活已老去,失去了色彩
there was less splendour to it as the years passed by
随着岁月的流逝,它不再那么辉煌
his life was gathering wrinkles and stains
他的生活充满了皱纹和污点
and hidden at bottom, disappointment and disgust were waiting
而隐藏在内心深处的失望和厌恶正在等待
they were showing their ugliness
他们展现了自己的丑陋
Siddhartha did not notice these things
悉达多没有注意到这些事情
he remembered the bright and reliable voice inside of him
他想起了内心那明亮而可靠的声音
he noticed the voice had become silent
他注意到声音已经消失了
the voice which had awoken in him at that time
当时他内心醒来的声音

the voice that had guided him in his best times
在他最美好的时候指引他的声音
he had been captured by the world
他已经被世界俘虏了
he had been captured by lust, covetousness, sloth
他被欲望、贪婪、懒惰所俘虏
and finally he had been captured by his most despised vice
最后他被他最鄙视的恶习所俘虏
the vice which he mocked the most
他最嘲笑的恶习
the most foolish one of all vices
最愚蠢的恶习
he had let greed into his heart
他让贪婪占据了他的心
Property, possessions, and riches also had finally captured him
财产、财物和财富也最终俘获了他
having things was no longer a game to him
拥有东西对他来说不再是一场游戏
his possessions had become a shackle and a burden
他的财产已经成为一种枷锁和负担
It had happened in a strange and devious way
事情发生的方式奇怪又曲折
Siddhartha had gotten this vice from the game of dice
悉达多从掷骰子游戏中染上了这种恶习
he had stopped being a Samana in his heart
他内心里已经不再是一个沙门了
and then he began to play the game for money
然后他开始玩游戏赚钱
first he joined the game with a smile
首先他面带微笑地加入游戏
at this time he only played casually
这时他只是随便玩玩
he wanted to join the customs of the childlike people

他想加入童真人的习俗

but now he played with an increasing rage and passion
但现在他打得越来越愤怒和激情

He was a feared gambler among the other merchants
他是其他商人所畏惧的赌徒

his stakes were so audacious that few dared to take him on
他的赌注太大胆了，几乎没有人敢跟他较量

He played the game due to a pain of his heart
他因为心痛而玩这个游戏

losing and wasting his wretched money brought him an angry joy
失去和浪费他的可怜的钱给他带来了愤怒的快乐

he could demonstrate his disdain for wealth in no other way
他没有其他方式来表达他对财富的蔑视

he could not mock the merchants' false god in a better way
他无法用更好的方式嘲讽商人的假神

so he gambled with high stakes
所以他下了很大的赌注

he mercilessly hated himself and mocked himself
他无情地憎恨自己，嘲笑自己

he won thousands, threw away thousands
他赢了数千，输了数千

he lost money, jewellery, a house in the country
他失去了金钱、珠宝和一栋乡间别墅

he won it again, and then he lost again
他又赢了，然后又输了

he loved the fear he felt while he was rolling the dice
他喜欢掷骰子时感受到的恐惧

he loved feeling worried about losing what he gambled
他喜欢担心失去赌注的感觉

he always wanted to get this fear to a slightly higher level
他总是想让这种恐惧上升到更高的水平

he only felt something like happiness when he felt this fear
他只有在感到恐惧时才会感到幸福

it was something like an intoxication
就像是喝醉了一样
something like an elevated form of life
类似于高级生命形式
something brighter in the midst of his dull life
平淡生活中的一些光明事物
And after each big loss, his mind was set on new riches
每次大亏损之后，他都一心想着获得新的财富
he pursued the trade more zealously
他更加热衷于从事贸易
he forced his debtors more strictly to pay
他更严格地要求债务人还款
because he wanted to continue gambling
因为他想继续赌博
he wanted to continue squandering
他想继续挥霍
he wanted to continue demonstrating his disdain of wealth
他想继续表现出对财富的蔑视
Siddhartha lost his calmness when losses occurred
悉达多在遭受损失时失去了冷静
he lost his patience when he was not paid on time
当他没有按时拿到工资时他失去了耐心
he lost his kindness towards beggars
他不再对乞丐仁慈
He gambled away tens of thousands at one roll of the dice
他一掷骰子就输掉了数万美元
he became more strict and more petty in his business
他在做事上变得更加严格，更加细心
occasionally, he was dreaming at night about money!
有时候，他晚上会梦到钱！
whenever he woke up from this ugly spell, he continued fleeing
每当他从这段可怕的咒语中醒来，他就会继续逃跑

whenever he found his face in the mirror to have aged, he found a new game
每当他发现镜子里的自己变老了,他就会找到一个新的游戏
whenever embarrassment and disgust came over him, he numbed his mind
每当尴尬和厌恶袭来时,他就麻痹自己的思想
he numbed his mind with sex and wine
他用性和酒来麻痹自己的头脑
and from there he fled back into the urge to pile up and obtain possessions
从那时起,他又回到了积累和获得财产的冲动中
In this pointless cycle he ran
在这个毫无意义的循环中,他
from his life he grow tired, old, and ill
他的一生变得疲惫、衰老、疾病

Then the time came when a dream warned him
后来,一个梦警告了他
He had spent the hours of the evening with Kamala
他和卡玛拉一起度过了晚上的时光
he had been in her beautiful pleasure-garden
他曾去过她美丽的游乐园
They had been sitting under the trees, talking
他们坐在树下聊天
and Kamala had said thoughtful words
卡玛拉说了一些深思熟虑的话
words behind which a sadness and tiredness lay hidden
话语背后隐藏着悲伤和疲惫
She had asked him to tell her about Gotama
她请他告诉她关于乔达摩的事
she could not hear enough of him
她对他百听不厌
she loved how clear his eyes were

她喜欢他清澈的眼神
she loved how still and beautiful his mouth was
她喜欢他那平静而美丽的嘴唇
she loved the kindness of his smile
她喜欢他那善意的微笑
she loved how peaceful his walk had been
她喜欢他平静的步行方式
For a long time, he had to tell her about the exalted Buddha
很长一段时间,他不得不向她讲述佛陀的故事
and Kamala had sighed, and spoke
卡玛拉叹了口气,说道
"One day, perhaps soon, I'll also follow that Buddha"
"有一天,或许很快,我也会追随那位佛陀"
"I'll give him my pleasure-garden for a gift"
"我要把我的花园送给他作为礼物"
"and I will take my refuge in his teachings"
"我将皈依他的教诲"
But after this, she had aroused him
但此后,她却让他兴奋不已
she had tied him to her in the act of making love
她把他绑在自己身上,让他做爱
with painful fervour, biting and in tears
带着痛苦的热情,咬着牙,流着泪
it was as if she wanted to squeeze the last sweet drop out of this wine
仿佛她想把这酒里的最后一滴甜味榨出来
Never before had it become so strangely clear to Siddhartha
悉达多从来没有如此清楚地意识到
he felt how close lust was akin to death
他感觉到欲望与死亡有多接近
he laid by her side, and Kamala's face was close to him
他躺在她身边,卡玛拉的脸靠近他
under her eyes and next to the corners of her mouth
眼睛下面和嘴角附近

it was as clear as never before
从未如此清晰
there read a fearful inscription
那里有一段令人恐惧的铭文
an inscription of small lines and slight grooves
小线条和细小凹槽的铭文
an inscription reminiscent of autumn and old age
让人联想到秋天和老年的题词
here and there, gray hairs among his black ones
这儿那儿,黑头发中间夹杂着白发
Siddhartha himself, who was only in his forties, noticed the same thing
悉达多本人,当时只有四十多岁,也注意到了同样的事情
Tiredness was written on Kamala's beautiful face
Kamala 美丽的脸上写满了疲惫
tiredness from walking a long path
走远路的疲惫
a path which has no happy destination
没有幸福终点的道路
tiredness and the beginning of withering
疲倦和枯萎的开始
fear of old age, autumn, and having to die
害怕衰老、害怕秋天、害怕死亡
With a sigh, he had bid his farewell to her
他叹了一口气,向她告别。
the soul full of reluctance, and full of concealed anxiety
充满不情愿的灵魂,充满隐藏的焦虑

Siddhartha had spent the night in his house with dancing girls
悉达多在他的家里和舞女们一起过夜
he acted as if he was superior to them
他表现得好像自己比他们优越

he acted superior towards the fellow-members of his caste
他对待同种姓的人表现得高人一等
but this was no longer true
但现在情况已不再如此
he had drunk much wine that night
那天晚上他喝了很多酒
and he went to bed a long time after midnight
他在午夜后很久才睡觉
tired and yet excited, close to weeping and despair
疲惫却又兴奋,几乎要哭出来,几乎要绝望
for a long time he sought to sleep, but it was in vain
他想睡了很久,但还是睡不着
his heart was full of misery
他心里充满痛苦
he thought he could not bear any longer
他觉得自己再也无法忍受
he was full of a disgust, which he felt penetrating his entire body
他感到厌恶,这种厌恶感渗透到他的整个身体
like the lukewarm repulsive taste of the wine
就像葡萄酒那温热而令人厌恶的味道
the dull music was a little too happy
沉闷的音乐有点太欢快了
the smile of the dancing girls was a little too soft
舞女的笑容有点太温柔了
the scent of their hair and breasts was a little too sweet
她们头发和乳房的气味有点太甜了
But more than by anything else, he was disgusted by himself
但最令他厌恶的是自己
he was disgusted by his perfumed hair
他对自己那头散发着香水味的头发感到厌恶
he was disgusted by the smell of wine from his mouth
他对自己嘴里的酒味感到恶心

he was disgusted by the listlessness of his skin
他对自己皮肤的萎靡不振感到厌恶

Like when someone who has eaten and drunk far too much
就像当某人吃得太多、喝得太多

they vomit it back up again with agonising pain
他们又痛苦地吐了出来

but they feel relieved by the vomiting
但呕吐后他们会感觉好受一些

this sleepless man wished to free himself of these pleasures
这个失眠的人希望摆脱这些享乐

he wanted to be rid of these habits
他想摆脱这些习惯

he wanted to escape all of this pointless life
他想逃离这种毫无意义的生活

and he wanted to escape from himself
他想逃避自己

it wasn't until the light of the morning when he had slightly fallen sleep
直到天亮他才稍微睡着了

the first activities in the street were already beginning
街道上的第一批活动已经开始

for a few moments he had found a hint of sleep
有一会儿,他似乎有点睡意了

In those moments, he had a dream
在那一刻,他做了一个梦

Kamala owned a small, rare singing bird in a golden cage
卡马拉有一只关在金笼子里的稀有小歌鸟

it always sung to him in the morning
它总是在早上唱歌给他听

but then he dreamt this bird had become mute
但后来他梦见这只鸟变得沉默了

since this arose his attention, he stepped in front of the cage
因为这引起了他的注意,他走到了笼子前面

he looked at the bird inside the cage

他看着笼子里的鸟
the small bird was dead, and lay stiff on the ground
小鸟死了,僵硬地躺在地上
He took the dead bird out of its cage
他把死鸟从笼子里拿出来。
he took a moment to weigh the dead bird in his hand
他花了一点时间掂量了一下手中的死鸟
and then threw it away, out in the street
然后把它扔到街上
in the same moment he felt terribly shocked
在同一时刻,他感到非常震惊
his heart hurt as if he had thrown away all value
他的心很痛,仿佛他已经抛弃了所有有价值的东西
everything good had been inside of this dead bird
一切美好的东西都在这个死鸟里面
Starting up from this dream, he felt encompassed by a deep sadness
从这个梦中醒来,他感到被一种深深的悲伤所包围
everything seemed worthless to him
对他来说一切都毫无价值
worthless and pointless was the way he had been going through life
他的人生一向毫无价值、毫无意义
nothing which was alive was left in his hands
他手中没有留下任何活物
nothing which was in some way delicious could be kept
美味的东西都无法保留
nothing worth keeping would stay
没有什么值得保留的
alone he stood there, empty like a castaway on the shore
他独自站在那里,像岸边的漂流者一样空虚

With a gloomy mind, Siddhartha went to his pleasure-garden

悉达多心情郁闷地来到他的花园。

he locked the gate and sat down under a mango-tree
他锁上门,坐在一棵芒果树下

he felt death in his heart and horror in his chest
他心里感到死亡,胸中感到恐惧

he sensed how everything died and withered in him
他感觉到他身上的一切都死去了,枯萎了

By and by, he gathered his thoughts in his mind
渐渐地,他集中了思想

once again, he went through the entire path of his life
又一次走完了他一生的路

he started with the first days he could remember
他从他有记忆的第一天开始

When was there ever a time when he had felt a true bliss?
他何时感受过真正的幸福?

Oh yes, several times he had experienced such a thing
哦,是的,他已经经历过好几次这样的事了

In his years as a boy he had had a taste of bliss
在他童年的岁月里,他曾尝过幸福的滋味

he had felt happiness in his heart when he obtained praise from the Brahmans
当他得到婆罗门的称赞时,他心里感到快乐

"There is a path in front of the one who has distinguished himself"
"出人头地的人,前面有一条路"

he had felt bliss reciting the holy verses
他背诵圣诗时感到幸福

he had felt bliss disputing with the learned ones
他觉得与博学之人辩论是件幸福的事

he had felt bliss when he was an assistant in the offerings
当他作为供奉助手时,他感到很幸福

Then, he had felt it in his heart
然后他心里感觉到了

"There is a path in front of you"

"你的面前有一条路"
"you are destined for this path"
"你注定要走这条路"
"the gods are awaiting you"
"众神正在等待你"
And again, as a young man, he had felt bliss
作为一个年轻人,他再次感受到幸福
when his thoughts separated him from those thinking on the same things
当他的思想与那些思考同样事情的人不同时
when he wrestled in pain for the purpose of Brahman
当他为了梵天而痛苦地挣扎时
when every obtained knowledge only kindled new thirst in him
当每获得的知识都只会在他心中激起新的渴望时
in the midst of the pain he felt this very same thing
在痛苦中他也感受到了同样的事情
"Go on! You are called upon!"
"继续!有人叫你!"
He had heard this voice when he had left his home
他离开家的时候听到过这个声音
he heard heard this voice when he had chosen the life of a Samana
当他选择沙门生活时,他听到了这个声音
and again he heard this voice when left the Samanas
当他离开沙门的时候,他又听到了这个声音
he had heard the voice when he went to see the perfected one
当他去见那位完美者时,他听到了声音
and when he had gone away from the perfected one, he had heard the voice
当他离开那位完美的人时,他听到了声音
he had heard the voice when he went into the uncertain
当他进入不确定的

For how long had he not heard this voice anymore?
他已经多久没有听到过这个声音了？

for how long had he reached no height anymore?
他有多久没有达到高度了？

how even and dull was the manner in which he went through life?
他的人生态度是怎样的平淡而又乏味？

for many long years without a high goal
多年来没有高目标

he had been without thirst or elevation
他没有口渴或兴奋

he had been content with small lustful pleasures
他满足于小小的性欲

and yet he was never satisfied!
但他从不满足！

For all of these years he had tried hard to become like the others
这些年来，他一直努力变得和其他人一样

he longed to be one of the childlike people
他渴望成为一个像孩子一样的人

but he didn't know that that was what he really wanted
但他不知道这才是他真正想要的

his life had been much more miserable and poorer than theirs
他的生活比他们悲惨得多，贫穷得多

because their goals and worries were not his
因为他们的目标和担忧与他无关

the entire world of the Kamaswami-people had only been a game to him
卡马斯瓦米族的整个世界对他来说只是一场游戏

their lives were a dance he would watch
他们的生活是一场舞蹈，他会观看

they performed a comedy he could amuse himself with
他们表演了一场他可以自娱自乐的喜剧

Only Kamala had been dear and valuable to him
只有卡玛拉对他来说是珍贵而宝贵的
but was she still valuable to him?
但她对他来说仍然有价值吗?
Did he still need her?
他还需要她吗?
Or did she still need him?
或者说她仍然需要他?
Did they not play a game without an ending?
他们不是在玩一场没有结局的游戏吗?
Was it necessary to live for this?
有必要为此而活吗?
No, it was not necessary!
不,没有必要!
The name of this game was Sansara
这款游戏的名字是 Sansara
a game for children which was perhaps enjoyable to play once
曾经很有趣的儿童游戏
maybe it could be played twice
也许可以播放两次
perhaps you could play it ten times
也许你可以玩十次
but should you play it for ever and ever?
但你应该永远玩下去吗?
Then, Siddhartha knew that the game was over
然后悉达多知道游戏结束了
he knew that he could not play it any more
他知道他不能再演奏了
Shivers ran over his body and inside of him
他浑身发抖,浑身发抖
he felt that something had died
他觉得有些东西已经死了

That entire day, he sat under the mango-tree
那天他整天坐在芒果树下
he was thinking of his father
他正在想念他的父亲
he was thinking of Govinda
他正在想着戈文达
and he was thinking of Gotama
他正在想着乔达摩
Did he have to leave them to become a Kamaswami?
他必须离开他们才能成为卡玛斯瓦米（Kamaswami）吗？
He was still sitting there when the night had fallen
夜幕降临，他仍然坐在那里
he caught sight of the stars, and thought to himself
他看见了星星，心里想着
"Here I'm sitting under my mango-tree in my pleasure-garden"
"我正坐在我花园里的芒果树下"
He smiled a little to himself
他暗自微笑
was it really necessary to own a garden?
拥有一座花园真的有必要吗？
was it not a foolish game?
这难道不是一场愚蠢的游戏吗？
did he need to own a mango-tree?
他需要拥有一棵芒果树吗？
He also put an end to this
他也结束了这一切
this also died in him
这也在他里面死了
He rose and bid his farewell to the mango-tree
他站起来，向芒果树告别。
he bid his farewell to the pleasure-garden
他向游乐园告别

Since he had been without food this day, he felt strong hunger
由于这一天没有吃东西,他感到饥饿难忍
and he thought of his house in the city
他想到了他在城里的房子
he thought of his chamber and bed
他想到了他的房间和床
he thought of the table with the meals on it
他想到了摆着饭菜的桌子
He smiled tiredly, shook himself, and bid his farewell to these things
他疲惫地笑了笑,摇了摇身子,向这些东西告别。
In the same hour of the night, Siddhartha left his garden
当天晚上,悉达多从花园里出来
he left the city and never came back
他离开了这座城市,再也没有回来

For a long time, Kamaswami had people look for him
很长一段时间,卡马斯瓦米都让人去寻找他
they thought he had fallen into the hands of robbers
他们以为他落入了强盗手中
Kamala had no one look for him
卡马拉没有人寻找他
she was not astonished by his disappearance
她对他的消失并不感到惊讶
Did she not always expect it?
她不是一直都期待着这一点吗?
Was he not a Samana?
难道他不是一个沙门吗?
a man who was at home nowhere, a pilgrim
一个无处安家的人,一个朝圣者
she had felt this the last time they had been together
上次他们在一起的时候她就感觉到了这一点
she was happy despite all the pain of the loss

尽管遭受了失去亲人的痛苦,她仍然很快乐
she was happy she had been with him one last time
她很高兴能最后一次和他在一起
she was happy she had pulled him so affectionately to her heart
她很高兴自己能如此深情地把他拥入怀中
she was happy she had felt completely possessed and penetrated by him
她很高兴自己感觉自己完全被他占有和渗透了
When she received the news, she went to the window
当她收到消息时,她走到窗前
at the window she held a rare singing bird
在窗边她抱着一只稀有的歌鸟
the bird was held captive in a golden cage
这只鸟被关在一个金笼子里
She opened the door of the cage
她打开了笼子的门
she took the bird out and let it fly
她把鸟拿出来并让它飞
For a long time, she gazed after it
她久久注视着它
From this day on, she received no more visitors
从此以后,她不再接待访客
and she kept her house locked
她把房子锁上了
But after some time, she became aware that she was pregnant
但过了一段时间,她意识到自己怀孕了
she was pregnant from the last time she was with Siddhartha
她最后一次和悉达多在一起时就怀孕了

By the River
河边

Siddhartha walked through the forest
悉达多穿过森林
he was already far from the city
他已经远离了城市
and he knew nothing but one thing
他只知道一件事
there was no going back for him
他已经没有回头路了
the life that he had lived for many years was over
他多年来过的生活结束了
he had tasted all of this life
他尝遍了人生的滋味
he had sucked everything out of this life
他已经耗尽了生命中的一切
until he was disgusted with it
直到他厌恶它
the singing bird he had dreamt of was dead
他梦到的那只歌唱的鸟死了
and the bird in his heart was dead too
他心里的那只鸟也死了
he had been deeply entangled in Sansara
他已经深深地陷入了轮回
he had sucked up disgust and death into his body
他把厌恶和死亡吸入体内
like a sponge sucks up water until it is full
就像海绵吸水，直到充满为止
he was full of misery and death
他充满了痛苦和死亡
there was nothing left in this world which could have attracted him
世界上再没有任何东西能吸引他了

nothing could have given him joy or comfort
没有什么能给他带来快乐或安慰

he passionately wished to know nothing about himself anymore
他迫切希望自己不再了解任何事

he wanted to have rest and be dead
他想休息并死去

he wished there was a lightning-bolt to strike him dead!
他真希望有一道闪电将他击毙！

If there only was a tiger to devour him!
如果有一只老虎来吞噬他的话！

If there only was a poisonous wine which would numb his senses
如果有一杯毒酒能使他麻木

a wine which brought him forgetfulness and sleep
一种能让他忘却烦恼、助人入睡的酒

a wine from which he wouldn't awake from
一杯他不会醒来的酒

Was there still any kind of filth he had not soiled himself with?
还有什么污秽他没有弄脏过吗？

was there a sin or foolish act he had not committed?
他还有哪些罪孽或愚蠢的行为没有犯过呢？

was there a dreariness of the soul he didn't know?
是否有一种他不知道的心灵的凄凉？

was there anything he had not brought upon himself?
还有什么不是他自己招来的呢？

Was it still at all possible to be alive?
还有可能活下去吗？

Was it possible to breathe in again and again?
是否可以再次呼吸？

Could he still breathe out?
他还能呼气吗？

was he able to bear hunger?

他能忍受饥饿吗？
was there any way to eat again?
有没有什么办法可以再吃？
was it possible to sleep again?
还能再睡着吗？
could he sleep with a woman again?
他还能和女人睡觉吗？
had this cycle not exhausted itself?
这个循环难道还没有结束吗？
were things not brought to their conclusion?
事情还没有结束吗？

Siddhartha reached the large river in the forest
悉达多来到森林里的大河边
it was the same river he crossed when he had still been a young man
那是他年轻时走过的同一条河
it was the same river he crossed from the town of Gotama
那是他从乔达摩城穿过的同一条河
he remembered a ferryman who had taken him over the river
他记得有一位渡船夫载他过河
By this river he stopped, and hesitantly he stood at the bank
他在这条河边停了下来，犹豫地站在岸边
Tiredness and hunger had weakened him
疲劳和饥饿使他虚弱不堪
"what should I walk on for?"
"我该为何而行？"
"to what goal was there left to go?"
"还有什么目标要实现呢？"
No, there were no more goals
不，没有更多进球
there was nothing left but a painful yearning to shake off this dream

剩下的只是痛苦的渴望摆脱这个梦想

he yearned to spit out this stale wine
他恨不得把这杯陈酒吐掉

he wanted to put an end to this miserable and shameful life
他想结束这悲惨而可耻的生活

a coconut-tree bent over the bank of the river
一棵椰子树弯向河岸

Siddhartha leaned against its trunk with his shoulder
悉达多用肩膀靠在树干上

he embraced the trunk with one arm
他用一只手臂抱住了树干

and he looked down into the green water
他低头看着绿色的水

the water ran under him
水从他身下流过

he looked down and found himself to be entirely filled with the wish to let go
他低下头,发现自己心中充满了放手的愿望

he wanted to drown in these waters
他想淹死在这些水中

the water reflected a frightening emptiness back at him
水反射出一种可怕的空虚

the water answered to the terrible emptiness in his soul
水回应了他灵魂中可怕的空虚

Yes, he had reached the end
是的,他已经到达了终点

There was nothing left for him, except to annihilate himself
他已经没有别的选择,只能自我毁灭

he wanted to smash the failure into which he had shaped his life
他想打破他一生所经历的失败

he wanted to throw his life before the feet of mockingly laughing gods
他想把自己的生命献给嘲笑的诸神

This was the great vomiting he had longed for; death
这是他渴望的大呕吐；死亡
the smashing to bits of the form he hated
把他讨厌的形式打碎
Let him be food for fishes and crocodiles
让他成为鱼和鳄鱼的食物
Siddhartha the dog, a lunatic
悉达多狗，一个疯子
a depraved and rotten body; a weakened and abused soul!
堕落腐烂的身体；虚弱受虐的灵魂！
let him be chopped to bits by the daemons
让他被恶魔砍成碎片
With a distorted face, he stared into the water
他面容扭曲，凝视着水面
he saw the reflection of his face and spat at it
他看见了镜子里自己的脸，就朝镜子里吐了口唾沫
In deep tiredness, he took his arm away from the trunk of the tree
他非常疲惫，把手从树干上拿开。
he turned a bit, in order to let himself fall straight down
他稍微转了转身，让自己垂直落下
in order to finally drown in the river
最终淹死在河里
With his eyes closed, he slipped towards death
他闭上双眼，滑向死亡
Then, out of remote areas of his soul, a sound stirred up
然后，从他灵魂深处传来一声声音
a sound stirred up out of past times of his now weary life
从他现在疲惫的生活中唤起的过去的声音
It was a singular word, a single syllable
这是一个单数词，一个音节
without thinking he spoke the voice to himself
他不假思索地自言自语

he slurred the beginning and the end of all prayers of the Brahmans
他把婆罗门的所有祈祷的开头和结尾都说得含糊不清
he spoke the holy Om
他念诵神圣的"Om"
"that what is perfect" or "the completion"
"完美"或"完成"
And in the moment he realized the foolishness of his actions
那一刻他意识到自己的行为很愚蠢
the sound of Om touched Siddhartha's ear
"嗡"的声音传入悉达多的耳朵
his dormant spirit suddenly woke up
他沉睡的灵魂突然醒来
Siddhartha was deeply shocked
悉达多深感震惊
he saw this was how things were with him
他看到自己的情况就是这样的
he was so doomed that he had been able to seek death
他已经注定要失败,以至于他可以寻求死亡
he had lost his way so much that he wished the end
他已经迷失了方向,他希望结束
the wish of a child had been able to grow in him
一个孩子的愿望在他心中得以实现
he had wished to find rest by annihilating his body!
他希望通过毁灭自己的身体来寻求安息!
all the agony of recent times
最近所有的痛苦
all sobering realizations that his life had created
他一生中所有令人清醒的认识
all the desperation that he had felt
他所感受到的所有绝望
these things did not bring about this moment
这些事情并没有带来这一刻

when the Om entered his consciousness he became aware of himself
当 Om 进入他的意识时,他开始意识到自己
he realized his misery and his error
他意识到了自己的痛苦和错误
Om! he spoke to himself
噢!他自言自语道
Om! and again he knew about Brahman
嗡!他又知道了婆罗门
Om! he knew about the indestructibility of life
噢!他知道生命的不可毁灭
Om! he knew about all that is divine, which he had forgotten
噢!他知道一切神圣的事物,但他却忘记了这些。
But this was only a moment that flashed before him
但这只是他眼前闪过的一瞬间
By the foot of the coconut-tree, Siddhartha collapsed
悉达多倒在椰子树下
he was struck down by tiredness
他疲惫不堪
mumbling "Om", he placed his head on the root of the tree
他一边念叨着"唵",一边把头靠在树根上
and he fell into a deep sleep
他陷入了沉睡
Deep was his sleep, and without dreams
他睡得很深,没有梦,
for a long time he had not known such a sleep any more
他已经很久没有睡过这样的觉了

When he woke up after many hours, he felt as if ten years had passed
几个小时后,他醒来时感觉好像已经过去了十年
he heard the water quietly flowing
他听到水静静地流淌

he did not know where he was
他不知道自己在哪里

and he did not know who had brought him here
他不知道是谁带他来的

he opened his eyes and looked with astonishment
他睁开眼睛，惊讶地看着

there were trees and the sky above him
他的上方有树木和天空

he remembered where he was and how he got here
他记得自己在哪里，以及他是如何来到这里

But it took him a long while for this
但他花了很长时间才做到这一点

the past seemed to him as if it had been covered by a veil
过去对他来说就像被一层面纱遮盖着

infinitely distant, infinitely far away, infinitely meaningless
无限遥远，无限遥远，无限无意义

He only knew that his previous life had been abandoned
他只知道，自己以前的生活已经被抛弃了

this past life seemed to him like a very old, previous incarnation
对他来说，过去的生活就像是一个非常古老的前世

this past life felt like a pre-birth of his present self
过去的生活感觉就像是现在的自己的预生

full of disgust and wretchedness, he had intended to throw his life away
他满怀厌恶和悲惨，打算放弃自己的生命

he had come to his senses by a river, under a coconut-tree
他在河边的一棵椰子树下恢复了理智

the holy word "Om" was on his lips
他的嘴唇上念着神圣的"Om"字

he had fallen asleep and had now woken up
他睡着了，现在醒了

he was looking at the world as a new man
他以一个新人的眼光看待世界

Quietly, he spoke the word "Om" to himself
他轻声地对自己念叨着"Om"这个词
the "Om" he was speaking when he had fallen asleep
他在睡着时念出的"Om"
his sleep felt like nothing more than a long meditative recitation of "Om"
他的睡眠感觉就像是长时间冥想吟诵"Om"
all his sleep had been a thinking of "Om"
他所有的睡眠都是在想着"Om"
a submergence and complete entering into "Om"
沉浸并完全进入"Om"
a going into the perfected and completed
进入完善和完成
What a wonderful sleep this had been!
这是多么美妙的一觉啊!
he had never before been so refreshed by sleep
他从来没有睡得这么精神
Perhaps, he really had died
或许,他真的死了
maybe he had drowned and was reborn in a new body?
也许他已经溺水身亡,然后在一个新的身体里重生了?
But no, he knew himself and who he was
但不,他了解自己,也知道他是谁。
he knew his hands and his feet
他认识他的手和他的脚
he knew the place where he lay
他知道他躺的地方
he knew this self in his chest
他心里清楚这个自我
Siddhartha the eccentric, the weird one
古怪的悉达多
but this Siddhartha was nevertheless transformed
但这个悉达多却改变了

he was strangely well rested and awake
奇怪的是，他休息得很好，而且很清醒
and he was joyful and curious
他很高兴也很好奇

Siddhartha straightened up and looked around
悉达多直起身子，环顾四周
then he saw a person sitting opposite to him
然后他看见一个人坐在他对面
a monk in a yellow robe with a shaven head
身穿黄色僧袍、剃着光头的僧人
he was sitting in the position of pondering
他正坐在那里思考
He observed the man, who had neither hair on his head nor a beard
他观察了那个没有头发也没有胡子的男人
he had not observed him for long when he recognised this monk
他没观察多久就认出了这位僧人
it was Govinda, the friend of his youth
那是他年轻时的朋友戈文达
Govinda, who had taken his refuge with the exalted Buddha
皈依佛陀的戈文达
Like Siddhartha, Govinda had also aged
和悉达多一样，戈文达也老了
but his face still bore the same features
但他的面容依然如旧
his face still expressed zeal and faithfulness
他的脸上仍然流露出热情和忠诚
you could see he was still searching, but timidly
你可以看到他还在寻找，但胆怯地
Govinda sensed his gaze, opened his eyes, and looked at him
戈文达感觉到他的目光，睁开眼睛，看着他

Siddhartha saw that Govinda did not recognise him
悉达多看到戈文达没有认出他
Govinda was happy to find him awake
戈文达很高兴看到他醒了
apparently, he had been sitting here for a long time
显然他已经在这里坐了很久了
he had been waiting for him to wake up
他一直在等他醒来
he waited, although he did not know him
他等待着，尽管他不认识他
"I have been sleeping" said Siddhartha
悉达多说："我一直在睡觉。"
"How did you get here?"
"你怎么会在这里？"
"You have been sleeping" answered Govinda
戈文达回答："你一直在睡觉。"
"It is not good to be sleeping in such places"
"在这种地方睡觉可不好"
"snakes and the animals of the forest have their paths here"
"蛇和森林里的动物都在这里行走"
"I, oh sir, am a follower of the exalted Gotama"
"先生，我是尊贵的乔达摩的追随者。"
"I was on a pilgrimage on this path"
"我在这条路上朝圣"
"I saw you lying and sleeping in a place where it is dangerous to sleep"
"我看到你躺在一个很危险的地方睡觉"
"Therefore, I sought to wake you up"
"因此，我试图唤醒你"
"but I saw that your sleep was very deep"
"但我看见你睡得很沉"
"so I stayed behind from my group"
"所以我留在了我的队伍里"
"and I sat with you until you woke up"

"我一直陪着你直到你醒来"

"And then, so it seems, I have fallen asleep myself"
"然后,看来我也睡着了"

"I, who wanted to guard your sleep, fell asleep"
"原本想守护你安睡的我,却睡着了"

"Badly, I have served you"
"不好意思,我服务你了"

"tiredness had overwhelmed me"
"疲倦已经淹没了我"

"But since you're awake, let me go to catch up with my brothers"
"既然你醒了,那就让我去追赶我的兄弟们吧。"

"I thank you, Samana, for watching out over my sleep" spoke Siddhartha
"我感谢你,沙门,照顾我的睡眠。"悉达多说道。

"You're friendly, you followers of the exalted one"
"你们很友善,尊贵的追随者们"

"Now you may go to them"
"现在你可以去找他们了"

"I'm going, sir. May you always be in good health"
"我走了,先生。祝您身体健康。"

"I thank you, Samana"
"谢谢你,沙门。"

Govinda made the gesture of a salutation and said "Farewell"
戈文达向他打了个招呼,说:"再见。"

"Farewell, Govinda" said Siddhartha
"再见,戈文达。"悉达多说。

The monk stopped as if struck by lightning
和尚如遭雷击般停了下来

"Permit me to ask, sir, from where do you know my name?"
"先生,请问您从哪里知道我的名字?"

Siddhartha smiled, "I know you, oh Govinda, from your father's hut"

悉达多微笑着说:"戈文达,我从你父亲的小屋里认识你。"

"and I know you from the school of the Brahmans"
"我认识你,是来自婆罗门学校的。"

"and I know you from the offerings"
"我从祭品中认识你"

"and I know you from our walk to the Samanas"
"我和你一起去萨马纳斯的时候就认识你了。"

"and I know you from when you took refuge with the exalted one"
"自从你投靠至高者以来,我就认识你了"

"You're Siddhartha," Govinda exclaimed loudly, "Now, I recognise you"
"你是悉达多,"戈文达大声喊道,"现在我认出你了。"

"I don't comprehend how I couldn't recognise you right away"
"我不明白为什么我没能立刻认出你"

"Siddhartha, my joy is great to see you again"
"悉达多,再次见到你我非常高兴"

"It also gives me joy, to see you again" spoke Siddhartha
悉达多说:"再次见到你,我也很高兴。"

"You've been the guard of my sleep"
"你一直是我睡眠的守护者"

"again, I thank you for this"
"再次感谢你"

"but I wouldn't have required any guard"
"但我不需要任何警卫"

"Where are you going to, oh friend?"
"你要去哪儿呢,朋友?"

"I'm going nowhere," answered Govinda
"我哪儿也不去。"戈文达回答

"We monks are always travelling"
"我们僧侣总是在旅行"

"whenever it is not the rainy season, we move from one place to another"

"只要不是雨季，我们就会从一个地方搬到另一个地方"

"we live according to the rules of the teachings passed on to us"

"我们按照所传授的教义生活"

"we accept alms, and then we move on"

"我们接受施舍，然后继续前进"

"It is always like this"

"一直都是这样"

"But you, Siddhartha, where are you going to?"

"可是悉达多，你要去哪里呢？"

"for me it is as it is with you"

"对我来说就像你一样"

"I'm going nowhere; I'm just travelling"

"我哪儿也不去，我只是在旅行"

"I'm also on a pilgrimage"

"我也在朝圣"

Govinda spoke "You say you're on a pilgrimage, and I believe you"

戈文达说："你说你在朝圣，我相信你。"

"But, forgive me, oh Siddhartha, you do not look like a pilgrim"

"但是，请原谅我，悉达多，你看上去不像一个朝圣者。"

"You're wearing a rich man's garments"

"你穿的是富人的衣服"

"you're wearing the shoes of a distinguished gentleman"

"你穿着一位杰出绅士的鞋子"

"and your hair, with the fragrance of perfume, is not a pilgrim's hair"

"你的头发散发着香水的香气，不像朝圣者的头发"

"you do not have the hair of a Samana"

"你没有沙门的头发。"

"you are right, my dear"
"你说得对,亲爱的"

"you have observed things well"
"你观察得很仔细"

"your keen eyes see everything"
"你敏锐的眼睛看透了一切"

"But I haven't said to you that I was a Samana"
"但我还没跟你说过我是个沙门呢。"

"I said I'm on a pilgrimage"
"我说我在朝圣"

"And so it is, I'm on a pilgrimage"
"所以,我正在朝圣"

"You're on a pilgrimage" said Govinda
戈文达说:"你正在朝圣。"

"But few would go on a pilgrimage in such clothes"
"但很少有人会穿着这样的衣服去朝圣"

"few would pilger in such shoes"
"很少有人愿意穿这样的鞋子"

"and few pilgrims have such hair"
"很少有朝圣者有这样的头发"

"I have never met such a pilgrim"
"我从未见过这样的朝圣者"

"and I have been a pilgrim for many years"
"我已经当了多年的朝圣者了"

"I believe you, my dear Govinda"
"我相信你,亲爱的戈文达。"

"But now, today, you've met a pilgrim just like this"
"但是今天,你遇到了这样的朝圣者"

"a pilgrim wearing these kinds of shoes and garment"
"穿着这种鞋子和衣服的朝圣者"

"Remember, my dear, the world of appearances is not eternal"
"记住,亲爱的,表象的世界不是永恒的"

"our shoes and garments are anything but eternal"
"我们的鞋子和衣服不是永恒的"

"our hair and bodies are not eternal either"
"我们的头发和身体也不是永恒的"

I'm wearing a rich man's clothes"
我穿的是富人的衣服"

"you've seen this quite right"
"你看得非常正确"

"I'm wearing them, because I have been a rich man"
"我戴着它们,因为我曾经是个有钱人"

"and I'm wearing my hair like the worldly and lustful people"
"我的发型也像世俗和淫荡的人一样"

"because I have been one of them"
"因为我曾经是他们中的一员"

"And what are you now, Siddhartha?" Govinda asked
"那么你现在是什么人呢,悉达多?"戈文达问

"I don't know it, just like you"
"我跟你一样,不知道"

"I was a rich man, and now I am not a rich man anymore"
"我曾经是一个有钱人,但现在我不再是一个有钱人了"

"and what I'll be tomorrow, I don't know"
"我不知道明天我会变成什么样"

"You've lost your riches?" asked Govinda
"你失去了财富?"戈文达问

"I've lost my riches, or they have lost me"
"我失去了财富,或者是财富失去了我"

"My riches somehow happened to slip away from me"
"我的财富不知何故从我身边溜走了"

"The wheel of physical manifestations is turning quickly, Govinda"
"物质显现之轮正在快速转动,戈文达"

"Where is Siddhartha the Brahman?"

"Where is Siddhartha the Samana?"
"婆罗门悉达多在哪儿？"

"Where is Siddhartha the rich man?"
"沙门悉达多在哪儿？"

"Non-eternal things change quickly, Govinda, you know it"
"富有的悉达多在哪儿？"

"非永恒的事物变化很快，戈文达，你知道的。"

Govinda looked at the friend of his youth for a long time
戈文达久久注视着他年轻时的朋友

he looked at him with doubt in his eyes
他用怀疑的眼神看着他

After that, he gave him the salutation which one would use on a gentleman
之后，他向他致以绅士般的敬意

and he went on his way, and continued his pilgrimage
他继续上路，继续他的朝圣之旅

With a smiling face, Siddhartha watched him leave
悉达多微笑地目送他离去

he loved him still, this faithful, fearful man
他仍然爱着他，这个忠诚而又敬畏的男人

how could he not have loved everybody and everything in this moment?
这一刻他怎么可能不爱每个人、每件事呢？

in the glorious hour after his wonderful sleep, filled with Om!
在他美妙的睡眠之后的光荣时刻，充满了 Om！

The enchantment, which had happened inside of him in his sleep
在他睡梦中发生的魔法

this enchantment was everything that he loved
这魔力就是他所爱的一切

he was full of joyful love for everything he saw
他对他所见的一切都充满了喜悦的爱

exactly this had been his sickness before

他以前也得过这种病
he had not been able to love anybody or anything
他无法爱任何人或任何事物
With a smiling face, Siddhartha watched the leaving monk
悉达多面带微笑地看着僧人离去

The sleep had strengthened him a lot
睡眠让他恢复了很多
but hunger gave him great pain
但饥饿给他带来了巨大的痛苦
by now he had not eaten for two days
到现在为止他已经两天没吃东西了
the times were long past when he could resist such hunger
他已经很久没有抵抗过这种饥饿了
With sadness, and yet also with a smile, he thought of that time
他既悲伤又微笑地想起那段时光
In those days, so he remembered, he had boasted of three things to Kamala
他记得,当时他曾向卡玛拉夸耀过三件事
he had been able to do three noble and undefeatable feats
他已经完成了三项崇高而不可战胜的壮举
he was able to fast, wait, and think
他能够禁食、等待和思考
These had been his possessions; his power and strength
这些都是他的财产,他的权力和力量
in the busy, laborious years of his youth, he had learned these three feats
在他忙碌、辛勤的青年时代,他学会了这三项技能
And now, his feats had abandoned him
现在,他的功绩抛弃了他
none of his feats were his any more
他的所有壮举都不再属于他
neither fasting, nor waiting, nor thinking

不禁食，不等待，不思考

he had given them up for the most wretched things
他为了最可悲的事情放弃了它们

what is it that fades most quickly?
什么东西消逝得最快？

sensual lust, the good life, and riches!
感官的欲望、美好的生活和财富！

His life had indeed been strange
他的生活确实很奇怪

And now, so it seemed, he had really become a childlike person
现在看来，他真的变成了一个孩子气的人

Siddhartha thought about his situation
悉达多思考了自己的处境

Thinking was hard for him now
现在他很难思考

he did not really feel like thinking
他确实不想思考

but he forced himself to think
但他强迫自己思考

"all these most easily perishing things have slipped from me"
"所有这些最容易消亡的东西都从我身边溜走了"

"again, now I'm standing here under the sun"
"现在我又站在阳光下"

"I am standing here just like a little child"
"我就像一个小孩子一样站在这里"

"nothing is mine, I have no abilities"
"没有什么是我的，我没有能力"

"there is nothing I could bring about"
"我什么也没做"

"I have learned nothing from my life"
"我的一生没有学到任何东西"

"How wondrous all of this is!"

"这一切多么奇妙啊！"

"it's wondrous that I'm no longer young"
"真奇妙，我不再年轻了"

"my hair is already half gray and my strength is fading"
"我的头发已经一半白了，我的力气也逐渐消退了"

"and now I'm starting again at the beginning, as a child!"
"而现在我又从头开始，像个孩子一样！"

Again, he had to smile to himself
他又一次暗自微笑

Yes, his fate had been strange!
是的，他的命运很奇怪！

Things were going downhill with him
他的情况每况愈下

and now he was again facing the world naked and stupid
现在他又赤身裸体、愚蠢地面对着世界

But he could not feel sad about this
但他无法为此感到难过

no, he even felt a great urge to laugh
不，他甚至感到很想笑

he felt an urge to laugh about himself
他感到很想嘲笑自己

he felt an urge to laugh about this strange, foolish world
他有一种想嘲笑这个奇怪而愚蠢的世界的冲动

"Things are going downhill with you!" he said to himself
"你的情况越来越糟了！"他自言自语道

and he laughed about his situation
他笑着谈论自己的处境

as he was saying it he happened to glance at the river
说话的时候他偶然瞥了一眼河流

and he also saw the river going downhill
他还看到河水顺坡而下

it was singing and being happy about everything
那是歌唱并对一切感到高兴

He liked this, and kindly he smiled at the river

他喜欢这样,他善意地对着河水微笑

Was this not the river in which he had intended to drown himself?

这难道不是他想自杀的那条河吗?

in past times, a hundred years ago

在过去,一百年前

or had he dreamed this?

或者说他梦见过这样的事?

"Wondrous indeed was my life" he thought

"我的生活真是奇妙",他想

"my life has taken wondrous detours"

"我的人生经历了许多奇妙的曲折"

"As a boy, I only dealt with gods and offerings"

"小时候我只和神灵和祭品打交道"

"As a youth, I only dealt with asceticism"

"年轻时我只与禁欲主义打交道"

"I spent my time in thinking and meditation"

"我花时间思考和冥想"

"I was searching for Brahman

"我在寻找梵天

"and I worshipped the eternal in the Atman"

"我崇拜阿特曼中的永恒"

"But as a young man, I followed the penitents"

"但作为一个年轻人,我追随了忏悔者的脚步"

"I lived in the forest and suffered heat and frost"

"我住在森林里,忍受着酷暑和严寒"

"there I learned how to overcome hunger"

"在那里我学会了如何克服饥饿"

"and I taught my body to become dead"

"我教会我的身体走向死亡"

"Wonderfully, soon afterwards, insight came towards me"

"奇妙的是,不久之后,我顿悟了。"

"insight in the form of the great Buddha's teachings"

"以佛陀的伟大教诲形式呈现的洞察力"

"I felt the knowledge of the oneness of the world"
"我感受到了世界大同的认知"

"I felt it circling in me like my own blood"
"我感觉它就像我自己的血液一样在我体内循环"

"But I also had to leave Buddha and the great knowledge"
"但我也必须离开佛陀和大智。"

"I went and learned the art of love with Kamala"
"我去和卡玛拉学习爱情的艺术"

"I learned trading and business with Kamaswami"
"我跟卡马斯瓦米学习贸易和做生意"

"I piled up money, and wasted it again"
"我攒了钱，又浪费了"

"I learned to love my stomach and please my senses"
"我学会了爱我的胃并取悦我的感官"

"I had to spend many years losing my spirit"
"我不得不花很多年的时间失去我的精神"

"and I had to unlearn thinking again"
"我必须再次忘记思考"

"there I had forgotten the oneness"
"我忘记了一体性"

"Isn't it just as if I had turned slowly from a man into a child"?
"这不就像我从一个男人慢慢变成了一个孩子吗？"

"from a thinker into a childlike person"
"从一个思想者变成一个孩子气的人"

"And yet, this path has been very good"
"但这条路一直都很好"

"and yet, the bird in my chest has not died"
"然而我胸中的那只鸟还没有死"

"what a path has this been!"
"这是怎样的一条路啊！"

"I had to pass through so much stupidity"
"我不得不经历这么多愚蠢的事情"

"I had to pass through so much vice"

"我不得不经历这么多恶习"
"I had to make so many errors"
"我犯了很多错误"
"I had to feel so much disgust and disappointment"
"我感到非常厌恶和失望"
"I had to do all this to become a child again"
"我必须做这一切才能再次成为一个孩子"
"and then I could start over again"
"然后我就可以重新开始"
"But it was the right way to do it"
"但这是正确的做法"
"my heart says yes to it and my eyes smile to it"
"我的心对此表示赞同,我的眼睛对此微笑"
"I've had to experience despair"
"我曾经历过绝望"
"I've had to sink down to the most foolish of all thoughts"
"我不得不陷入最愚蠢的想法"
"I've had to think to the thoughts of suicide"
"我不得不考虑自杀"
"only then would I be able to experience divine grace"
"只有这样我才能感受到神的恩典"
"only then could I hear Om again"
"只有那时我才能再次听到Om"
"only then would I be able to sleep properly and awake again"
"这样我才能安然入睡,然后再次醒来"
"I had to become a fool, to find Atman in me again"
"我必须变成一个傻子,才能再次找到我内心的阿特曼"
"I had to sin, to be able to live again"
"为了重获新生,我必须犯下罪孽"
"Where else might my path lead me to?"
"我的道路还会把我引向何方?"
"It is foolish, this path, it moves in loops"

"这条路很愚蠢，它在循环往复"
"perhaps it is going around in a circle"
"也许它正在绕圈子"
"Let this path go where it likes"
"让这条路随意发展"
"where ever this path goes, I want to follow it"
"无论这条路通向何方，我都想追随它"
he felt joy rolling like waves in his chest
他感到胸中的喜悦如潮水般翻腾。
he asked his heart, "from where did you get this happiness?"
他问自己的心："你的幸福是从哪里来的？"
"does it perhaps come from that long, good sleep?"
"这可能是因为长时间的良好睡眠造成的吗？"
"the sleep which has done me so much good"
"睡眠对我有很大帮助"
"or does it come from the word Om, which I said?"
"或者它来自我说的 Om 这个词？"
"Or does it come from the fact that I have escaped?"
"还是因为我逃脱了？"
"does this happiness come from standing like a child under the sky?"
"这种幸福是不是来自于像孩子一样站在天空之下？"

"Oh how good is it to have fled"
"哦，逃离真好"
"it is great to have become free!"
"获得自由真是太好了！"
"How clean and beautiful the air here is"
"这里的空气多么清新、美丽啊"
"the air is good to breath"
"空气清新，适合呼吸"
"where I ran away from everything smelled of ointments"
"我逃离的地方，到处都是药膏的味道"
"spices, wine, excess, sloth"

"香料、葡萄酒、过剩、懒惰"
"How I hated this world of the rich"
"我多么讨厌这个有钱人的世界"
"I hated those who revel in fine food and the gamblers!"
"我讨厌那些沉迷于美食和赌徒的人!"
"I hated myself for staying in this terrible world for so long!
"我恨自己在这个可怕的世界里呆了这么久!"
"I have deprived, poisoned, and tortured myself"
"我剥夺了自己、毒害了自己、折磨了自己"
"I have made myself old and evil!"
"我让自己变得又老又邪恶了!"
"No, I will never again do the things I liked doing so much"
"不,我再也不会做我那么喜欢做的事情了"
"I won't delude myself into thinking that Siddhartha was wise!"
"我不会欺骗自己,以为悉达多很聪明!"
"But this one thing I have done well"
"但有一件事我做得很好"
"this I like, this I must praise"
"我喜欢这个,我必须赞扬这个"
"I like that there is now an end to that hatred against myself"
"我很高兴现在对自己的仇恨终于结束了"
"there is an end to that foolish and dreary life!"
"这愚蠢而又沉闷的生活终究会有尽头!"
"I praise you, Siddhartha, after so many years of foolishness"
"悉达多,我赞美你,你愚蠢了这么多年。"
"you have once again had an idea"
"你又有主意了"
"you have heard the bird in your chest singing"
"你听到了你胸中鸟儿的歌唱"
"and you followed the song of the bird!"
"你就跟着鸟儿的歌声走吧!"
with these thoughts he praised himself
他用这些想法称赞自己

he had found joy in himself again
他又找到了快乐

he listened curiously to his stomach rumbling with hunger
他好奇地听着肚子饿得咕咕叫

he had tasted and spat out a piece of suffering and misery
他尝到了又吐出了一片痛苦和不幸

in these recent times and days, this is how he felt
最近这些日子里,他的感受是这样的

he had devoured it up to the point of desperation and death
他已经将它吞噬,直到绝望和死亡的地步

how everything had happened was good
发生的一切都是好的

he could have stayed with Kamaswami for much longer
他本可以和卡马斯瓦米在一起更长时间

he could have made more money, and then wasted it
他本可以赚更多的钱,然后却浪费了它

he could have filled his stomach and let his soul die of thirst
他本可以填饱肚子,让灵魂渴死

he could have lived in this soft upholstered hell much longer
他本可以在这个柔软的地狱里生活更长时间

if this had not happened, he would have continued this life
如果这件事没有发生,他将继续这样的生活

the moment of complete hopelessness and despair
完全绝望的时刻

the most extreme moment when he hung over the rushing waters
最极端的时刻,他悬在湍急的水面上

the moment he was ready to destroy himself
在他准备毁灭自己的那一刻

the moment he had felt this despair and deep disgust
当他感受到这种绝望和深深的厌恶时

he had not succumbed to it
他没有屈服于它

the bird was still alive after all
这只鸟毕竟还活着
this was why he felt joy and laughed
这就是他感到快乐和大笑的原因
this was why his face was smiling brightly under his hair
这就是为什么他的脸上露出灿烂的笑容
his hair which had now turned gray
他的头发已经变白了
"It is good," he thought, "to get a taste of everything for oneself"
"亲自尝遍一切，真好，"他想。
"everything which one needs to know"
"人们需要知道的一切"
"lust for the world and riches do not belong to the good things"
"贪爱世间和财富不属于善事"
"I have already learned this as a child"
"我从小就学会了这一点"
"I have known it for a long time"
"我早就知道了"
"but I hadn't experienced it until now"
"但直到现在我才体验到它"
"And now that I I've experienced it I know it"
"现在我经历了这一切，我知道了这一切"
"I don't just know it in my memory, but in my eyes, heart, and stomach"
"我不只在记忆中知道，而且在我的眼睛、心里和胃里也知道。"
"it is good for me to know this!"
"知道这个对我很有帮助！"

For a long time, he pondered his transformation
他花了很长时间思考自己的转变
he listened to the bird, as it sang for joy

他听着鸟儿欢快地歌唱

Had this bird not died in him?

难道这只鸟还没有在他心中死去吗？

had he not felt this bird's death?

难道他没有感受到这只鸟的死亡吗？

No, something else from within him had died

不，他体内的其他东西已经死了

something which yearned to die had died

渴望死亡的东西已经死了

Was it not this that he used to intend to kill?

这难道不是他以前想要杀死的吗？

Was it not his his small, frightened, and proud self that had died?

死去的难道不是他那个渺小、恐惧、骄傲的自我吗？

he had wrestled with his self for so many years

他已经与自我斗争了很多年

the self which had defeated him again and again

那个一次又一次打败他的自我

the self which was back again after every killing

每次杀戮之后重新回归的自我

the self which prohibited joy and felt fear?

禁止欢乐并感到恐惧的自我？

Was it not this self which today had finally come to its death?

难道这个自我今天不已经终于走向了死亡吗？

here in the forest, by this lovely river

这片森林，在这条美丽的河边

Was it not due to this death, that he was now like a child?

不就是因为这次死亡，才让他现在变得像个孩子一样吗？

so full of trust and joy, without fear

充满信任和喜悦，毫无畏惧

Now Siddhartha also got some idea of why he had fought this self in vain

现在悉达多也明白了为什么他要徒劳地与这个自我斗争

he knew why he couldn't fight his self as a Brahman
他知道为什么他不能作为婆罗门与自己斗争

Too much knowledge had held him back
太多的知识阻碍了他

too many holy verses, sacrificial rules, and self-castigation
太多的圣训、祭祀规则和自我惩罚

all these things held him back
所有这些事情都阻碍了他

so much doing and striving for that goal!
为了这个目标付出了很多努力!

he had been full of arrogance
他一直很傲慢

he was always the smartest
他总是最聪明的

he was always working the most
他总是工作最努力

he had always been one step ahead of all others
他总是比别人领先一步

he was always the knowing and spiritual one
他总是知识渊博、充满灵性

he was always considered the priest or wise one
他一直被认为是牧师或智者

his self had retreated into being a priest, arrogance, and spirituality
他的自我已经退缩为牧师、傲慢和灵性

there it sat firmly and grew all this time
它一直稳稳地生长在那里

and he had thought he could kill it by fasting
他以为他可以通过禁食来杀死它

Now he saw his life as it had become
现在他看到自己的生活已经变成了这样

he saw that the secret voice had been right

他发现那个秘密声音说得对

no teacher would ever have been able to bring about his salvation

没有老师能够拯救他

Therefore, he had to go out into the world

因此他必须走出去

he had to lose himself to lust and power

他必须迷失自己，沉迷于欲望和权力

he had to lose himself to women and money

他不得不迷失自己去追求女人和金钱

he had to become a merchant, a dice-gambler, a drinker

他必须成为一名商人、一名赌徒、一名酒鬼

and he had to become a greedy person

他必须成为一个贪婪的人

he had to do this until the priest and Samana in him was dead

他必须这样做，直到他内心的祭司和沙门身份消失

Therefore, he had to continue bearing these ugly years

因此，他必须继续忍受这些不堪的岁月

he had to bear the disgust and the teachings

他必须忍受厌恶和教诲

he had to bear the pointlessness of a dreary and wasted life

他必须忍受无意义的沉闷和浪费的人生

he had to conclude it up to its bitter end

他必须把它坚持到底

he had to do this until Siddhartha the lustful could also die

他必须这样做，直到好色的悉达多也死去

He had died and a new Siddhartha had woken up from the sleep

他已死，一个新的悉达多已从沉睡中醒来

this new Siddhartha would also grow old

这个新的悉达多也会变老

he would also have to die eventually

他最终也会死去

Siddhartha was still mortal, as is every physical form
悉达多仍是凡人，就像一切物质形态一样
But today he was young and a child and full of joy
但今天他年轻，还是个孩子，充满欢乐
He thought these thoughts to himself
他心里想着这些事情
he listened with a smile to his stomach
他笑着听着，肚子也跟着一起
he listened gratefully to a buzzing bee
他感激地听着蜜蜂嗡嗡叫
Cheerfully, he looked into the rushing river
他高兴地望着湍急的河水
he had never before liked a water as much as this one
他从来没有像现在这样喜欢过水
he had never before perceived the voice so stronger
他从未听到过如此强烈的声音
he had never understood the parable of the moving water so strongly
他从来没有如此深刻地理解过流动的水的寓言
he had never before noticed how beautifully the river moved
他以前从未注意到河流流动得如此美丽
It seemed to him, as if the river had something special to tell him
他觉得这条河好像有特别的事情要告诉他
something he did not know yet, which was still awaiting him
有些事情他还不知道，还在等待着他
In this river, Siddhartha had intended to drown himself
悉达多曾想在这条河里自尽
in this river the old, tired, desperate Siddhartha had drowned today
今天，年老、疲惫、绝望的悉达多已淹死在这条河里

But the new Siddhartha felt a deep love for this rushing water
但新的悉达多却对这湍急的水流怀有深深的爱
and he decided for himself, not to leave it very soon
他决定自己不要这么快离开

The Ferryman
摆渡人

"By this river I want to stay," thought Siddhartha
　"我想留在这条河边。" 悉达多想

"it is the same river which I have crossed a long time ago"
　"这是我很久以前走过的同一条河"

"I was on my way to the childlike people"
　"我正走向那些童心未泯的人们"

"a friendly ferryman had guided me across the river"
　"一位友善的渡船者带我过河"

"he is the one I want to go to"
　"他就是我想要去的人"

"starting out from his hut, my path led me to a new life"
　"从他的小屋出发，我的道路引领我走向新生活"

"a path which had grown old and is now dead"
　"一条已经老旧且死寂的道路"

"my present path shall also take its start there!"
　"我现在的道路也将从那里开始！"

Tenderly, he looked into the rushing water
他温柔地望着湍急的水流

he looked into the transparent green lines the water drew
他看着水画出的透明绿线

the crystal lines of water were rich in secrets
水的晶莹线条蕴藏着丰富的秘密

he saw bright pearls rising from the deep
他看到明亮的珍珠从深海中升起

quiet bubbles of air floating on the reflecting surface
反射面上漂浮着安静的气泡

the blue of the sky depicted in the bubbles
气泡中描绘的天空的蓝色

the river looked at him with a thousand eyes
河流用千只眼睛注视着他

the river had green eyes and white eyes

河流有绿色的眼睛和白色的眼睛
the river had crystal eyes and sky-blue eyes
河流有水晶般的眼睛和天蓝色的眼睛
he loved this water very much, it delighted him
他非常喜欢这种水,它让他很开心
he was grateful to the water
他很感激水
In his heart he heard the voice talking
他听到心里有声音在说话
"Love this water! Stay near it!"
"喜欢这水!待在它附近吧!"
"Learn from the water!" his voice commanded him
"向水学习!" 他的声音命令道
Oh yes, he wanted to learn from it
哦,是的,他想从中吸取教训
he wanted to listen to the water
他想听听水声
He who would understand this water's secrets
了解这水的秘密的人
he would also understand many other things
他也会理解很多其他的事情
this is how it seemed to him
他觉得是这样
But out of all secrets of the river, today he only saw one
但在这条河的所有秘密中,今天他只看到了一个
this secret touched his soul
这个秘密触动了他的灵魂
this water ran and ran, incessantly
这水流啊流啊,不停地
the water ran, but nevertheless it was always there
水流着,但无论如何它总是在那里
the water always, at all times, was the same
水总是一成不变
and at the same time it was new in every moment

同时每时每刻都是新的
he who could grasp this would be great
能领悟这一点的人将会很伟大
but he didn't understand or grasp it
但他不理解也不领会
he only felt some idea of it stirring
他只感觉到一些念头在涌动
it was like a distant memory, a divine voices
就像遥远的记忆，神圣的声音

Siddhartha rose as the workings of hunger in his body became unbearable
悉达多因身体里的饥饿感难以忍受而起身
In a daze he walked further away from the city
他迷迷糊糊地走远了
he walked up the river along the path by the bank
他沿着河岸边的小路向上游走去
he listened to the current of the water
他聆听着水流的声音
he listened to the rumbling hunger in his body
他听着身体里传来的饥饿感
When he reached the ferry, the boat was just arriving
当他到达渡口时，船正好到。
the same ferryman who had once transported the young Samana across the river
那个曾经把年轻的沙门渡过河的摆渡人
he stood in the boat and Siddhartha recognised him
他站在船上，悉达多认出了他
he had also aged very much
他也老了很多
the ferryman was astonished to see such an elegant man walking on foot
船夫惊讶地看到如此优雅的男子步行
"Would you like to ferry me over?" he asked

"你愿意载我过去吗？"他问

he took him into his boat and pushed it off the bank
他把他带到自己的船上，并把船推离岸边

"It's a beautiful life you have chosen for yourself" the passenger spoke
"这是你自己选择的美好生活"乘客说道

"It must be beautiful to live by this water every day"
"每天住在这水边一定很美好"

"and it must be beautiful to cruise on it on the river"
"在河上航行一定很美"

With a smile, the man at the oar moved from side to side
桨手微笑着左右摇动

"It is as beautiful as you say, sir"
"正如您所说的那样美丽，先生"

"But isn't every life and all work beautiful?"
"但每个生命和所有工作不是都是美好的吗？"

"This may be true" replied Siddhartha
"也许确实如此。"悉达多回答道。

"But I envy you for your life"
"但我羡慕你的生活"

"Ah, you would soon stop enjoying it"
"啊，你很快就会不再享受它了"

"This is no work for people wearing fine clothes"
"这不是穿着华丽衣服的人能干的工作"

Siddhartha laughed at the observation
悉达多听了这番话，哈哈大笑起来

"Once before, I have been looked upon today because of my clothes"
"今天我曾因我的穿着而被人瞧不起。"

"I have been looked upon with distrust"
"人们一直对我抱有不信任的态度"

"they are a nuisance to me"
"他们对我来说很烦人"

"Wouldn't you, ferryman, like to accept these clothes"

"船夫,你不想接受这些衣服吗?"

"because you must know, I have no money to pay your fare"
"因为你知道,我没有钱付你的车费"

"You're joking, sir," the ferryman laughed
"先生,您开玩笑呢。" 船夫笑着说。

"I'm not joking, friend"
"我不是在开玩笑,朋友"

"once before you have ferried me across this water in your boat"
"你曾用你的船把我渡过这片水域"

"you did it for the immaterial reward of a good deed"
"你这样做是为了获得善行的非物质奖励"

"ferry me across the river and accept my clothes for it"
"渡我过河,收我衣服"

"And do you, sir, intent to continue travelling without clothes?"
"那么,先生,您还想不穿衣服继续旅行吗?"

"Ah, most of all I wouldn't want to continue travelling at all"
"啊,我最不想继续旅行了"

"I would rather you gave me an old loincloth"
"我宁愿你给我一条旧缠腰布"

"I would like it if you kept me with you as your assistant"
"如果您能让我做您的助手,那就太好了"

"or rather, I would like if you accepted me as your trainee"
"或者说,我希望你能接受我为你的学生。"

"because first I'll have to learn how to handle the boat"
"因为我首先得学会怎么驾驶这艘船"

For a long time, the ferryman looked at the stranger
船夫久久地注视着这个陌生人

he was searching in his memory for this strange man
他在记忆中寻找这个陌生的男人

"Now I recognise you," he finally said
"现在我认出你了," 他终于说道。

"At one time, you've slept in my hut"

"有一次,你在我的小屋里睡过觉"
"this was a long time ago, possibly more than twenty years"
"这已经是很久以前的事了,可能有二十多年了"
"and you've been ferried across the river by me"
"而你已经渡过我这条河了"
"that day we parted like good friends"
"那天我们像好朋友一样分手"
"Haven't you been a Samana?"
"你不是曾经当过沙门吗?"
"I can't think of your name anymore"
"我再也想不起你的名字了"
"My name is Siddhartha, and I was a Samana"
"我的名字是悉达多,我以前是一个沙门。"
"I had still been a Samana when you last saw me"
"你上次见到我的时候,我还是个沙门。"
"So be welcome, Siddhartha. My name is Vasudeva"
"欢迎你,悉达多。我叫瓦苏戴瓦。"
"You will, so I hope, be my guest today as well"
"我希望你今天也能成为我的客人。"
"and you may sleep in my hut"
"你可以睡在我的小屋里"
"and you may tell me, where you're coming from"
"你可以告诉我你从哪里来"
"and you may tell me why these beautiful clothes are such a nuisance to you"
"你可以告诉我为什么这些漂亮的衣服对你来说这么麻烦"
They had reached the middle of the river
他们已经到达河中央
Vasudeva pushed the oar with more strength
瓦苏戴瓦更加用力地划桨
in order to overcome the current
为了克服当前
He worked calmly, with brawny arms

他用强壮的手臂冷静地工作
his eyes were fixed in on the front of the boat
他的眼睛一直盯着船头
Siddhartha sat and watched him
悉达多坐着看着他
he remembered his time as a Samana
他回忆起自己当沙门的时光
he remembered how love for this man had stirred in his heart
他记得对这个男人的爱是如何在他心中激起的
Gratefully, he accepted Vasudeva's invitation
他满怀感激地接受了瓦苏戴瓦的邀请
When they had reached the bank, he helped him to tie the boat to the stakes
当他们到达岸边时，他帮助他把船绑在木桩上
after this, the ferryman asked him to enter the hut
之后，船夫请他进屋
he offered him bread and water, and Siddhartha ate with eager pleasure
他给悉达多端来面包和水，悉达多吃得津津有味。
and he also ate with eager pleasure of the mango fruits Vasudeva offered him
他也兴致勃勃地吃了瓦苏戴瓦给他的芒果。

Afterwards, it was almost the time of the sunset
之后，快到日落的时候了
they sat on a log by the bank
他们坐在河岸边的一根木头上
Siddhartha told the ferryman about where he originally came from
悉达多向船夫讲述了他的故乡
he told him about his life as he had seen it today
他向他讲述了今天所见所闻的生活。
the way he had seen it in that hour of despair

他在那个绝望的时刻所看到的情况

the tale of his life lasted late into the night
他的人生故事持续到深夜

Vasudeva listened with great attention
瓦苏戴瓦全神贯注地听着

Listening carefully, he let everything enter his mind
他仔细聆听,把一切都记在脑子里

birthplace and childhood, all that learning
出生地和童年,所有的学习

all that searching, all joy, all distress
所有的寻找,所有的欢乐,所有的苦恼

This was one of the greatest virtues of the ferryman
这是摆渡人最伟大的美德之一

like only a few, he knew how to listen
像少数人一样,他懂得倾听

he did not have to speak a word
他不必说一句话

but the speaker sensed how Vasudeva let his words enter his mind
但演讲者感觉到瓦苏戴瓦让他的话进入了他的脑海

his mind was quiet, open, and waiting
他的心很平静,很开放,在等待

he did not lose a single word
他没有漏掉一个字

he did not await a single word with impatience
他没有焦急地等待一句话

he did not add his praise or rebuke
他没有加上赞扬或责备

he was just listening, and nothing else
他只是在听,没有做其他事

Siddhartha felt what a happy fortune it is to confess to such a listener
悉达多觉得,能向这样的听众坦白,是多么幸福的事。

he felt fortunate to bury in his heart his own life
他感到很幸运,因为他把自己的生命埋在了心里
he buried his own search and suffering
他埋葬了自己的寻找和痛苦
he told the tale of Siddhartha's life
他讲述了悉达多的一生
when he spoke of the tree by the river
当他谈到河边的那棵树时
when he spoke of his deep fall
当他谈到他的深深的失落时
when he spoke of the holy Om
当他讲到神圣的 Om 时
when he spoke of how he had felt such a love for the river
当他谈到他对这条河的热爱时
the ferryman listened to these things with twice as much attention
船夫更加专心地听着这些话
he was entirely and completely absorbed by it
他完全被它迷住了
he was listening with his eyes closed
他闭着眼睛听
when Siddhartha fell silent a long silence occurred
当悉达多沉默时,出现了长时间的沉默
then Vasudeva spoke "It is as I thought"
然后瓦苏戴瓦说:"正如我所想的。"
"The river has spoken to you"
"河流对你说话了"
"the river is your friend as well"
"河流也是你的朋友"
"the river speaks to you as well"
"河流也对你说话"
"That is good, that is very good"
"那很好,那非常好"
"Stay with me, Siddhartha, my friend"

"留在我身边吧,悉达多,我的朋友。"

"I used to have a wife"
"我曾经有一个妻子"

"her bed was next to mine"
"她的床就在我的旁边"

"but she has died a long time ago"
"但她早就去世了"

"for a long time, I have lived alone"
"很长一段时间以来,我都独自生活"

"Now, you shall live with me"
"现在,你就跟我一起生活吧"

"there is enough space and food for both of us"
"这里有足够的空间和食物供我们两人居住"

"I thank you," said Siddhartha
悉达多说道:"谢谢您。"

"I thank you and accept"
"我感谢你并接受"

"And I also thank you for this, Vasudeva"
"我也为此感谢你,瓦苏戴瓦。"

"I thank you for listening to me so well"
"谢谢你这么认真地听我说话"

"people who know how to listen are rare"
"懂得倾听的人很少见"

"I have not met a single person who knew it as well as you do"
"我还没见过一个像你这么了解的人"

"I will also learn in this respect from you"
"我也会向你学习这方面的东西"

"You will learn it," spoke Vasudeva
"你会学会的," 瓦苏戴瓦说

"but you will not learn it from me"
"但你不会从我这里学到"

"The river has taught me to listen"
"河流教会了我倾听"

"you will learn to listen from the river as well"
"你也会学会倾听河流的声音"

"It knows everything, the river"
"河流无所不知"

"everything can be learned from the river"
"一切都可以从河流中学到"

"See, you've already learned this from the water too"
"你看,你也从水中学到了这一点"

"you have learned that it is good to strive downwards"
"你已经知道努力往下是好的"

"you have learned to sink and to seek depth"
"你已经学会了沉沦并寻求深度"

"The rich and elegant Siddhartha is becoming an oarsman's servant"
"富有而优雅的悉达多正在成为一名桨手的仆人"

"the learned Brahman Siddhartha becomes a ferryman"
"博学的婆罗门悉达多成为了一名摆渡人"

"this has also been told to you by the river"
"河流也告诉了你这一点"

"You'll learn the other thing from it as well"
"你还会从中学到其他东西"

Siddhartha spoke after a long pause
悉达多沉默了许久,然后说道

"What other things will I learn, Vasudeva?"
"我还能学到什么呢,瓦苏戴瓦?"

Vasudeva rose. "It is late," he said
瓦苏戴瓦站起来。"天色已晚,"他说。

and Vasudeva proposed going to sleep
瓦苏戴瓦建议去睡觉

"I can't tell you that other thing, oh friend"
"我不能告诉你那件事,哦朋友"

"You'll learn the other thing, or perhaps you know it already"
"你会学到另一件事,或者也许你已经知道了"

"See, I'm no learned man"
"你看，我不是一个有学问的人"

"I have no special skill in speaking"
"我没有特别的演讲技巧"

"I also have no special skill in thinking"
"我也没有特别的思考能力"

"All I'm able to do is to listen and to be godly"
"我能做的就是倾听并保持虔诚"

"I have learned nothing else"
"我什么也没学到"

"If I was able to say and teach it, I might be a wise man"
"如果我能说并教它，我可能会成为一个智者"

"but like this I am only a ferryman"
"但我现在只是一个摆渡人"

"and it is my task to ferry people across the river"
"我的任务就是渡河"

"I have transported many thousands of people"
"我已经运送了数千人"

"and to all of them, my river has been nothing but an obstacle"
"对他们所有人来说，我的河流只不过是一个障碍"

"it was something that got in the way of their travels"
"这阻碍了他们的旅行"

"they travelled to seek money and business"
"他们旅行是为了寻求金钱和生意"

"they travelled for weddings and pilgrimages"
"他们为了参加婚礼和朝圣而旅行"

"and the river was obstructing their path"
"河水阻挡了他们的去路"

"the ferryman's job was to get them quickly across that obstacle"
"摆渡人的工作是让他们迅速越过那个障碍"

"But for some among thousands, a few, the river has stopped being an obstacle"

"但对于数千人中的少数人来说,河流已不再是一个障碍"

"they have heard its voice and they have listened to it"
"他们听到了它的声音,他们听从了它"

"and the river has become sacred to them"
"这条河对他们来说已成为圣河"

"it become sacred to them as it has become sacred to me"
"它对他们来说变得神圣,就像它对我来说变得神圣一样"

"for now, let us rest, Siddhartha"
"现在让我们休息一下吧,悉达多。"

Siddhartha stayed with the ferryman and learned to operate the boat
悉达多和船夫呆在一起,学会了开船

when there was nothing to do at the ferry, he worked with Vasudeva in the rice-field
当渡口没什么事可做时,他就和瓦苏戴瓦一起在稻田里工作

he gathered wood and plucked the fruit off the banana-trees
他收集木材,摘下香蕉树上的果实

He learned to build an oar and how to mend the boat
他学会了造桨和修船

he learned how to weave baskets and repaid the hut
他学会了编织篮子并偿还了小屋

and he was joyful because of everything he learned
他因所学的一切而感到快乐

the days and months passed quickly
日子一天天过去

But more than Vasudeva could teach him, he was taught by the river
但瓦苏戴瓦教给他的远不止这些,河流也教给了他

Incessantly, he learned from the river
他不断地向河流学习

Most of all, he learned to listen
最重要的是，他学会了倾听

he learned to pay close attention with a quiet heart
他学会了用平静的心去密切关注

he learned to keep a waiting, open soul
他学会了保持一颗等待、开放的心

he learned to listen without passion
他学会了不带感情地倾听

he learned to listen without a wish
他学会了不带任何期望地倾听

he learned to listen without judgement
他学会了不加评判地倾听

he learned to listen without an opinion
他学会了不带任何意见地倾听

In a friendly manner, he lived side by side with Vasudeva
他与瓦苏戴瓦友好地生活在一起

occasionally they exchanged some words
偶尔他们会交谈几句

then, at length, they thought about the words
然后，他们终于思考了这些话

Vasudeva was no friend of words
瓦苏戴瓦不喜欢言语

Siddhartha rarely succeeded in persuading him to speak
悉达多很少能说服他开口说话

"did you too learn that secret from the river?"
"你也从河流中得知了那个秘密吗？"

"the secret that there is no time?"
"没有时间的秘密？"

Vasudeva's face was filled with a bright smile
瓦苏戴瓦的脸上洋溢着灿烂的笑容

"Yes, Siddhartha," he spoke
"是的，悉达多。"他说道。

"I learned that the river is everywhere at once"

"it is at the source and at the mouth of the river"
"它位于河流的源头和河口"
"it is at the waterfall and at the ferry"
"它位于瀑布和渡口处"
"it is at the rapids and in the sea"
"它位于急流和大海中"
"it is in the mountains and everywhere at once"
"它存在于山中,并且无处不在"
"and I learned that there is only the present time for the river"
"我意识到河流只有现在的时间"
"it does not have the shadow of the past"
"它没有过去的影子"
"and it does not have the shadow of the future"
"而且它没有未来的影子"
"is this what you mean?" he asked
"这就是你的意思吗?"他问
"This is what I meant," said Siddhartha
悉达多说:"我就是这个意思。"
"And when I had learned it, I looked at my life"
"当我明白这一点后,我审视了自己的人生"
"and my life was also a river"
"我的生活也是一条河"
"the boy Siddhartha was only separated from the man Siddhartha by a shadow"
"少年悉达多和成年悉达多之间只隔着一个影子"
"and a shadow separated the man Siddhartha from the old man Siddhartha"
"一个影子把男人悉达多和老人悉达多分开了"
"things are separated by a shadow, not by something real"
"事物被影子分开,而不是被真实的东西分开"
"Also, Siddhartha's previous births were not in the past"
"此外,悉达多的前世并不发生在过去。"

"and his death and his return to Brahma is not in the future"
"他的死亡和回归梵天并不在未来"

"nothing was, nothing will be, but everything is"
"什么都没有发生，什么也不会发生，但一切都存在"

"everything has existence and is present"
"万事万物皆有存在，皆在当下"

Siddhartha spoke with ecstasy
悉达多欣喜若狂地说道

this enlightenment had delighted him deeply
这种启示让他深感欣喜

"was not all suffering time?"
"难道所有苦难不都是时间吗？"

"were not all forms of tormenting oneself a form of time?"
"难道所有折磨自己的方式不都是时间的一种形式吗？"

"was not everything hard and hostile because of time?"
"是不是所有的事情都因为时间而变得艰难和充满敌意？"

"is not everything evil overcome when one overcomes time?"
"当一个人战胜了时间，难道一切邪恶就都被战胜了吗？"

"as soon as time leaves the mind, does suffering leave too?"
"一旦时间离开心灵，痛苦也会离开吗？"

Siddhartha had spoken in ecstatic delight
悉达多欣喜若狂地说

but Vasudeva smiled at him brightly and nodded in confirmation
但瓦苏戴瓦却对他灿烂地微笑，并点头表示同意

silently he nodded and brushed his hand over Siddhartha's shoulder
他默默地点点头，用手抚过悉达多的肩膀

and then he turned back to his work
然后他又回去工作了

And Siddhartha asked Vasudeva again another time
悉达多又问瓦苏戴瓦

the river had just increased its flow in the rainy season
雨季河水流量刚刚增加

and it made a powerful noise
并发出巨大的噪音

"Isn't it so, oh friend, the river has many voices?"
"是不是这样，朋友，这条河有很多种声音？"

"Hasn't it the voice of a king and of a warrior?"
"这难道不是国王和战士的声音吗？"

"Hasn't it the voice of of a bull and of a bird of the night?"
"这不是公牛和夜鸟的声音吗？"

"Hasn't it the voice of a woman giving birth and of a sighing man?"
"这不是妇人生产的声音和男人叹息的声音吗？"

"and does it not also have a thousand other voices?"
"它不是还有一千种其他的声音吗？"

"it is as you say it is," Vasudeva nodded
"正如你所说，" 瓦苏戴瓦点点头

"all voices of the creatures are in its voice"
"所有生物的声音都在它的声音里"

"And do you know..." Siddhartha continued
"你知道吗……" 悉达多继续说道。

"what word does it speak when you succeed in hearing all of voices at once?"
"当你成功同时听到所有声音时，它会说些什么词？"

Happily, Vasudeva's face was smiling
瓦苏戴瓦脸上露出了幸福的笑容

he bent over to Siddhartha and spoke the holy Om into his ear
他俯身向悉达多，在他耳边念诵神圣的"唵"。

And this had been the very thing which Siddhartha had also been hearing
而这正是悉达多所听到的

time after time, his smile became more similar to the ferryman's
一次又一次,他的笑容越来越像船夫的

his smile became almost just as bright as the ferryman's
他的笑容变得几乎和摆渡人的一样灿烂

it was almost just as thoroughly glowing with bliss
它几乎同样闪耀着幸福的光芒

shining out of thousand small wrinkles
闪耀着千万条细小皱纹的光辉

just like the smile of a child
就像孩子的微笑

just like the smile of an old man
就像一位老人的微笑

Many travellers, seeing the two ferrymen, thought they were brothers
许多旅客看到这两个摆渡人,都以为他们是兄弟

Often, they sat in the evening together by the bank
他们经常晚上一起坐在银行旁边

they said nothing and both listened to the water
他们什么也没说,只是听着水声

the water, which was not water to them
对他们来说那根本不是水

it wasn't water, but the voice of life
那不是水,而是生命的声音

the voice of what exists and what is eternally taking shape
存在和永恒形成的声音

it happened from time to time that both thought of the same thing
有时,他们会想到同一件事

they thought of a conversation from the day before

他们想起了前一天的一次谈话
they thought of one of their travellers
他们想到了其中一位旅行者
they thought of death and their childhood
他们想到了死亡和童年
they heard the river tell them the same thing
他们听到河流告诉他们同样的事情
both delighted about the same answer to the same question
都对同一个问题的同一个答案感到高兴
There was something about the two ferrymen which was transmitted to others
两名摆渡人身上有一些特质,并传递给了其他人
it was something which many of the travellers felt
这是许多旅行者的感受
travellers would occasionally look at the faces of the ferrymen
旅人们偶尔会看看渡船夫的脸
and then they told the story of their life
然后他们讲述了他们的生活故事
they confessed all sorts of evil things
他们承认了各种邪恶的事情
and they asked for comfort and advice
他们寻求安慰和建议
occasionally someone asked for permission to stay for a night
偶尔有人请求允许留宿一晚
they also wanted to listen to the river
他们还想听听河水
It also happened that curious people came
也有一些好奇的人来
they had been told that there were two wise men
有人告诉他们有两位贤士
or they had been told there were two sorcerers
或者他们被告知有两个巫师

The curious people asked many questions
好奇的人们问了很多问题
but they got no answers to their questions
但他们的问题没有得到答案
they found neither sorcerers nor wise men
他们既没有找到巫师，也没有找到智者
they only found two friendly little old men, who seemed to be mute
他们只发现了两个友善的小老头，他们似乎哑口无言
they seemed to have become a bit strange in the forest by themselves
它们似乎独自在森林里变得有点奇怪
And the curious people laughed about what they had heard
好奇的人们听到后哈哈大笑
they said common people were foolishly spreading empty rumours
他们说普通民众愚蠢地传播谣言

The years passed by, and nobody counted them
岁月流逝，无人统计
Then, at one time, monks came by on a pilgrimage
后来，有一次，僧侣们朝圣而来
they were followers of Gotama, the Buddha
他们是佛陀乔达摩的追随者
they asked to be ferried across the river
他们要求渡河
they told them they were in a hurry to get back to their wise teacher
他们告诉他们急着要回到他们明智的老师身边
news had spread the exalted one was deadly sick
消息传开，尊贵的人病危
he would soon die his last human death
他很快就会死去
in order to become one with the salvation

为了与救赎合一

It was not long until a new flock of monks came
不久之后,又来了一批新的僧侣

they were also on their pilgrimage
他们也正在朝圣

most of the travellers spoke of nothing other than Gotama
大多数旅行者只谈论乔达摩

his impending death was all they thought about
他们唯一想的就是他即将死去

if there had been war, just as many would travel
如果发生战争,许多人也会去旅行

just as many would come to the coronation of a king
就像许多人会来参加国王的加冕典礼一样

they gathered like ants in droves
他们像蚂蚁一样聚集在一起

they flocked, like being drawn onwards by a magic spell
它们像被魔法吸引一样蜂拥而至

they went to where the great Buddha was awaiting his death
他们去了佛祖等待圆寂的地方

the perfected one of an era was to become one with the glory
一个时代的完美者,就是与荣耀合二为一

Often, Siddhartha thought in those days of the dying wise man
那时,悉达多常常想起那位垂死的智者

the great teacher whose voice had admonished nations
伟大的导师,他的声音告诫各国人民

the one who had awoken hundreds of thousands
唤醒了数十万人的人

a man whose voice he had also once heard
他也曾听过其声音

a teacher whose holy face he had also once seen with respect
他也曾尊敬地见过老师的圣容

Kindly, he thought of him
他真心地想到了他

he saw his path to perfection before his eyes
他看到了通往完美的道路
and he remembered with a smile those words he had said to him
他微笑着回忆起他对他说的话
when he was a young man and spoke to the exalted one
当他还是个年轻人，对至高者说话的时候
They had been, so it seemed to him, proud and precious words
在他看来，这些话是值得骄傲和珍贵的。
with a smile, he remembered the the words
他微笑着想起了那句话
he knew that there was nothing standing between Gotama and him any more
他知道，乔达摩和他之间已经没有任何阻碍
he had known this for a long time already
他早就知道了
though he was still unable to accept his teachings
尽管他仍然无法接受他的教导
there was no teaching a truly searching person
没有教导一个真正探索的人
someone who truly wanted to find, could accept
一个真正想要找到并能接受的人
But he who had found the answer could approve of any teaching
但找到答案的人可以认可任何教学
every path, every goal, they were all the same
每条道路，每个目标，都是一样的
there was nothing standing between him and all the other thousands any more
再也没有任何东西阻挡他和其他成千上万的人
the thousands who lived in that what is eternal
生活在永恒中的数千人
the thousands who breathed what is divine

成千上万的人呼吸着神圣的空气

On one of these days, Kamala also went to him
有一天,卡玛拉也去找他。
she used to be the most beautiful of the courtesans
她曾是最美丽的妓女
A long time ago, she had retired from her previous life
很久以前,她就从以前的生活中退休了
she had given her garden to the monks of Gotama as a gift
她将自己的花园作为礼物送给了乔达摩的僧侣
she had taken her refuge in the teachings
她皈依了教义
she was among the friends and benefactors of the pilgrims
她是朝圣者的朋友和恩人之一
she was together with Siddhartha, the boy
她和悉达多在一起,
Siddhartha the boy was her son
悉达多是她的儿子
she had gone on her way due to the news of the near death of Gotama
她因为得知乔达摩即将去世的消息而上路
she was in simple clothes and on foot
她衣着朴素,步行
and she was With her little son
她带着她的小儿子
she was travelling by the river
她正在河边旅行
but the boy had soon grown tired
但男孩很快就累了
he desired to go back home
他想回家
he desired to rest and eat
他想休息和吃饭
he became disobedient and started whining

他变得不听话，开始抱怨

Kamala often had to take a rest with him

卡玛拉经常不得不和他一起休息

he was accustomed to getting what he wanted

他习惯于得到他想要的东西

she had to feed him and comfort him

她必须喂他并安慰他

she had to scold him for his behaviour

她不得不责骂他的行为

He did not comprehend why he had to go on this exhausting pilgrimage

他不明白自己为什么要踏上这段令人精疲力尽的朝圣之旅

he did not know why he had to go to an unknown place

他不知道自己为什么要去一个陌生的地方

he did know why he had to see a holy dying stranger

他确实知道为什么他必须看到一个圣洁的垂死陌生人

"So what if he died?" he complained

他抱怨道："死了又怎么样？"

why should this concern him?

这跟他有什么关系？

The pilgrims were getting close to Vasudeva's ferry

朝圣者们正接近瓦苏戴瓦的渡口

little Siddhartha once again forced his mother to rest

小悉达多又一次强迫母亲休息

Kamala had also become tired

卡马拉也累了

while the boy was chewing a banana, she crouched down on the ground

当男孩正在嚼香蕉时，她蹲在地上

she closed her eyes a bit and rested

她闭上眼睛休息了一下

But suddenly, she uttered a wailing scream

但突然间，她发出一声尖叫

the boy looked at her in fear
男孩害怕地看着她

he saw her face had grown pale from horror
他看到她脸色因恐惧而变得苍白

and from under her dress, a small, black snake fled
一条小黑蛇从她的衣服下面跑了出来

a snake by which Kamala had been bitten
卡玛拉被一条蛇咬过

Hurriedly, they both ran along the path, to reach people
他们俩急忙沿着小路跑去，找到人们

they got near to the ferry and Kamala collapsed
他们靠近渡口，卡马拉倒下了

she was not able to go any further
她无法再往前走了

the boy started crying miserably
男孩开始伤心地哭泣

his cries were only interrupted when he kissed his mother
只有当他亲吻母亲时，他的哭声才会停止

she also joined his loud screams for help
她也加入了他的大声呼救

she screamed until the sound reached Vasudeva's ears
她尖叫，直到声音传到瓦苏戴瓦的耳朵里

Vasudeva quickly came and took the woman on his arms
瓦苏戴瓦赶紧过来，把女人抱在怀里

he carried her into the boat and the boy ran along
他把她抱上船，男孩跟着跑了

soon they reached the hut, where Siddhartha stood by the stove
他们很快就到了小屋，悉达多站在炉边。

he was just lighting the fire
他只是在点火

He looked up and first saw the boy's face
他抬起头，首先看到的是男孩的脸

it wondrously reminded him of something

这让他惊奇地想起了某件事
like a warning to remember something he had forgotten
就像警告他要记住他忘记的事情
Then he saw Kamala, whom he instantly recognised
然后他看到了卡玛拉,他立刻认出了她
she lay unconscious in the ferryman's arms
她昏迷地躺在船夫的怀里
now he knew that it was his own son
现在他知道这是他自己的儿子
his son whose face had been such a warning reminder to him
儿子的面容一直对他警示不已
and the heart stirred in his chest
他的心在胸膛里激动
Kamala's wound was washed, but had already turned black
卡玛拉的伤口被清洗了,但已经变黑
and her body was swollen
她的身体肿胀了
she was made to drink a healing potion
她被要求喝下治疗药水
Her consciousness returned and she lay on Siddhartha's bed
她恢复了意识,躺在悉达多的床上
Siddhartha stood over Kamala, who he used to love so much
悉达多站在他曾经深爱过的卡玛拉身边
It seemed like a dream to her
对她来说这就像一场梦
with a smile, she looked at her friend's face
她微笑着看着朋友的脸
slowly she realized her situation
她慢慢意识到了自己的处境
she remembered she had been bitten
她记得她被咬过
and she timidly called for her son
她胆怯地呼唤儿子

"He's with you, don't worry," said Siddhartha
"他和你在一起,别担心。"悉达多说。

Kamala looked into his eyes
卡马拉看着他的眼睛

She spoke with a heavy tongue, paralysed by the poison
她说话时舌头沉重,因为中毒而麻木

"You've become old, my dear," she said
她说:"亲爱的,你老了。"

"you've become gray," she added
"你变灰了,"她补充道

"But you are like the young Samana, who came without clothes"
"但你就像那位没有穿衣服的年轻沙门一样。"

"you're like the Samana who came into my garden with dusty feet"
"你就像走进我花园的沙门,脚上沾满灰尘"

"You are much more like him than you were when you left me"
"你比离开我的时候更像他了"

"In the eyes, you're like him, Siddhartha"
"从眼睛上看,你和他很像,悉达多。"

"Alas, I have also grown old"
"唉呀,我也老了"

"could you still recognise me?"
"你还能认出我吗?"

Siddhartha smiled, "Instantly, I recognised you, Kamala, my dear"
悉达多微笑道:"我一眼就认出了你,卡玛拉,我亲爱的。"

Kamala pointed to her boy
卡玛拉指着她的儿子

"Did you recognise him as well?"
"你也认出他了吗?"

"He is your son," she confirmed

她确认道："他是你的儿子。"
Her eyes became confused and fell shut
她的眼睛变得迷茫,然后闭上了
The boy wept and Siddhartha took him on his knees
男孩哭了,悉达多把他抱到膝盖上
he let him weep and petted his hair
他任由他哭泣,抚摸着他的头发
at the sight of the child's face, a Brahman prayer came to his mind
看到孩子的脸,他的脑海里浮现出婆罗门的祈祷
a prayer which he had learned a long time ago
这是他很久以前学会的祈祷
a time when he had been a little boy himself
那时他自己也还只是个小男孩
Slowly, with a singing voice, he started to speak
他慢慢地用歌唱般的声音开始说话
from his past and childhood, the words came flowing to him
来自他的过去和童年,这些话语涌入他的脑海
And with that song, the boy became calm
听了那首歌,男孩变得平静下来
he was only now and then uttering a sob
他只是偶尔抽泣一下
and finally he fell asleep
最后他睡着了
Siddhartha placed him on Vasudeva's bed
悉达多把他放在瓦苏戴瓦的床上
Vasudeva stood by the stove and cooked rice
瓦苏戴瓦站在炉边煮饭
Siddhartha gave him a look, which he returned with a smile
悉达多看了他一眼,他也报以微笑
"She'll die," Siddhartha said quietly
"她会死的。"悉达多平静地说。
Vasudeva knew it was true, and nodded
瓦苏戴瓦知道这是真的,于是点了点头

over his friendly face ran the light of the stove's fire
炉火的光芒照在他友善的脸上
once again, Kamala returned to consciousness
卡玛拉再次恢复意识
the pain of the poison distorted her face
毒药的痛苦扭曲了她的脸
Siddhartha's eyes read the suffering on her mouth
悉达多的眼睛读出了她嘴里的痛苦
from her pale cheeks he could see that she was suffering
从她苍白的脸颊上,他可以看出她很痛苦
Quietly, he read the pain in her eyes
他静静地读着她眼中的痛苦
attentively, waiting, his mind become one with her suffering
专注地等待,他的心与她的痛苦融为一体
Kamala felt it and her gaze sought his eyes
卡玛拉感觉到了,她的目光追寻着他的眼睛
Looking at him, she spoke
她看着他,说道
"Now I see that your eyes have changed as well"
"现在我发现你的眼睛也变了"
"They've become completely different"
"他们已经变得完全不同了"
"what do I still recognise in you that is Siddhartha?
"我还能认出你身上有什么是悉达多吗?"
"It's you, and it's not you"
"是你,又不是你"
Siddhartha said nothing, quietly his eyes looked at hers
悉达多什么也没说,只是静静地看着她
"You have achieved it?" she asked
她问:"你做到了吗?"
"You have found peace?"
"你找到平静了吗?"
He smiled and placed his hand on hers
他微笑着把手放在她的手上

"I'm seeing it" she said
"我看到了,"她说

"I too will find peace"
"我也会找到平静"

"You have found it," Siddhartha spoke in a whisper
"你找到了。"悉达多低声说道。

Kamala never stopped looking into his eyes
Kamala 从未停止注视着他的眼睛

She thought about her pilgrimage to Gotama
她想起了去乔达摩朝圣的旅程

the pilgrimage which she wanted to take
她想去朝圣

in order to see the face of the perfected one
为了看到完美者的面容

in order to breathe his peace
为了呼吸他的平静

but she had now found it in another place
但她现在在另一个地方找到了它

and this she thought that was good too
她认为这也很好

it was just as good as if she had seen the other one
就像她看到另一个一样好

She wanted to tell this to him
她想告诉他这件事

but her tongue no longer obeyed her will
但她的舌头不再听从她的意志

Without speaking, she looked at him
她不说话,看着他

he saw the life fading from her eyes
他看到她眼中的光彩渐渐消逝

the final pain filled her eyes and made them grow dim
最后的痛苦充斥着她的双眼,使它们变得暗淡

the final shiver ran through her limbs
最后的颤抖传遍了她的四肢

his finger closed her eyelids
他的手指合上了她的眼睑

For a long time, he sat and looked at her peacefully dead face
他久久地坐在那里,看着她平静而死气沉沉的脸
For a long time, he observed her mouth
他长时间观察着她的嘴
her old, tired mouth, with those lips, which had become thin
她那张苍老、疲倦的嘴和那双变得薄薄的嘴唇,
he remembered he used to compare this mouth with a freshly cracked fig
他记得他曾经把这张嘴比作一颗刚裂开的无花果
this was in the spring of his years
这是他人生的春天
For a long time, he sat and read the pale face
他坐了许久,看着那张苍白的脸
he read the tired wrinkles
他读着疲惫的皱纹
he filled himself with this sight
他满眼都是这一幕
he saw his own face in the same manner
他也以同样的方式看到了自己的脸
he saw his face was just as white
他看见他的脸色也一样苍白
he saw his face was just as quenched out
他看到他的脸也同样冷淡
at the same time he saw his face and hers being young
同时他看到他的脸和她的脸都很年轻
their faces with red lips and fiery eyes
她们嘴唇红润、眼神炽烈
the feeling of both being real at the same time
两者同时真实的感觉

the feeling of eternity completely filled every aspect of his being
永恒的感觉充满了他生命的每一个方面
in this hour he felt more deeply than than he had ever felt before
此刻他的感受比以往任何时候更加深刻。
he felt the indestructibility of every life
他感受到每一个生命的不可毁灭
he felt the eternity of every moment
他感受到了每一刻的永恒
When he rose, Vasudeva had prepared rice for him
当他起床时,瓦苏戴瓦已经为他准备好了米饭
But Siddhartha did not eat that night
但悉达多当晚没有吃饭
In the stable their goat stood
他们的山羊站在马厩里
the two old men prepared beds of straw for themselves
两位老人给自己准备了稻草床
Vasudeva laid himself down to sleep
瓦苏戴瓦躺下睡觉
But Siddhartha went outside and sat before the hut
但悉达多却走出去,坐在茅屋前
he listened to the river, surrounded by the past
他聆听着河流,被过去包围着
he was touched and encircled by all times of his life at the same time
他同时被生命中的所有时刻所感动和包围
occasionally he rose and he stepped to the door of the hut
偶尔他站起来,走到小屋门口
he listened whether the boy was sleeping
他听男孩是否在睡觉

before the sun could be seen, Vasudeva came out of the stable

太阳还没升起来，瓦苏戴瓦就从马厩里出来了
he walked over to his friend
他走向他的朋友
"You haven't slept," he said
他说："你还没睡觉。"
"No, Vasudeva. I sat here"
"不，瓦苏戴瓦。我坐在这里。"
"I was listening to the river"
"我正在聆听河流的声音"
"the river has told me a lot"
"这条河告诉了我很多东西"
"it has deeply filled me with the healing thought of oneness"
"它让我深深地感受到合一的治愈力量"
"You've experienced suffering, Siddhartha"
"你经历过痛苦，悉达多"
"but I see no sadness has entered your heart"
"但我看不出你的心里有任何悲伤"
"No, my dear, how should I be sad?"
"不，亲爱的，我怎么会伤心呢？"
"I, who have been rich and happy"
"我，曾经富有和快乐"
"I have become even richer and happier now"
"我现在变得更加富有和快乐了"
"My son has been given to me"
"我的儿子已被赐给我"
"Your son shall be welcome to me as well"
"我也欢迎你的儿子"
"But now, Siddhartha, let's get to work"
"但是现在，悉达多，我们开始工作吧。"
"there is much to be done"
"还有很多事情要做"
"Kamala has died on the same bed on which my wife had died"
"卡玛拉和我妻子死在同一张床上"

"Let us build Kamala's funeral pile on the hill"
"让我们在山上为卡玛拉修建葬礼"
"the hill on which I my wife's funeral pile is"
"我妻子的葬礼堆就位于这座山上"
While the boy was still asleep, they built the funeral pile
当男孩还在睡觉的时候,他们堆起了葬礼堆

The Son
儿子

Timid and weeping, the boy had attended his mother's funeral
这个男孩羞怯地哭泣着参加了母亲的葬礼
gloomy and shy, he had listened to Siddhartha
他心情阴郁而害羞,听悉达多说话
Siddhartha greeted him as his son
悉达多迎接他,就像迎接他的儿子
he welcomed him at his place in Vasudeva's hut
他在瓦苏戴瓦的小屋里迎接了他
Pale, he sat for many days by the hill of the dead
他脸色苍白,在亡灵山边坐了好几天
he did not want to eat
他不想吃
he did not look at anyone
他没有看任何人
he did not open his heart
他没有敞开心扉
he met his fate with resistance and denial
他以反抗和拒绝面对自己的命运
Siddhartha spared giving him lessons
悉达多没有教他什么
and he let him do as he pleased
他让他为所欲为
Siddhartha honoured his son's mourning
悉达多尊重儿子的哀悼
he understood that his son did not know him
他明白儿子不认识他
he understood that he could not love him like a father
他明白自己不能像父亲一样爱他
Slowly, he also understood that the eleven-year-old was a pampered boy

慢慢地，他也明白了，这个十一岁的孩子是个被宠坏的男孩

he saw that he was a mother's boy
他看到他是一个妈妈的儿子

he saw that he had grown up in the habits of rich people
他发现自己是在富人的习惯下长大的

he was accustomed to finer food and a soft bed
他习惯了精致的食物和柔软的床

he was accustomed to giving orders to servants
他习惯于向仆人发号施令

the mourning child could not suddenly be content with a life among strangers
悲伤的孩子无法突然满足于在陌生人中的生活

Siddhartha understood the pampered child would not willingly be in poverty
悉达多明白，被宠坏的孩子不会甘愿生活在贫困之中

He did not force him to do these these things
他没有强迫他做这些事

Siddhartha did many chores for the boy
悉达多为这个男孩做了很多家务

he always saved the best piece of the meal for him
他总是把最好的部分留给自己

Slowly, he hoped to win him over, by friendly patience
他希望通过友善的耐心慢慢地赢得他的支持

Rich and happy, he had called himself, when the boy had come to him
当男孩来到他身边时，他称自己为富有和幸福

Since then some time had passed
从那时起已经过去了一段时间

but the boy remained a stranger and in a gloomy disposition
但男孩依然是个陌生人，而且心情阴郁

he displayed a proud and stubbornly disobedient heart
他表现出一颗骄傲和顽固不顺从的心

he did not want to do any work

他不想做任何工作
he did not pay his respect to the old men
他没有向老人表示敬意
he stole from Vasudeva's fruit-trees
他从瓦苏戴瓦的果树上偷走了
his son had not brought him happiness and peace
他的儿子没有给他带来幸福和平安
the boy had brought him suffering and worry
这个男孩给他带来了痛苦和烦恼
slowly Siddhartha began to understand this
悉达多慢慢开始明白这一点
But he loved him regardless of the suffering he brought him
但他爱他，无论他给他带来多少痛苦
he preferred the suffering and worries of love over
happiness and joy without the boy
他宁愿承受爱情的痛苦和忧虑，也不愿承受没有儿子的幸福和快乐
from when young Siddhartha was in the hut the old men had split the work
从小悉达多还在茅屋时起，老人们就开始分工
Vasudeva had again taken on the job of the ferryman
瓦苏戴瓦又担任了摆渡人的工作
and Siddhartha, in order to be with his son, did the work in the hut and the field
为了陪伴儿子，悉达多在屋里和田里干活。

for long months Siddhartha waited for his son to understand him
悉达多花了好几个月等待儿子理解他
he waited for him to accept his love
他等他接受他的爱
and he waited for his son to perhaps reciprocate his love
他等待儿子回报他的爱
For long months Vasudeva waited, watching

瓦苏戴瓦等待了好几个月，观察着
he waited and said nothing
他等待着，什么也没说
One day, young Siddhartha tormented his father very much
有一天，年轻的悉达多非常折磨他的父亲
he had broken both of his rice-bowls
他把两个饭碗都打碎了
Vasudeva took his friend aside and talked to him
瓦苏戴瓦把他的朋友拉到一边，和他说话
"Pardon me," he said to Siddhartha
"请原谅我，" 他对悉达多说。
"from a friendly heart, I'm talking to you"
"我怀着友好的心情和你谈话"
"I'm seeing that you are tormenting yourself"
"我看你正在折磨自己"
"I'm seeing that you're in grief"
"我看到你很悲伤"
"Your son, my dear, is worrying you"
"亲爱的，你的儿子让你担心了"
"and he is also worrying me"
"他也让我担心"
"That young bird is accustomed to a different life"
"那只小鸟已经习惯了不同的生活"
"he is used to living in a different nest"
"他已经习惯了住在不同的窝里"
"he has not, like you, run away from riches and the city"
"他没有像你一样逃离财富和城市"
"he was not disgusted and fed up with the life in Sansara"
"他并没有对轮回的生活感到厌恶和厌倦"
"he had to do all these things against his will"
"他不得不违背自己的意愿做这些事"
"he had to leave all this behind"
"他必须抛弃这一切"
"I asked the river, oh friend"

"我问过河流,哦朋友"
"many times I have asked the river"
"我曾多次询问河流"
"But the river laughs at all of this"
"但河水却嘲笑这一切"
"it laughs at me and it laughs at you"
"它嘲笑我,也嘲笑你"
"the river is shaking with laughter at our foolishness"
"我们的愚蠢让河水都笑得颤抖了"
"Water wants to join water as youth wants to join youth"
"水想加入水,就像年轻人想加入年轻人一样"
"your son is not in the place where he can prosper"
"你的儿子还没有找到可以发迹的地方"
"you too should ask the river"
"你也应该问问河流"
"you too should listen to it!"
"你也应该听一听!"
Troubled, Siddhartha looked into his friendly face
悉达多心烦意乱地看着他友善的面孔
he looked at the many wrinkles in which there was incessant cheerfulness
他看着那些皱纹,但皱纹里却洋溢着无尽的快乐
"How could I part with him?" he said quietly, ashamed
他羞愧地轻声说:"我怎么能和他分开呢?"
"Give me some more time, my dear"
"再给我一点时间吧亲爱的"
"See, I'm fighting for him"
"看,我在为他而战"
"I'm seeking to win his heart"
"我想赢得他的心"
"with love and with friendly patience I intend to capture it"
"我打算用爱和友善的耐心去捕捉它"
"One day, the river shall also talk to him"
"有一天,河流也会和他说话"

"he also is called upon"
"他也被呼召"

Vasudeva's smile flourished more warmly
瓦苏戴瓦的笑容更加温暖

"Oh yes, he too is called upon"
"哦,是的,他也被召唤了"

"he too is of the eternal life"
"他也是属于永生的"

"But do we, you and me, know what he is called upon to do?"
"但是你和我,我们是否知道他被要求做什么?"

"we know what path to take and what actions to perform"
"我们知道该走哪条路、该采取什么行动"

"we know what pain we have to endure"
"我们知道我们必须忍受什么样的痛苦"

"but does he know these things?"
"但是他知道这些事情吗?"

"Not a small one, his pain will be"
"这不是小事,他的痛苦将是"

"after all, his heart is proud and hard"
"毕竟,他的内心骄傲又冷酷"

"people like this have to suffer and err a lot"
"像这样的人必须忍受很多痛苦并且犯很多错误"

"they have to do much injustice"
"他们必须做很多不公正的事情"

"and they have burden themselves with much sin"
"他们背负着许多罪孽"

"Tell me, my dear," he asked of Siddhartha
"告诉我,亲爱的," 他问悉达多

"you're not taking control of your son's upbringing?"
"你就不能掌控你儿子的成长吗?"

"You don't force him, beat him, or punish him?"
"你没有强迫他、殴打他或者惩罚他吗?"

"No, Vasudeva, I don't do any of these things"

"不，瓦苏戴瓦，我不会做这些事"
"I knew it. You don't force him"
"我就知道。你别逼他。"
"you don't beat him and you don't give him orders"
"你不要打他，也不要命令他"
"because you know softness is stronger than hard"
"因为你知道柔软比坚硬更强大"
"you know water is stronger than rocks"
"你知道水比石头更坚固"
"and you know love is stronger than force"
"你知道爱比武力更强大"
"Very good, I praise you for this"
"非常好，我表扬你了"
"But aren't you mistaken in some way?"
"但你是不是有些搞错了？"
"don't you think that you are forcing him?"
"你不觉得你是在强迫他吗？"
"don't you perhaps punish him a different way?"
"你难道不能用不同的方法惩罚他吗？"
"Don't you shackle him with your love?"
"难道你没有用你的爱束缚住他吗？"
"Don't you make him feel inferior every day?"
"你这不是让他天天自卑吗？"
"doesn't your kindness and patience make it even harder for him?"
"你的善良和耐心不是让他更加难受吗？"
"aren't you forcing him to live in a hut with two old banana-eaters?"
"你不是强迫他和两个吃香蕉的老家伙住在一间小屋里吗？"
"old men to whom even rice is a delicacy"
"对老人来说，米饭也是美味"
"old men whose thoughts can't be his"
"老人的想法无法与他一致"

"old men whose hearts are old and quiet"
"心地善良、沉静的老人"

"old men whose hearts beat in a different pace than his"
"那些心跳速度和他不一样的老人"

"Isn't he forced and punished by all this?""
"这一切难道不是他被迫接受和受到的惩罚吗？"

Troubled, Siddhartha looked to the ground
悉达多心烦意乱，低头看着地面

Quietly, he asked, "What do you think should I do?"
他轻声问道："你认为我该怎么做？"

Vasudeva spoke, "Bring him into the city"
瓦苏戴瓦说："把他带进城里。"

"bring him into his mother's house"
"带他回他母亲家去"

"there'll still be servants around, give him to them"
"周围还会有仆人，把他交给他们吧"

"And if there aren't any servants, bring him to a teacher"
"如果没有仆人，就带他去见老师"

"but don't bring him to a teacher for teachings' sake"
"但不要带他去见老师以求教诲"

"bring him to a teacher so that he is among other children"
"带他去见老师，让他和其他孩子在一起"

"and bring him to the world which is his own"
"并带他进入他自己的世界"

"have you never thought of this?"
"你就没想过这个吗？"

"you're seeing into my heart," Siddhartha spoke sadly
"你看透了我的心，" 悉达多悲伤地说

"Often, I have thought of this"
"我经常想到这一点"

"but how can I put him into this world?"
"但是我怎样才能把他带到这个世界上呢？"

"Won't he become exuberant?"
"他不会变得兴奋吗？"

"won't he lose himself to pleasure and power?"
"他不会沉迷于享乐和权力吗？"
"won't he repeat all of his father's mistakes?"
"他不会重蹈他父亲的覆辙吗？"
"won't he perhaps get entirely lost in Sansara?"
"他是不是会彻底迷失在轮回之中呢？"
Brightly, the ferryman's smile lit up
船夫的笑容灿烂地绽放
softly, he touched Siddhartha's arm
他轻轻地触摸悉达多的手臂
"Ask the river about it, my friend!"
"去向河流询问吧，我的朋友！"
"Hear the river laugh about it!"
"听听河水在嘲笑我！"
"Would you actually believe that you had committed your foolish acts?
"你真的会相信你犯下了这些愚蠢的罪行吗？
"in order to spare your son from committing them too"
"为了防止你儿子也犯同样的错误"
"And could you in any way protect your son from Sansara?"
"你能用什么方法保护你的儿子免受Sansara的伤害吗？"
"How could you protect him from Sansara?"
"你怎么能保护他免受Sansara的伤害呢？"
"By means of teachings, prayer, admonition?"
"通过教导、祈祷、劝诫？"
"My dear, have you entirely forgotten that story?"
"亲爱的，你完全忘记那个故事了吗？"
"the story containing so many lessons"
"这个故事包含了很多教训"
"the story about Siddhartha, a Brahman's son"
"婆罗门之子悉达多的故事"
"the story which you once told me here on this very spot?"
"你曾经在这个地方给我讲过的故事？"

"Who has kept the Samana Siddhartha safe from Sansara?"
"是谁保护了沙门悉达多免受轮回之苦？"
"who has kept him from sin, greed, and foolishness?"
"谁使他远离罪恶、贪婪和愚蠢？"
"Were his father's religious devotion able to keep him safe?
"他父亲的宗教信仰能保护他的安全吗？
"were his teacher's warnings able to keep him safe?"
"老师的警告能保证他的安全吗？"
"could his own knowledge keep him safe?"
"他自己的知识能保证他的安全吗？"
"was his own search able to keep him safe?"
"他自己的搜寻能保证他的安全吗？"
"What father has been able to protect his son?"
"哪个父亲能保护自己的儿子呢？"
"what father could keep his son from living his life for himself?"
"哪个父亲能阻止他的儿子为自己而活呢？"
"what teacher has been able to protect his student?"
"哪个老师能保护自己的学生呢？"
"what teacher can stop his student from soiling himself with life?"
"哪个老师能阻止自己的学生玷污自己的生命呢？"
"who could stop him from burdening himself with guilt?"
"谁能阻止他背负罪感呢？"
"who could stop him from drinking the bitter drink for himself?"
"谁能阻止他自己喝下这杯苦酒呢？"
"who could stop him from finding his path for himself?"
"谁能阻止他寻找自己的道路呢？"
"did you think anybody could be spared from taking this path?"
"你认为有人能避免走这条路吗？"
"did you think that perhaps your little son would be spared?"

"你认为你的小儿子也许能幸免于难吗?"
"did you think your love could do all that?"
"你认为你的爱可以做到这一切吗?"
"did you think your love could keep him from suffering"
"你认为你的爱能让他免受痛苦吗?"
"did you think your love could protect him from pain and disappointment?
"你认为你的爱可以保护他免受痛苦和失望吗?
"you could die ten times for him"
"你可以为他死十次"
"but you could take no part of his destiny upon yourself"
"但你不能左右他的命运"
Never before, Vasudeva had spoken so many words
瓦苏戴瓦从来没有说过这么多话
Kindly, Siddhartha thanked him
悉达多亲切地向他道谢
he went troubled into the hut
他心烦意乱地走进小屋

he could not sleep for a long time
他很久没睡着
Vasudeva had told him nothing he had not already thought and known
瓦苏戴瓦没有告诉他任何他已经想到和知道的事情
But this was a knowledge he could not act upon
但他无法根据这一认识采取行动
stronger than knowledge was his love for the boy
他对男孩的爱比知识更强烈
stronger than knowledge was his tenderness
他的温柔比知识更强大
stronger than knowledge was his fear to lose him
比知识更强烈的是他害怕失去他
had he ever lost his heart so much to something?
他曾经对某件事如此痴心吗?

had he ever loved any person so blindly?
他曾经如此盲目地爱过一个人吗？
had he ever suffered for someone so unsuccessfully?
他曾经为某人受过如此痛苦却又如此无奈的苦吗？
had he ever made such sacrifices for anyone and yet been so unhappy?
他曾为任何人做出过如此大的牺牲，却依然如此不快乐吗？
Siddhartha could not heed his friend's advice
悉达多没有听从朋友的劝告
he could not give up the boy
他不能放弃这个男孩
He let the boy give him orders
他让男孩给他发号施令
he let him disregard him
他让他无视他
He said nothing and waited
他什么也没说，只是等待
daily, he attempted the struggle of friendliness
每天，他都试图努力保持友好
he initiated the silent war of patience
他发起了无声的耐心战争
Vasudeva also said nothing and waited
瓦苏戴瓦也没有说话，只是等待
They were both masters of patience
他们都是耐心大师

one time the boy's face reminded him very much of Kamala
有一次，男孩的脸让他想起了卡玛拉
Siddhartha suddenly had to think of something Kamala had once said
悉达多突然想起了卡玛拉曾经说过的一句话
"You cannot love" she had said to him
她曾对他说："你无法去爱"

and he had agreed with her
他同意了她的观点
and he had compared himself with a star
他曾将自己比作一颗明星
and he had compared the childlike people with falling leaves
他把孩子般的人比作落叶
but nevertheless, he had also sensed an accusation in that line
但尽管如此,他也感觉到这句话里有指责
Indeed, he had never been able to love
事实上,他从来没有能够爱
he had never been able to devote himself completely to another person
他从来没有能够完全把自己奉献给另一个人
he had never been able to to forget himself
他从来没能忘记自己
he had never been able to commit foolish acts for the love of another person
他从来没能为了爱别人而做出愚蠢的事情
at that time it seemed to set him apart from the childlike people
那时,他似乎与那些孩子气的人不同
But ever since his son was here, Siddhartha also become a childlike person
但自从儿子来了以后,悉达多也变成了一个孩子气的人
he was suffering for the sake of another person
他是为了别人而受苦
he was loving another person
他爱上了另一个人
he was lost to a love for someone else
他爱上了别人
he had become a fool on account of love

他因爱而变傻

Now he too felt the strongest and strangest of all passions
现在他也感受到了最强烈、最奇怪的激情

he suffered from this passion miserably
他因这种激情而痛苦不堪

and he was nevertheless in bliss
但他仍然很幸福

he was nevertheless renewed in one respect
然而,他在一个方面焕然一新

he was enriched by this one thing
这件事让他受益匪浅

He sensed very well that this blind love for his son was a passion
他很清楚地感觉到,对儿子这种盲目的爱是一种激情

he knew that it was something very human
他知道这是非常人性化的事情

he knew that it was Sansara
他知道这是轮回

he knew that it was a murky source, dark waters
他知道那是一处浑浊的源头,黑暗的水域

but he felt it was not worthless, but necessary
但他认为这并非毫无价值,而且是必要的

it came from the essence of his own being
它来自他自身的本质

This pleasure also had to be atoned for
这种快乐也必须得到补偿

this pain also had to be endured
这种痛苦也必须忍受

these foolish acts also had to be committed
这些愚蠢的行为也必须发生

Through all this, the son let him commit his foolish acts
儿子通过这一切,让他做了蠢事

he let him court for his affection
他让他向他求爱

he let him humiliate himself every day
他让他每天都受辱

he gave in to the moods of his son
他屈服于儿子的情绪

his father had nothing which could have delighted him
他的父亲没有什么能让他高兴

and he nothing that the boy feared
他什么也不怕

He was a good man, this father
他是一个好人,这个父亲

he was a good, kind, soft man
他是一个善良、温和的男人

perhaps he was a very devout man
也许他是一个非常虔诚的人

perhaps he was a saint, the boy thought
也许他是一位圣人,男孩想

but all these attributes could not win the boy over
但所有这些特点都无法赢得男孩的芳心

He was bored by this father, who kept him imprisoned
他对这个把他囚禁的父亲感到厌烦

a prisoner in this miserable hut of his
在他这个简陋的小屋里

he was bored of him answering every naughtiness with a smile
他厌倦了他用微笑回答每一个顽皮的问题

he didn't appreciate insults being responded to by friendliness
他不喜欢用友好的态度来回应侮辱

he didn't like viciousness returned in kindness
他不喜欢以恶报善

this very thing was the hated trick of this old sneak
这正是这个老流氓的恶作剧

Much more the boy would have liked it if he had been threatened by him

如果他能威胁这个男孩,他会更高兴
he wanted to be abused by him
他想被他虐待

A day came when young Siddhartha had had enough
有一天,年轻的悉达多受够了
what was on his mind came bursting forth
他心里想的都涌现出来了
and he openly turned against his father
他公开反对他的父亲
Siddhartha had given him a task
悉达多给了他一个任务
he had told him to gather brushwood
他叫他去收集灌木丛
But the boy did not leave the hut
但男孩没有离开小屋
in stubborn disobedience and rage, he stayed where he was
他固执地抗拒,愤怒地留在原地
he thumped on the ground with his feet
他用脚重重地敲打地面
he clenched his fists and screamed in a powerful outburst
他握紧拳头,大声尖叫
he screamed his hatred and contempt into his father's face
他对着父亲的脸大声喊出他的仇恨和蔑视
"Get the brushwood for yourself!" he shouted, foaming at the mouth
"自己去把柴火拿来!"他大叫,口吐白沫
"I'm not your servant"
"我不是你的仆人"
"I know that you won't hit me, you wouldn't dare"
"我知道你不会打我,你不敢"
"I know that you constantly want to punish me"
"我知道你总是想惩罚我"

"you want to put me down with your religious devotion and your indulgence"
"你想用你的宗教信仰和你的纵容来贬低我"
"You want me to become like you"
"你想让我变得像你一样"
"you want me to be just as devout, soft, and wise as you"
"你希望我和你一样虔诚、温柔、睿智"
"but I won't do it, just to make you suffer"
"但我不会这么做,只是为了让你受苦"
"I would rather become a highway-robber than be as soft as you"
"我宁愿当劫匪,也不愿像你这么软弱"
"I would rather be a murderer than be as wise as you"
"我宁愿当杀人犯,也不愿像你一样聪明"
"I would rather go to hell, than to become like you!"
"我宁愿下地狱,也不愿变成像你一样!"
"I hate you, you're not my father
"我恨你,你不是我父亲
"even if you've slept with my mother ten times, you are not my father!"
"就算你和我妈妈睡过十次,你也不是我爸爸!"
Rage and grief boiled over in him
他心中充满愤怒和悲伤
he foamed at his father in a hundred savage and evil words
他用上百种粗鲁恶毒的言语向他父亲怒不可遏
Then the boy ran away into the forest
然后男孩跑进了森林
it was late at night when the boy returned
男孩回来的时候已经很晚了
But the next morning, he had disappeared
但第二天早上,他却消失了
What had also disappeared was a small basket
同样消失的还有一个小篮子

the basket in which the ferrymen kept those copper and silver coins
摆渡人用来装铜币和银币的篮子
the coins which they received as a fare
他们收到的车费硬币
The boat had also disappeared
船也失踪了
Siddhartha saw the boat lying by the opposite bank
悉达多看见船停在对岸
Siddhartha had been shivering with grief
悉达多一直因悲伤而颤抖
the ranting speeches the boy had made touched him
男孩的夸夸其谈让他感动
"I must follow him," said Siddhartha
悉达多说："我必须跟随他。"
"A child can't go through the forest all alone, he'll perish"
"孩子不能独自穿过森林,否则他会死的"
"We must build a raft, Vasudeva, to get over the water"
"我们必须造一只木筏,瓦苏戴瓦,才能渡过水面。"

"We will build a raft" said Vasudeva
"我们将建造一个木筏," 瓦苏戴瓦说
"we will build it to get our boat back"
"我们会修好它,把我们的船夺回来"
"But you shall not run after your child, my friend"
"但你不应该追赶你的孩子,我的朋友。"
"he is no child anymore"
"他不再是一个孩子了"
"he knows how to get around"
"他知道如何出行"
"He's looking for the path to the city"
"他正在寻找通往城市的道路"
"and he is right, don't forget that"
"他是对的,别忘了这一点"

"he's doing what you've failed to do yourself"
"他正在做你自己没能做到的事"
"he's taking care of himself"
"他正在照顾自己"
"he's taking his course for himself"
"他正在为自己选择道路"
"Alas, Siddhartha, I see you suffering"
"哎呀,悉达多,我看见你在受苦。"
"but you're suffering a pain at which one would like to laugh"
"但你正在经受一种让人想笑的痛苦"
"you're suffering a pain at which you'll soon laugh yourself"
"你正在经受痛苦,但很快你自己也会笑出来的"
Siddhartha did not answer his friend
悉达多没有回答他的朋友
He already held the axe in his hands
他已经把斧头握在手中
and he began to make a raft of bamboo
他开始用竹子做木筏
Vasudeva helped him to tie the canes together with ropes of grass
瓦苏戴瓦帮他用草绳把藤条绑在一起
When they crossed the river they drifted far off their course
当他们过河时,他们偏离了航线
they pulled the raft upriver on the opposite bank
他们把木筏拉到对岸
"Why did you take the axe along?" asked Siddhartha
"你为什么带着斧头呢?"悉达多问。
"It might have been possible that the oar of our boat got lost"
"我们的船桨可能丢了"
But Siddhartha knew what his friend was thinking
但是悉达多知道他的朋友在想什么
He thought, the boy would have thrown away the oar
他想,男孩会扔掉桨

in order to get some kind of revenge
为了报复
and in order to keep them from following him
为了阻止他们跟随他
And in fact, there was no oar left in the boat
事实上,船上已经没有桨了
Vasudeva pointed to the bottom of the boat
瓦苏戴瓦指着船底
and he looked at his friend with a smile
他微笑着看着他的朋友
he smiled as if he wanted to say something
他微笑着,好像想说些什么
"Don't you see what your son is trying to tell you?"
"你不明白你的儿子想告诉你什么吗?"
"Don't you see that he doesn't want to be followed?"
"你没看出来他不想被人跟踪吗?"
But he did not say this in words
但他没有用言语表达
He started making a new oar
他开始制作一只新桨
But Siddhartha bid his farewell, to look for the run-away
但悉达多告别了,去寻找逃跑的人
Vasudeva did not stop him from looking for his child
瓦苏戴瓦没有阻止他寻找他的孩子

Siddhartha had been walking through the forest for a long time
悉达多在森林里走了很久
the thought occurred to him that his search was useless
他突然想到他的搜寻是无用的
Either the boy was far ahead and had already reached the city
要么男孩已经走得很远,到达了城市
or he would conceal himself from him

或者他会向他隐瞒自己
he continued thinking about his son
他继续想念他的儿子
he found that he was not worried for his son
他发现自己并不担心儿子
he knew deep inside that he had not perished
他内心深处知道他没有死
nor was he in any danger in the forest
他在森林里也没有遇到任何危险
Nevertheless, he ran without stopping
尽管如此,他还是不停地奔跑
he was not running to save him
他并没有跑去救他
he was running to satisfy his desire
他跑步是为了满足自己的欲望
he wanted to perhaps see him one more time
他也许想再见他一次
And he ran up to just outside of the city
他跑到城外
When, near the city, he reached a wide road
当他靠近城市时,他来到一条宽阔的道路
he stopped, by the entrance of the beautiful pleasure-garden
他停在了美丽的游乐园入口处
the garden which used to belong to Kamala
曾经属于卡马拉的花园
the garden where he had seen her for the first time
他第一次见到她的花园
when she was sitting in her sedan-chair
当她坐在轿子里的时候
The past rose up in his soul
往事浮现在他的心里
again, he saw himself standing there
他又看见自己站在那里
a young, bearded, naked Samana

一位留着胡须、裸体的年轻沙门

his hair hair was full of dust
他的头发上满是灰尘

For a long time, Siddhartha stood there
悉达多久久地站在那里

he looked through the open gate into the garden
他透过敞开的大门向花园望去

he saw monks in yellow robes walking among the beautiful trees
他看到身穿黄色僧袍的僧侣在美丽的树林间行走

For a long time, he stood there, pondering
他站在那里,沉思良久

he saw images and listened to the story of his life
他看到了图像,听到了他的人生故事

For a long time, he stood there looking at the monks
他久久地站在那里,看着僧侣们

he saw young Siddhartha in their place
他看到年轻的悉达多站在他们的位置上

he saw young Kamala walking among the high trees
他看见年轻的卡玛拉在高大的树林中行走

Clearly, he saw himself being served food and drink by Kamala
显然,他看到卡玛拉正在给自己端来食物和饮料

he saw himself receiving his first kiss from her
他看见自己从她那里得到了初吻

he saw himself looking proudly and disdainfully back on his life as a Brahman
他看到自己骄傲而又轻蔑地回顾自己作为婆罗门的生活

he saw himself beginning his worldly life, proudly and full of desire
他看到自己开始了他的世俗生活,骄傲而充满欲望

He saw Kamaswami, the servants, the orgies
他看到了卡玛斯瓦米、仆人和狂欢

he saw the gamblers with the dice
他看到赌徒们拿着骰子
he saw Kamala's song-bird in the cage
他看见卡玛拉的歌鸟在笼子里
he lived through all this again
他又经历了这一切
he breathed Sansara and was once again old and tired
他呼吸着轮回,又一次变得苍老和疲惫
he felt the disgust and the wish to annihilate himself again
他感到厌恶,想要再次毁灭自己
and he was healed again by the holy Om
他又被神圣的 Om 治愈了
for a long time Siddhartha had stood by the gate
悉达多在门口站了许久
he realised his desire was foolish
他意识到自己的愿望是愚蠢的
he realized it was foolishness which had made him go up to this place
他意识到自己来到这里是愚蠢的
he realized he could not help his son
他意识到自己无法帮助儿子
and he realized that he was not allowed to cling to him
他意识到自己不被允许依附于他
he felt the love for the run-away deeply in his heart
他内心深处感受到了对逃跑的爱
the love for his son felt like a wound
对儿子的爱就像一道伤口
but this wound had not been given to him in order to turn the knife in it
但他受了这伤,并不是为了把刀子插进去
the wound had to become a blossom
伤口必须化作花朵
and his wound had to shine
他的伤口必须发光

That this wound did not blossom or shine yet made him sad
这伤口未开花未发光却让他伤心
Instead of the desired goal, there was emptiness
目标没有实现，只有空虚
emptiness had drawn him here, and sadly he sat down
空虚把他吸引到这里，他悲伤地坐了下来
he felt something dying in his heart
他感到心里有什么东西死去了
he experienced emptiness and saw no joy any more
他感到空虚，再也看不到快乐
there was no goal for which to aim for
没有目标
He sat lost in thought and waited
他坐在那里沉思，等待着
This he had learned by the river
这是他在河边学到的
waiting, having patience, listening attentively
等待、耐心、认真倾听
And he sat and listened, in the dust of the road
他坐在路上的尘土中，聆听着
he listened to his heart, beating tiredly and sadly
他听着自己的心跳，疲倦而悲伤
and he waited for a voice
他等待着一个声音
Many an hour he crouched, listening
他常常蹲着，听
he saw no images any more
他再也看不到任何图像
he fell into emptiness and let himself fall
他陷入空虚，任由自己堕落
he could see no path in front of him
他看不到前面的路
And when he felt the wound burning, he silently spoke the Om

当他感到伤口灼痛时，他默念着"嗡"
he filled himself with Om
他心中充满了Om
The monks in the garden saw him
花园里的僧侣们看见了他
dust was gathering on his gray hair
他的灰白头发上积满灰尘
since he crouched for many hours, one of monks placed two bananas in front of him
因为他蹲了好几个小时，一个僧人把两根香蕉放在他面前
The old man did not see him
老人没有看见他

From this petrified state, he was awoken by a hand touching his shoulder
一只手触碰了他的肩膀，把他从惊恐状态中唤醒。
Instantly, he recognised this tender bashful touch
他立刻认出了这温柔而羞涩的触感
Vasudeva had followed him and waited
瓦苏戴瓦跟着他，等待着
he regained his senses and rose to greet Vasudeva
他恢复了理智，站起来迎接瓦苏戴瓦
he looked into Vasudeva's friendly face
他看着瓦苏戴瓦友善的脸
he looked into the small wrinkles
他看着那些小皱纹
his wrinkles were as if they were filled with nothing but his smile
他的皱纹仿佛被他的微笑填满
he looked into the happy eyes, and then he smiled too
他看着那双幸福的眼睛，然后他也笑了
Now he saw the bananas lying in front of him
现在他看到香蕉摆在他面前

he picked the bananas up and gave one to the ferryman
他捡起香蕉,给了船夫一个
After eating the bananas, they silently went back into the forest
吃完香蕉后,他们默默地回到了森林里
they returned home to the ferry
他们回到渡口
Neither one talked about what had happened that day
两人都没有谈论那天发生的事情
neither one mentioned the boy's name
没有人提到男孩的名字
neither one spoke about him running away
没人谈论他逃跑的事
neither one spoke about the wound
没有人谈论伤口
In the hut, Siddhartha lay down on his bed
在茅屋里,悉达多躺在床上
after a while Vasudeva came to him
过了一会儿,瓦苏戴瓦来到他身边
he offered him a bowl of coconut-milk
他给他端来一碗椰奶
but he was already asleep
但他已经睡着了

Om
唵

For a long time the wound continued to burn
伤口持续灼烧了很长时间
Siddhartha had to ferry many travellers across the river
悉达多必须渡很多旅客过河
many of the travellers were accompanied by a son or a daughter
许多旅行者都带着儿子或女儿
and he saw none of them without envying them
他看到她们,总是羡慕不已。
he couldn't see them without thinking about his lost son
每当看到它们,他就会想起他失踪的儿子
"So many thousands possess the sweetest of good fortunes"
"成千上万的人拥有最甜蜜的好运"
"why don't I also possess this good fortune?"
"我怎么就不具备这个福气呢?"
"even thieves and robbers have children and love them"
"即使是小偷和强盗也会有孩子并且爱他们"
"and they are being loved by their children"
"他们也深受孩子们的喜爱"
"all are loved by their children except for me"
"除了我之外,所有人都深受孩子们的喜爱"
he now thought like the childlike people, without reason
他现在的思维方式就像孩子一样,没有理由
he had become one of the childlike people
他已经成为一个孩子气的人
he looked upon people differently than before
他以不同于以前的方式看待人们
he was less smart and less proud of himself
他不那么聪明,也不那么自负
but instead, he was warmer and more curious
但相反,他更加热情,更加好奇

when he ferried travellers, he was more involved than before
当他载客时,他比以前更加投入

childlike people, businessmen, warriors, women
童心未泯的人、商人、战士、妇女

these people did not seem alien to him, as they used to
这些人对他来说并不像以前那样陌生,

he understood them and shared their life
他理解他们并分享他们的生活

a life which was not guided by thoughts and insight
没有思想和洞察力指导的生活

but a life guided solely by urges and wishes
而是一种仅受冲动和愿望引导的生活

he felt like the the childlike people
他感觉就像孩子般的人

he was bearing his final wound
他正承受着最后的伤痛

he was nearing perfection
他已经接近完美

but the childlike people still seemed like his brothers
但那些孩子般的人仍然像他的兄弟一样

their vanities, desires for possession were no longer ridiculous to him
他们的虚荣心和占有欲对他来说不再是可笑的

they became understandable and lovable
他们变得可以理解和可爱

they even became worthy of veneration to him
他们甚至值得他崇拜

The blind love of a mother for her child
母亲对孩子盲目的爱

the stupid, blind pride of a conceited father for his only son
一个自负的父亲对自己唯一的儿子的愚蠢、盲目的骄傲

the blind, wild desire of a young, vain woman for jewellery

一个年轻虚荣的女人对珠宝的盲目、狂野的欲望
her wish for admiring glances from men
她渴望得到男人赞赏的目光
all of these simple urges were not childish notions
所有这些简单的渴望都不是幼稚的想法
but they were immensely strong, living, and prevailing urges
但它们是极其强烈、鲜活和普遍的冲动
he saw people living for the sake of their urges
他看到人们为了满足自己的欲望而活着
he saw people achieving rare things for their urges
他看到人们为了实现自己的愿望而取得了罕见的成就
travelling, conducting wars, suffering
旅行、打仗、受苦
they bore an infinite amount of suffering
他们承受了无限的痛苦
and he could love them for it, because he saw life
他因此而爱他们，因为他看到了生命
that what is alive was in each of their passions
每个人的激情中都充满着活力
that what is indestructible was in their urges, the Brahman
不可毁灭的东西在他们的欲望中，婆罗门
these people were worthy of love and admiration
这些人值得爱和钦佩
they deserved it for their blind loyalty and blind strength
他们因盲目的忠诚和盲目的力量而应得这一结果
there was nothing that they lacked
他们什么都不缺
Siddhartha had nothing which would put him above the rest, except one thing
悉达多没有什么能使他出类拔萃，除了一件事
there still was a small thing he had which they didn't
他还有一件小东西，而他们没有
he had the conscious thought of the oneness of all life

他意识到所有生命都是一体的
but Siddhartha even doubted whether this knowledge should be valued so highly
但悉达多甚至怀疑这种知识是否值得如此重视
it might also be a childish idea of the thinking people
这也可能是思想人士的幼稚想法
the worldly people were of equal rank to the wise men
世俗之人和智者地位平等
animals too can in some moments seem to be superior to humans
动物在某些时候也会显得比人类优越
they are superior in their tough, unrelenting performance of what is necessary
他们以坚韧不拔、不懈怠的态度完成必要的任务，
an idea slowly blossomed in Siddhartha
一个想法在悉达多心中慢慢萌芽
and the idea slowly ripened in him
这个想法在他心中逐渐成熟
he began to see what wisdom actually was
他开始明白智慧到底是什么
he saw what the goal of his long search was
他看到了他长期寻找的目标
his search was nothing but a readiness of the soul
他的寻找只不过是灵魂的准备
a secret art to think every moment, while living his life
生活中时刻思考的秘密艺术
it was the thought of oneness
这是合一的思想
to be able to feel and inhale the oneness
能够感受到并吸入合一
Slowly this awareness blossomed in him
慢慢地，他意识到了这一点
it was shining back at him from Vasudeva's old, childlike face

瓦苏戴瓦那张稚嫩的脸上闪耀着光芒
harmony and knowledge of the eternal perfection of the world
和谐与对世界永恒完美的认识
smiling and to be part of the oneness
微笑并成为一体的一部分
But the wound still burned
但伤口仍在灼痛
longingly and bitterly Siddhartha thought of his son
悉达多怀念他的儿子
he nurtured his love and tenderness in his heart
他心中滋养着爱与温柔
he allowed the pain to gnaw at him
他任由痛苦折磨着自己
he committed all foolish acts of love
他做了所有愚蠢的爱之举
this flame would not go out by itself
火焰不会自行熄灭

one day the wound burned violently
有一天伤口剧烈烧灼
driven by a yearning, Siddhartha crossed the river
悉达多在渴望的驱使下,渡过了河流
he got off the boat and was willing to go to the city
他下了船,愿意去城里
he wanted to look for his son again
他想再次寻找他的儿子
The river flowed softly and quietly
河水静静地流淌
it was the dry season, but its voice sounded strange
那是旱季,但它的声音听起来很奇怪
it was clear to hear that the river laughed
可以清楚地听到河水在笑
it laughed brightly and clearly at the old ferryman

它向老船夫开怀大笑

he bent over the water, in order to hear even better
他俯身靠近水面，以便听得更清楚

and he saw his face reflected in the quietly moving waters
他看见自己的脸倒映在静静流动的水面上

in this reflected face there was something
在这张倒映的脸上，有某种东西

something which reminded him, but he had forgotten
有件事让他想起了，但他忘了

as he thought about it, he found it
当他思考的时候，他发现

this face resembled another face which he used to know and love
这张脸很像他曾经熟悉和喜爱的另一张脸

but he also used to fear this face
但他也曾经害怕这张脸

It resembled his father's face, the Brahman
它与他父亲的脸很像，婆罗门

he remembered how he had forced his father to let him go
他记得他是如何强迫父亲放他走的

he remembered how he had bid his farewell to him
他记得他是如何向他告别的

he remembered how he had gone and had never come back
他记得自己走了之后就再也没有回来

Had his father not also suffered the same pain for him?
他的父亲不也为他承受了同样的痛苦吗？

was his father's pain not the pain Siddhartha is suffering now?
父亲的痛苦难道不是悉达多现在所遭受的痛苦吗？

Had his father not long since died?
他的父亲不是刚去世不久吗？

had he died without having seen his son again?
他难道没有再见到儿子就去世了？

Did he not have to expect the same fate for himself?

难道他自己就不会遭遇同样的命运吗？
Was it not a comedy in a fateful circle?
这何尝不是命运轮回中的一出喜剧呢？
The river laughed about all of this
河水嘲笑这一切
everything came back which had not been suffered
一切未受过损失的都回来了
everything came back which had not been solved
一切尚未解决的问题又回来了
the same pain was suffered over and over again
同样的痛苦一次又一次地遭受
Siddhartha went back into the boat
悉达多回到船上
and he returned back to the hut
然后他回到了小屋
he was thinking of his father and of his son
他想念他的父亲和他的儿子
he thought of having been laughed at by the river
他想到自己被河水嘲笑
he was at odds with himself and tending towards despair
他与自己格格不入，趋向绝望
but he was also tempted to laugh
但他也忍不住笑了起来
he could laugh at himself and the entire world
他可以嘲笑自己和整个世界
Alas, the wound was not blossoming yet
唉，伤口还没有开花
his heart was still fighting his fate
他的心仍在与命运抗争
cheerfulness and victory were not yet shining from his suffering
他的痛苦中还未闪耀出快乐和胜利的光芒
Nevertheless, he felt hope along with the despair
尽管如此，他在绝望的同时，也感到了希望

once he returned to the hut he felt an undefeatable desire to open up to Vasudeva
回到小屋后，他感到一种无法抑制的渴望，想向瓦苏戴瓦敞开心扉

he wanted to show him everything
他想向他展示一切

he wanted to say everything to the master of listening
他想把一切都告诉倾听大师

Vasudeva was sitting in the hut, weaving a basket
瓦苏戴瓦坐在小屋里，编织着篮子

He no longer used the ferry-boat
他不再使用渡船

his eyes were starting to get weak
他的眼睛开始变得无力

his arms and hands were getting weak as well
他的手臂和手也变得虚弱

only the joy and cheerful benevolence of his face was unchanging
只有他脸上的喜悦和开朗仁慈是不变的

Siddhartha sat down next to the old man
悉达多坐在老人身边

slowly, he started talking about what they had never spoke about
慢慢地，他开始谈论他们从未谈论过的事情

he told him of his walk to the city
他告诉他自己步行去城里

he told at him of the burning wound
他向他讲述了灼烧的伤口

he told him about the envy of seeing happy fathers
他告诉他看到父亲们幸福的情景，他感到很羡慕

his knowledge of the foolishness of such wishes
他知道这种愿望是愚蠢的

his futile fight against his wishes

他徒劳地与自己的意愿抗争

he was able to say everything, even the most embarrassing parts

他能说出一切,甚至最尴尬的部分

he told him everything he could tell him

他把能说的都告诉了他。

he showed him everything he could show him

他向他展示了他所能展示的一切。

He presented his wound to him

他向他展示了自己的伤口

he also told him how he had fled today

他还告诉他今天是如何逃跑的

he told him how he ferried across the water

他告诉他如何渡过水面

a childish run-away, willing to walk to the city

一个孩子气的离家出走者,愿意步行去城里

and he told him how the river had laughed

他告诉他河水曾如何大笑

he spoke for a long time

他讲了很长时间

Vasudeva was listening with a quiet face

瓦苏戴瓦一脸平静地听着

Vasudeva's listening gave Siddhartha a stronger sensation than ever before

瓦苏戴瓦的倾听让悉达多比以往任何时候都更加激动

he sensed how his pain and fears flowed over to him

他感觉到自己的痛苦和恐惧如何蔓延到他身上

he sensed how his secret hope flowed over him

他感觉到他的秘密希望如何涌上心头

To show his wound to this listener was the same as bathing it in the river

向这位听众展示他的伤口,就如同在河里洗澡一样

the river would have cooled Siddhartha's wound

河水会冷却悉达多的伤口

the quiet listening cooled Siddhartha's wound
静静地聆听，让悉达多的伤口冷却下来
it cooled him until he become one with the river
它让他冷静下来，直到他与河流融为一体
While he was still speaking, still admitting and confessing
当他还在说话、还在承认和坦白时
Siddhartha felt more and more that this was no longer Vasudeva
悉达多越来越觉得，这不再是瓦苏戴瓦了
it was no longer a human being who was listening to him
听他说话的已经不再是一个人了。
this motionless listener was absorbing his confession into himself
这位一动不动的听众正在将他的忏悔融入自己的内心
this motionless listener was like a tree the rain
这一动不动的倾听者就像一棵树，雨
this motionless man was the river itself
这个一动不动的男人就是河流本身
this motionless man was God himself
这个一动不动的男人就是上帝本人
the motionless man was the eternal itself
一动不动的人本身就是永恒
Siddhartha stopped thinking of himself and his wound
悉达多不再想着自己和他的伤口
this realisation of Vasudeva's changed character took possession of him
他意识到瓦苏戴瓦的性格已经改变
and the more he entered into it, the less wondrous it became
他越深入其中，就越不觉得奇妙
the more he realised that everything was in order and natural
他越发意识到一切都井然有序、自然而然
he realised that Vasudeva had already been like this for a long time

他意识到 Vasudeva 已经这样很久了
he had just not quite recognised it yet
他只是还没有完全意识到
yes, he himself had almost reached the same state
是的,他自己也几乎达到了同样的境界
He felt, that he was now seeing old Vasudeva as the people see the gods
他感觉,他现在看到老瓦苏戴瓦就像人们看到神一样
and he felt that this could not last
他觉得这种情况不会持续下去
in his heart, he started bidding his farewell to Vasudeva
他心里开始向瓦苏戴瓦告别
Throughout all this, he talked incessantly
在这整个过程中,他不停地说话
When he had finished talking, Vasudeva turned his friendly eyes at him
当他讲完话后,瓦苏戴瓦友善地望着他
the eyes which had grown slightly weak
眼睛变得有点无力
he said nothing, but let his silent love and cheerfulness shine
他什么也没说,只是让自己无声的爱和快乐闪耀
his understanding and knowledge shone from him
他的理解和知识从他身上散发出来
He took Siddhartha's hand and led him to the seat by the bank
他牵着悉达多的手,领他到银行旁边的座位上。
he sat down with him and smiled at the river
他和他一起坐下,对着河面微笑
"You've heard it laugh," he said
"你听到了它的笑声," 他说
"But you haven't heard everything"
"但你还没有听到一切"
"Let's listen, you'll hear more"

"让我们听一听,你会听到更多"

Softly sounded the river, singing in many voices
河水轻轻地流淌,用许多声音歌唱

Siddhartha looked into the water
悉达多望向水面

images appeared to him in the moving water
流动的水中出现了图像

his father appeared, lonely and mourning for his son
他的父亲出现了,他感到孤独,为儿子哀悼

he himself appeared in the moving water
他自己出现在流动的水中

he was also being tied with the bondage of yearning to his distant son
他也被对远方儿子的思念所束缚

his son appeared, lonely as well
他的儿子也孤独地出现了

the boy, greedily rushing along the burning course of his young wishes
男孩,贪婪地沿着年轻愿望的燃烧之路奔跑

each one was heading for his goal
每个人都在朝着自己的目标前进

each one was obsessed by the goal
每个人都痴迷于这个目标

each one was suffering from the pursuit
每个人都在遭受追捕

The river sang with a voice of suffering
河流用痛苦的声音歌唱

longingly it sang and flowed towards its goal
它渴望地歌唱,流向它的目标

"Do you hear?" Vasudeva asked with a mute gaze
"你听见了吗?" 瓦苏戴瓦用无声的目光问道

Siddhartha nodded in reply
悉达多点头回答。

"Listen better!" Vasudeva whispered

"听好了！"瓦苏戴瓦低声说

Siddhartha made an effort to listen better
悉达多努力倾听

The image of his father appeared
父亲的形象浮现出来

his own image merged with his father's
他的形象与他父亲的形象融为一体

the image of his son merged with his image
儿子的形象与他的形象融为一体

Kamala's image also appeared and was dispersed
卡玛拉的形象也出现并消散了

and the image of Govinda, and other images
以及戈文达的像，以及其他像

and all the imaged merged with each other
所有的图像都融合在一起

all the imaged turned into the river
所有想象都化作了河流

being the river, they all headed for the goal
成为河流，他们都朝着目标前进

longing, desiring, suffering flowed together
渴望、欲望、痛苦汇聚在一起

and the river's voice sounded full of yearning
河水的声音充满渴望

the river's voice was full of burning woe
河水的声音充满着灼热的悲伤

the river's voice was full of unsatisfiable desire
河流的声音充满了无法满足的欲望

For the goal, the river was heading
为了进球，河流正流向

Siddhartha saw the river hurrying towards its goal
悉达多看到河流奔向目的地

the river of him and his loved ones and of all people he had ever seen
他和他的亲人以及他所见过的所有人的河流

all of these waves and waters were hurrying
所有这些波浪和水都在奔腾
they were all suffering towards many goals
他们都在为实现多个目标而努力
the waterfall, the lake, the rapids, the sea
瀑布、湖泊、急流、大海
and all goals were reached
所有目标均已实现
and every goal was followed by a new one
每实现一个目标都会有一个新目标
and the water turned into vapour and rose to the sky
水变成蒸汽,升上天空
the water turned into rain and poured down from the sky
水变成了雨,从天上倾泻而下
the water turned into a source
水变成了源头
then the source turned into a stream
然后源头变成了溪流
the stream turned into a river
小溪变成了河流
and the river headed forwards again
河水又向前流去
But the longing voice had changed
但渴望的声音已经改变
It still resounded, full of suffering, searching
它依然回荡着,充满痛苦,寻找
but other voices joined the river
但其他声音也加入进来
there were voices of joy and of suffering
有欢乐的声音,也有痛苦的声音
good and bad voices, laughing and sad ones
好声音和坏声音,笑声和悲伤声
a hundred voices, a thousand voices
一百个声音,一千个声音

Siddhartha listened to all these voices
悉达多聆听了这些声音

He was now nothing but a listener
他现在只是一个听众

he was completely concentrated on listening
他全神贯注地倾听

he was completely empty now
他现在完全空了

he felt that he had now finished learning to listen
他觉得自己现在已经学会了倾听

Often before, he had heard all this
以前他经常听到这样的事情,

he had heard these many voices in the river
他听到河里有很多声音

today the voices in the river sounded new
今天河里的声音听起来很新

Already, he could no longer tell the many voices apart
他已经无法分辨出这么多的声音了

there was no difference between the happy voices and the weeping ones
快乐的声音和哭泣的声音没有区别

the voices of children and the voices of men were one
孩子们的声音和男人的声音是一样的

all these voices belonged together
所有这些声音都属于一起

the lamentation of yearning and the laughter of the knowledgeable one
思念的悲叹和知识分子的笑声

the scream of rage and the moaning of the dying ones
愤怒的尖叫和垂死者的呻吟

everything was one and everything was intertwined
一切都是一体,一切都是交织在一起的

everything was connected and entangled a thousand times
一切都千丝万缕地联系在一起

everything together, all voices, all goals
一切在一起,所有的声音,所有的目标
all yearning, all suffering, all pleasure
所有的渴望,所有的痛苦,所有的快乐
all that was good and evil
一切善与恶
all of this together was the world
所有这些加在一起就是世界
All of it together was the flow of events
所有这些加在一起就是事件的流程
all of it was the music of life
这一切都是生命的音乐
when Siddhartha was listening attentively to this river
当悉达多专心聆听这条河水的时候
the song of a thousand voices
千声之歌
when he neither listened to the suffering nor the laughter
当他既不听痛苦,也不听笑声时
when he did not tie his soul to any particular voice
当他没有将自己的灵魂与任何特定的声音联系在一起时
when he submerged his self into the river
当他把自己沉入河中时
but when he heard them all he perceived the whole, the oneness
但当他听完所有的声音时,他意识到了整体,意识到了统一
then the great song of the thousand voices consisted of a single word
那么,千声歌唱的伟大歌曲就由一个词组成
this word was Om; the perfection
这个词是Om;完美

"Do you hear" Vasudeva's gaze asked again

"你听见了吗？" 瓦苏戴瓦再次问道

Brightly, Vasudeva's smile was shining
瓦苏戴瓦的笑容灿烂

it was floating radiantly over all the wrinkles of his old face
它闪耀着光芒，笼罩着他苍老的脸上的所有皱纹

the same way the Om was floating in the air over all the voices of the river
就像 Om 飘荡在空气中，覆盖着河流的声音

Brightly his smile was shining, when he looked at his friend
当他看着他的朋友时，他的笑容灿烂

and brightly the same smile was now starting to shine on Siddhartha's face
悉达多的脸上又开始绽放出灿烂的笑容。

His wound had blossomed and his suffering was shining
他的伤口开花了，他的痛苦闪耀着光芒

his self had flown into the oneness
他的自我已经飞入了一体

In this hour, Siddhartha stopped fighting his fate
此时，悉达多不再与命运抗争

at the same time he stopped suffering
与此同时，他不再受苦

On his face flourished the cheerfulness of a knowledge
他的脸上洋溢着知识的喜悦

a knowledge which was no longer opposed by any will
一种不再受到任何意志反对的知识

a knowledge which knows perfection
完美的知识

a knowledge which is in agreement with the flow of events
与事件进程相一致的知识

a knowledge which is with the current of life
伴随生命潮流的知识

full of sympathy for the pain of others
对他人的痛苦充满同情

full of sympathy for the pleasure of others

对他人的快乐充满同情
devoted to the flow, belonging to the oneness
专注于流动,属于一体
Vasudeva rose from the seat by the bank
瓦苏戴瓦从银行的座位上站起来
he looked into Siddhartha's eyes
他看着悉达多的眼睛
and he saw the cheerfulness of the knowledge shining in his eyes
他看到他的眼睛里闪烁着知识的喜悦
he softly touched his shoulder with his hand
他用手轻轻地触摸他的肩膀
"I've been waiting for this hour, my dear"
"亲爱的,我一直在等待这个时刻"
"Now that it has come, let me leave"
"既然来了,就让我离开吧"
"For a long time, I've been waiting for this hour"
"我等待这一刻已经很久了"
"for a long time, I've been Vasudeva the ferryman"
"长期以来,我一直是摆渡人瓦苏戴瓦"
"Now it's enough. Farewell"
"现在够了。再见。"
"farewell river, farewell Siddhartha!"
"再见了河流,再见了悉达多!"
Siddhartha made a deep bow before him who bid his farewell
悉达多深深地向他鞠躬,他向他告别。
"I've known it," he said quietly
他平静地说:"我早就知道了。"
"You'll go into the forests?"
"你要去森林里吗?"
"I'm going into the forests"
"我要去森林里"

"I'm going into the oneness" spoke Vasudeva with a bright smile
"我要进入合一" 瓦苏戴瓦带着灿烂的笑容说道
With a bright smile, he left
带着灿烂的笑容，他离开了
Siddhartha watched him leaving
悉达多目送他离去
With deep joy, with deep solemnity he watched him leave
他怀着深深的喜悦和庄严，目送他离开
he saw his steps were full of peace
他看到他的脚步充满平安
he saw his head was full of lustre
他看到他的头上充满光泽
he saw his body was full of light
他看到他的身体充满光芒

Govinda
戈文达

Govinda had been with the monks for a long time
戈文达和僧侣们在一起已经很长时间了
when not on pilgrimages, he spent his time in the pleasure-garden
不朝圣时,他就在游乐园里消磨时光
the garden which the courtesan Kamala had given the followers of Gotama
妓女卡玛拉送给乔达摩信徒的花园
he heard talk of an old ferryman, who lived a day's journey away
他听到一位住在离这里一天路程远的老船夫的故事
he heard many regarded him as a wise man
他听说很多人认为他是一个智者
When Govinda went back, he chose the path to the ferry
当戈文达回去的时候,他选择了去渡口的路
he was eager to see the ferryman
他急切地想见到渡船夫
he had lived his entire life by the rules
他一生都按规矩生活
he was looked upon with veneration by the younger monks
他受到年轻僧侣的崇敬
they respected his age and modesty
他们尊重他的年龄和谦虚
but his restlessness had not perished from his heart
但他内心的不安感还没有消失
he was searching for what he had not found
他正在寻找他尚未找到的东西
He came to the river and asked the old man to ferry him over
他来到河边,请老人渡他过去
when they got off the boat on the other side, he spoke with the old man

当他们在另一边下船时,他和老人交谈

"You're very good to us monks and pilgrims"
"你对我们僧侣和朝圣者非常好"

"you have ferried many of us across the river"
"你帮助我们很多人渡过了这条河"

"Aren't you too, ferryman, a searcher for the right path?"
"摆渡人,你不也是在寻找正确道路的人吗?"

smiling from his old eyes, Siddhartha spoke
悉达多老眼里露出微笑,说道

"oh venerable one, do you call yourself a searcher?"
"噢,尊者,您称自己为搜索者吗?"

"are you still a searcher, although already well in years?"
"尽管已经年事已高,您还是一个搜索者吗?"

"do you search while wearing the robe of Gotama's monks?"
"你穿着乔达摩僧侣的僧袍去搜寻吗?"

"It's true, I'm old," spoke Govinda
"是啊,我老了。" 戈文达说。

"but I haven't stopped searching"
"但我没有停止寻找"

"I will never stop searching"
"我永远不会停止寻找"

"this seems to be my destiny"
"这似乎就是我的命运"

"You too, so it seems to me, have been searching"
"在我看来,你也一直在寻找"

"Would you like to tell me something, oh honourable one?"
"尊敬的先生,您愿意告诉我一些事情吗?"

"What might I have that I could tell you, oh venerable one?"
"我可以告诉您什么呢,尊敬的先生?"

"Perhaps I could tell you that you're searching far too much?"
"或许我可以告诉你,你搜索得太多了?"

"Could I tell you that you don't make time for finding?"

"我能告诉你,你没有时间去寻找吗?"

"How come?" asked Govinda

"怎么会这样?"戈文达问

"When someone is searching they might only see what they search for"

"当有人进行搜索时,他们可能只会看到他们所搜索的内容"

"he might not be able to let anything else enter his mind"

"他可能无法再让其他事情进入他的脑海"

"he doesn't see what he is not searching for"

"他看不到他没有寻找的东西"

"because he always thinks of nothing but the object of his search"

"因为他总是只想着他要寻找的东西"

"he has a goal, which he is obsessed with"

"他有一个目标,并且为之痴迷"

"Searching means having a goal"

"寻找就意味着有目标"

"But finding means being free, open, and having no goal"

"但寻找意味着自由、开放、没有目标"

"You, oh venerable one, are perhaps indeed a searcher"

"尊者,您也许确实是一位探索者。"

"because, when striving for your goal, there are many things you don't see"

"因为,当你为目标而奋斗时,有很多事情你看不到"

"you might not see things which are directly in front of your eyes"

"你可能看不到眼前的东西"

"I don't quite understand yet," said Govinda, "what do you mean by this?"

"我还不太明白,"戈文达说,"你这是什么意思?"

"oh venerable one, you've been at this river before, a long time ago"
"噢，尊者，您很久以前就来过这条河。"

"and you have found a sleeping man by the river"
"你在河边发现了一个熟睡的男人"

"you have sat down with him to guard his sleep"
"你已经坐在他旁边，守护他的睡眠"

"but, oh Govinda, you did not recognise the sleeping man"
"但是，哦，戈文达，你没有认出那个正在睡觉的人"

Govinda was astonished, as if he had been the object of a magic spell
戈文达惊呆了，仿佛他被施了魔法

the monk looked into the ferryman's eyes
僧人看着船夫的眼睛

"Are you Siddhartha?" he asked with a timid voice
"你是悉达多吗？" 他怯生生地问道。

"I wouldn't have recognised you this time either!"
"这次我肯定也认不出你了！"

"from my heart, I'm greeting you, Siddhartha"
"我衷心地问候你，悉达多"

"from my heart, I'm happy to see you once again!"
"我从心底里很高兴再次见到你！"

"You've changed a lot, my friend"
"你改变了很多，我的朋友"

"and you've now become a ferryman?"
"现在你成了摆渡人了？"

In a friendly manner, Siddhartha laughed
悉达多友好地笑了

"yes, I am a ferryman"
"是的，我是一名摆渡人"

"Many people, Govinda, have to change a lot"
"许多人，戈文达，必须做出很大改变"

"they have to wear many robes"

"他们必须穿很多长袍"

"I am one of those who had to change a lot"
"我是那些必须做出很大改变的人之一"

"Be welcome, Govinda, and spend the night in my hut"
"欢迎你，戈文达，在我的小屋里过夜吧。"

Govinda stayed the night in the hut
戈文达在小屋里过夜

he slept on the bed which used to be Vasudeva's bed
他睡在曾经是 Vasudeva 的床上

he posed many questions to the friend of his youth
他向年轻时的朋友提出了很多问题

Siddhartha had to tell him many things from his life
悉达多必须告诉他自己生活中的许多事情

then the next morning came
然后第二天早上

the time had come to start the day's journey
是时候开始一天的旅程了

without hesitation, Govinda asked one more question
戈文达毫不犹豫地又问了一个问题

"Before I continue on my path, Siddhartha, permit me to ask one more question"
"在我继续赶路之前，悉达多，请允许我再问一个问题。"

"Do you have a teaching that guides you?"
"你有指导你的教义吗？"

"Do you have a faith or a knowledge you follow"
"你有信仰或者遵循的知识吗？"

"is there a knowledge which helps you to live and do right?"
"是否有一种知识可以帮助你正确生活并做正确的事？"

"You know well, my dear, I have always been distrustful of teachers"
"亲爱的，你知道的，我一直不信任老师。"

"as a young man I already started to doubt teachers"
"当我年轻的时候，我就开始怀疑老师了"
"when we lived with the penitents in the forest, I distrusted their teachings"
"当我们和忏悔者一起住在森林里时，我不相信他们的教义"
"and I turned my back to them"
"然后我就背对着他们"
"I have remained distrustful of teachers"
"我一直不信任老师"
"Nevertheless, I have had many teachers since then"
"尽管如此，从那时起我有过很多老师"
"A beautiful courtesan has been my teacher for a long time"
"一位美丽的妓女曾是我的老师"
"a rich merchant was my teacher"
"我的老师是一位富商"
"and some gamblers with dice taught me"
"一些赌徒用骰子教我"
"Once, even a follower of Buddha has been my teacher"
"曾经，佛陀的弟子也曾是我的老师"
"he was travelling on foot, pilgering"
"他正在徒步旅行，四处奔波"
"and he sat with me when I had fallen asleep in the forest"
"当我在森林里睡着的时候，他坐在我身边"
"I've also learned from him, for which I'm very grateful"
"我也从他身上学到了很多东西，对此我非常感激"
"But most of all, I have learned from this river"
"但最重要的是，我从这条河里学到了很多东西"
"and I have learned most from my predecessor, the ferryman Vasudeva"
"我从我的前任船夫瓦苏戴瓦那里学到最多。"
"He was a very simple person, Vasudeva, he was no thinker"
"他是一个非常简单的人，瓦苏戴瓦，他不是一个思想家"

"but he knew what is necessary just as well as Gotama"
"但他和乔达摩一样清楚什么是必要的"

"he was a perfect man, a saint"
"他是一个完美的人,一个圣人"

"Siddhartha still loves to mock people, it seems to me"
"在我看来,悉达多仍然喜欢嘲笑别人"

"I believe in you and I know that you haven't followed a teacher"
"我相信你,我知道你没有跟随老师"

"But haven't you found something by yourself?"
"可是你自己没有发现什么东西吗?"

"though you've found no teachings, you still found certain thoughts"
"尽管你没有找到任何教义,但你仍然找到了某些想法"

"certain insights, which are your own"
"某些见解,属于你自己的"

"insights which help you to live"
"帮助你生活的见解"

"Haven't you found something like this?"
"你没发现这样的东西吗?"

"If you would like to tell me, you would delight my heart"
"如果你愿意告诉我,你会让我心满意足"

"you are right, I have had thoughts and gained many insights"
"你说得对,我有很多思考,也有很多感悟"

"Sometimes I have felt knowledge in me for an hour"
"有时我会在一个小时内感受到知识的滋润"

"at other times I have felt knowledge in me for an entire day"
"其他时候,我感觉自己一整天都充满了知识"

"the same knowledge one feels when one feels life in one's heart"

"当一个人在心中感受到生命时,他所感受到的也是同样的认识"

"There have been many thoughts"
"有很多想法"

"but it would be hard for me to convey these thoughts to you"
"但我很难向你传达这些想法"

"my dear Govinda, this is one of my thoughts which I have found"
"亲爱的戈文达,这是我发现的一个想法"

"wisdom cannot be passed on"
"智慧无法传承"

"Wisdom which a wise man tries to pass on always sounds like foolishness"
"智者试图传授的智慧总是听起来很愚蠢"

"Are you kidding?" asked Govinda
"你在开玩笑吗?" 戈文达问

"I'm not kidding, I'm telling you what I have found"
"我不是在开玩笑,我只是告诉你我发现了什么"

"Knowledge can be conveyed, but wisdom can't"
"知识可以传达,但智慧不能"

"wisdom can be found, it can be lived"
"智慧是可以找到的,智慧是可以实践的"

"it is possible to be carried by wisdom"
"有可能被智慧所承载"

"miracles can be performed with wisdom"
"智慧可以创造奇迹"

"but wisdom cannot be expressed in words or taught"
"但智慧无法用言语表达或传授"

"This was what I sometimes suspected, even as a young man"
"我年轻时也曾怀疑过这一点"

"this is what has driven me away from the teachers"
"这就是我离开老师的原因"

"I have found a thought which you'll regard as foolishness"
"我发现了一个你会认为很愚蠢的想法"

"but this thought has been my best"
"但这个想法是我最好的"

"The opposite of every truth is just as true!"
"每一个真理的反面也同样真实！"

"any truth can only be expressed when it is one-sided"
"任何真理只有片面性才能表达出来"

"only one sided things can be put into words"
"只有片面的事情才能用语言表达"

"Everything which can be thought is one-sided"
"一切可以思考的事物都是片面的"

"it's all one-sided, so it's just one half"
"都是片面的，所以只有一半"

"it all lacks completeness, roundness, and oneness"
"一切都缺乏完整性、圆度和统一性"

"the exalted Gotama spoke in his teachings of the world"
"高贵的乔达摩在他的世界教义中说道"

"but he had to divide the world into Sansara and Nirvana"
"但他必须把世界分为轮回和涅槃"

"he had divided the world into deception and truth"
"他把世界分为欺骗和真相"

"he had divided the world into suffering and salvation"
"他将世界分为苦难和救赎"

"the world cannot be explained any other way"
"世界无法用任何其他方式来解释"

"there is no other way to explain it, for those who want to teach"
"对于那些想教书的人来说，没有其他方法可以解释这一点"

"But the world itself is never one-sided"
"但世界本身从来都不是一边倒的"

"the world exists around us and inside of us"
"世界存在于我们周围和我们的内心"

"A person or an act is never entirely Sansara or entirely Nirvana"
"一个人或一个行为不可能完全是轮回或完全是涅槃"

"a person is never entirely holy or entirely sinful"
"一个人不可能完全圣洁，也不可能完全有罪"

"It seems like the world can be divided into these opposites"
"世界似乎可以分为这些对立面"

"but that's because we are subject to deception"
"但那是因为我们容易受骗"

"it's as if the deception was something real"
"就好像欺骗是真实存在的一样"

"Time is not real, Govinda"
"时间不是真实的，戈文达"

"I have experienced this often and often again"
"我经常遇到这种情况"

"when time is not real, the gap between the world and the eternity is also a deception"
"当时间不真实时，世界与永恒之间的差距也是一种欺骗"

"the gap between suffering and blissfulness is not real"
"痛苦与幸福之间的差距并不是真实的"

"there is no gap between evil and good"
"善与恶之间没有界限"

"all of these gaps are deceptions"
"所有这些差距都是欺骗"

"but these gaps appear to us nonetheless"
"但我们仍然看到这些差距"

"How come?" asked Govinda timidly
"怎么会这样？"戈文达胆怯地问。

"Listen well, my dear," answered Siddhartha
"听好了，亲爱的。"悉达多回答道。

"The sinner, which I am and which you are, is a sinner"
"我是罪人，你们也是罪人"

"but in times to come the sinner will be Brahma again"
"但在未来的时代，罪人将再次成为梵天"
"he will reach the Nirvana and be Buddha"
"他将证得涅槃，成为佛。"
"the times to come are a deception"
"未来的时代是一个骗局"
"the times to come are only a parable!"
"将来的日子只不过是一个比喻！"
"The sinner is not on his way to become a Buddha"
"罪人无法成佛"
"he is not in the process of developing"
"他还没有发展"
"our capacity for thinking does not know how else to picture these things"
"我们的思维能力不知道如何用其他方式来描绘这些事物"
"No, within the sinner there already is the future Buddha"
"不，罪人心中已经有了未来佛。"
"his future is already all there"
"他的未来已经在那里了"
"you have to worship the Buddha in the sinner"
"你必须在罪人身上拜佛"
"you have to worship the Buddha hidden in everyone"
"你必须崇拜每个人心中隐藏的佛陀"
"the hidden Buddha which is coming into being the possible"
"隐秘的佛陀正在成为可能"
"The world, my friend Govinda, is not imperfect"
"我的朋友戈文达，这个世界并不完美"
"the world is on no slow path towards perfection"
"世界正在一步步走向完美"
"no, the world is perfect in every moment"
"不，世界每一刻都是完美的"
"all sin already carries the divine forgiveness in itself"

"一切罪孽都已得到神的宽恕"
"all small children already have the old person in themselves"
"所有小孩心里都已经有一个老人了"
"all infants already have death in them"
"所有婴儿的体内都已经存在死亡"
"all dying people have the eternal life"
"所有垂死的人都有永生"
"we can't see how far another one has already progressed on his path"
"我们看不到另一个人在他的道路上已经走了多远"
"in the robber and dice-gambler, the Buddha is waiting"
"在强盗和赌徒的心里,佛陀正在等待"
"in the Brahman, the robber is waiting"
"在婆罗门教中,强盗正在等待"
"in deep meditation, there is the possibility to put time out of existence"
"在深度冥想中,时间有可能不复存在"
"there is the possibility to see all life simultaneously"
"有可能同时看到所有生命"
"it is possible to see all life which was, is, and will be"
"我们可以看到过去、现在和将来的所有生命"
"and there everything is good, perfect, and Brahman"
"那里一切都是美好的、完美的、梵天的"
"Therefore, I see whatever exists as good"
"因此,我认为一切存在的东西都是好的"
"death is to me like life"
"对我来说,死亡就如同生命一样"
"to me sin is like holiness"
"对我而言,罪恶就如同圣洁"
"wisdom can be like foolishness"
"智慧可以像愚昧一样"
"everything has to be as it is"
"一切必须按照原样"

"everything only requires my consent and willingness"
"一切只需要我的同意和意愿"

"all that my view requires is my loving agreement to be good for me"
"我的观点所需要的只是我的爱心同意对我好"

"my view has to do nothing but work for my benefit"
"我的观点只能为我带来利益"

"and then my perception is unable to ever harm me"
"那么我的感知就无法伤害我了"

"I have experienced that I needed sin very much"
"我体验到我非常需要罪"

"I have experienced this in my body and in my soul"
"我的身体和灵魂都经历过这种事"

"I needed lust, the desire for possessions, and vanity"
"我需要欲望、对财产的渴望和虚荣心"

"and I needed the most shameful despair"
"我需要最可耻的绝望"

"in order to learn how to give up all resistance"
"为了学会放弃一切抵抗"

"in order to learn how to love the world"
"为了学会如何爱这个世界"

"in order to stop comparing things to some world I wished for"
"为了不再拿事物与我所希望的世界作比较"

"I imagined some kind of perfection I had made up"
"我想象着自己所创造的某种完美"

"but I have learned to leave the world as it is"
"但我已经学会了接受这个世界现状"

"I have learned to love the world as it is"
"我已学会热爱这个世界"

"and I learned to enjoy being a part of it"
"我也学会了享受其中的乐趣"

"These, oh Govinda, are some of the thoughts which have come into my mind"

"哦,戈文达,这些就是我脑子里浮现的一些想法。"

Siddhartha bent down and picked up a stone from the ground
悉达多弯下腰,从地上捡起一块石头
he weighed the stone in his hand
他用手掂量着石头
"This here," he said playing with the rock, "is a stone"
"这个,"他一边玩石头一边说,"是一块石头。"
"this stone will, after a certain time, perhaps turn into soil"
"这块石头经过一段时间也许会变成土壤"
"it will turn from soil into a plant or animal or human being"
"它将从土壤变成植物、动物或人类"
"In the past, I would have said this stone is just a stone"
"以前我会说这块石头只是一块石头"
"I might have said it is worthless"
"我可能会说它毫无价值"
"I would have told you this stone belongs to the world of the Maya"
"我会告诉你这块石头属于玛雅世界"
"but I wouldn't have seen that it has importance"
"但我没想到它有这么重要"
"it might be able to become a spirit in the cycle of transformations"
"也许它可以在变化的循环中变成一种精神"
"therefore I also grant it importance"
"因此我也认为它很重要"
"Thus, I would perhaps have thought in the past"
"因此,我过去也许会这么想"
"But today I think differently about the stone"
"但今天我对这块石头的看法不同了"
"this stone is a stone, and it is also animal, god, and Buddha"
"此石为石,亦兽,亦神,亦佛"

"I do not venerate and love it because it could turn into this or that"
"我并不是因为它会变成这样或那样而崇拜和喜爱它"

"I love it because it is those things"
"我喜欢它,因为它就是这些东西"

"this stone is already everything"
"这块石头已经是一切了"

"it appears to me now and today as a stone"
"现在在我看来它就是一块石头"

"that is why I love this"
"这就是我喜欢它的原因"

"that is why I see worth and purpose in each of its veins and cavities"
"这就是为什么我看到了它的每一条血管和腔体的价值和目的"

"I see value in its yellow, gray, and hardness"
"我从它的黄色、灰色和坚硬中看到了价值"

"I appreciated the sound it makes when I knock at it"
"我很欣赏敲门时发出的声音"

"I love the dryness or wetness of its surface"
"我喜欢它表面的干燥或湿润"

"There are stones which feel like oil or soap"
"有些石头摸起来感觉像油或肥皂"

"and other stones feel like leaves or sand"
"其他石头摸起来感觉像树叶或沙子"

"and every stone is special and prays the Om in its own way"
"每块石头都是独一无二的,并以自己的方式祈祷Om"

"each stone is Brahman"
"每块石头都是梵天"

"but simultaneously, and just as much, it is a stone"
"但同时,它又是一块石头"

"it is a stone regardless of whether it's oily or juicy"

"不管油腻还是多汁,它都是石头"
"and this why I like and regard this stone"
"这就是我喜欢并尊重这块石头的原因"
"it is wonderful and worthy of worship"
"它很奇妙,值得崇拜"
"But let me speak no more of this"
"但我不要再说了"
"words are not good for transmitting the secret meaning"
"语言无法传达秘密的意思"
"everything always becomes a bit different, as soon as it is put into words"
"一旦用语言表达出来,一切就会变得有些不同"
"everything gets distorted a little by words"
"一切都因言语而稍稍扭曲"
"and then the explanation becomes a bit silly"
"然后解释就变得有点愚蠢了"
"yes, and this is also very good, and I like it a lot"
"是的,这个也很好,我很喜欢"
"I also very much agree with this"
"我也非常同意这一点"
"one man's treasure and wisdom always sounds like foolishness to another person"
"一个人的财富和智慧在另一个人看来总是愚蠢的"
Govinda listened silently to what Siddhartha was saying
戈文达默默地听着悉达多说话
there was a pause and Govinda hesitantly asked a question
沉默了一会儿,戈文达犹豫地问了一个问题
"Why have you told me this about the stone?"
"你为什么要告诉我有关这块石头的事?"
"I did it without any specific intention"
"我这么做并没有什么特别的目的"
"perhaps what I meant was, that I love this stone and the river"
"也许我的意思是,我爱这块石头和这条河"

"and I love all these things we are looking at"
"我喜欢我们正在看的这些东西"

"and we can learn from all these things"
"我们可以从这些事情中学到东西"

"I can love a stone, Govinda"
"我可以爱一块石头，戈文达"

"and I can also love a tree or a piece of bark"
"我也可以爱一棵树或一片树皮"

"These are things, and things can be loved"
"这些都是事物，而事物是可以被爱的"

"but I cannot love words"
"但我无法热爱文字"

"therefore, teachings are no good for me"
"因此，教诲对我没有用处"

"teachings have no hardness, softness, colours, edges, smell, or taste"
"教法无刚、无柔、无色、无边、无香、无味"

"teachings have nothing but words"
"教诲无非是言辞"

"perhaps it is words which keep you from finding peace"
"也许是语言让你无法找到平静"

"because salvation and virtue are mere words"
"因为救赎和美德只是空谈"

"Sansara and Nirvana are also just mere words, Govinda"
"轮回和涅槃也只是空谈而已，哥文达。"

"there is no thing which would be Nirvana"
"没有任何东西可以成为涅槃"

"therefore Nirvana is just the word"
"因此涅槃只是一个词"

Govinda objected, "Nirvana is not just a word, my friend"
戈文达反驳道："涅槃不只是一个词，我的朋友。"

"Nirvana is a word, but also it is a thought"
"涅槃是一个词语，更是一个思想"

Siddhartha continued, "it might be a thought"

悉达多继续说，"这可能是一个想法。"

"I must confess, I don't differentiate much between thoughts and words"

"我必须承认，我不太区分思想和言语"

"to be honest, I also have no high opinion of thoughts"

"说实话，我对思想的评价也不高"

"I have a better opinion of things than thoughts"

"我对事物的看法比对想法的看法更好"

"Here on this ferry-boat, for instance, a man has been my predecessor"

"例如，在这艘渡船上，有一个人是我的前任"

"he was also one of my teachers"

"他也是我的老师之一"

"a holy man, who has for many years simply believed in the river"

"一位多年来一直坚信河流的圣人"

"and he believed in nothing else"

"他不相信其他任何东西"

"He had noticed that the river spoke to him"

"他注意到河流在对他说话"

"he learned from the river"

"他从河流中学到"

"the river educated and taught him"

"河流教育了他，教会了他"

"the river seemed to be a god to him"

"对他来说，这条河就像是神"

"for many years he did not know that everything was as divine as the river"

"多年来他并不知道一切都像河流一样神圣"

"the wind, every cloud, every bird, every beetle"

"风，每一朵云，每只鸟，每只甲虫"

"they can teach just as much as the river"

"它们能教给我们的东西和河流一样多"

"But when this holy man went into the forests, he knew everything"
"但当这位圣人走进森林时,他知道了一切"
"he knew more than you and me, without teachers or books"
"无需老师或书籍,他知道的比你我都多"
"he knew more than us only because he had believed in the river"
"他比我们知道得更多,只是因为他相信河流"

Govinda still had doubts and questions
Govinda 仍然有疑问和问题
"But is that what you call things actually something real?"
"但是你所说的东西真的是真实存在的吗?"
"do these things have existence?"
"这些东西存在吗?"
"Isn't it just a deception of the Maya"
"这难道不是玛雅人的骗局吗?"
"aren't all these things an image and illusion?"
"这一切难道不是映像和幻象吗?"
"Your stone, your tree, your river"
"你的石头,你的树,你的河流"
"are they actually a reality?"
"它们真的是现实吗?"
"This too," spoke Siddhartha, "I do not care very much about"
"这个我也不太在意,"悉达多说。
"Let the things be illusions or not"
"让这些事情成为幻觉或者不是"
"after all, I would then also be an illusion"
"毕竟,我也会是个幻象"
"and if these things are illusions then they are like me"
"如果这些东西都是幻象,那么它们就和我一样"
"This is what makes them so dear and worthy of veneration for me"

"这就是为什么他们对我来说如此珍贵和值得尊敬"
"these things are like me and that is how I can love them"
"这些东西就像我,这就是我爱它们的原因"
"this is a teaching you will laugh about"
"这是一个你会发笑的教导"
"love, oh Govinda, seems to me to be the most important thing of all"
"哦,戈文达,爱情对我来说是最重要的"
"to thoroughly understand the world may be what great thinkers do"
"彻底理解世界也许是伟大的思想家所做的事情"
"they explain the world and despise it"
"他们解释世界,却又鄙视它"
"But I'm only interested in being able to love the world"
"但我只对能够爱这个世界感兴趣"
"I am not interested in despising the world"
"我对鄙视世界不感兴趣"
"I don't want to hate the world"
"我不想憎恨这个世界"
"and I don't want the world to hate me"
"我不想让全世界恨我"
"I want to be able to look upon the world and myself with love"
"我希望能够用爱来看待世界和自己"
"I want to look upon all beings with admiration"
"我要以敬畏的眼光看待一切众生"
"I want to have a great respect for everything"
"我希望对一切事物都抱有极大的敬意"
"This I understand," spoke Govinda
"我明白了。"戈文达说。
"But this very thing was discovered by the exalted one to be a deception"
"但高贵者发现这其实是个骗局"
"He commands benevolence, clemency, sympathy, tolerance"

"他要求仁慈、宽容、同情、宽容"
"but he does not command love"
"但他并不命令爱"
"he forbade us to tie our heart in love to earthly things"
"他禁止我们把爱心寄托于世俗事物"
"I know it, Govinda," said Siddhartha, and his smile shone golden
"我知道,戈文达。" 悉达多说,他的笑容闪着金光。

"And behold, with this we are right in the thicket of opinions"
"看哪,我们正处于意见的丛林之中"
"now we are in the dispute about words"
"现在我们陷入了词语争论"
"For I cannot deny, my words of love are a contradiction"
"我无法否认,我的爱语是矛盾的"
"they seem to be in contradiction with Gotama's words"
"它们似乎与乔达摩的话相矛盾"
"For this very reason, I distrust words so much"
"正因为如此,我才如此不相信言语"
"because I know this contradiction is a deception"
"因为我知道这种矛盾是一种欺骗"
"I know that I am in agreement with Gotama"
"我知道我同意乔达摩的观点"
"How could he not know love when he has discovered all elements of human existence"
"当他发现了人类存在的所有要素时,他怎么会不懂爱呢?"
"he has discovered their transitoriness and their meaninglessness"
"他发现了它们的短暂性和无意义"
"and yet he loved people very much"
"但他仍然非常爱人们"
"he used a long, laborious life only to help and teach them!"

"他用漫长、辛劳的一生只是为了帮助和教导他们！"

"Even with your great teacher, I prefer things over the words"
"即使有伟大的老师,我还是更喜欢事物而不是语言"

"I place more importance on his acts and life than on his speeches"
"我更看重他的行为和生活,而不是他的演讲"

"I value the gestures of his hand more than his opinions"
"我更看重他的手势而不是他的观点"

"for me there was nothing in his speech and thoughts"
"对我来说,他的言语和思想毫无意义"

"I see his greatness only in his actions and in his life"
"我只在他的行为和生活中看到他的伟大"

For a long time, the two old men said nothing
两位老人许久没有说话

Then Govinda spoke, while bowing for a farewell
然后戈文达一边鞠躬告别,一边开口说道

"I thank you, Siddhartha, for telling me some of your thoughts"
"我感谢你,悉达多,愿意告诉我你的想法。"

"These thoughts are partially strange to me"
"这些想法对我来说有些奇怪"

"not all of these thoughts have been instantly understandable to me"
"并非所有这些想法我都能立即理解"

"This being as it may, I thank you"
"无论如何,我还是感谢你"

"and I wish you to have calm days"
"祝你度过平静的日子"

But secretly he thought something else to himself
但他心里却在想别的事

"This Siddhartha is a bizarre person"
"这个悉达多真是个奇怪的人"

"he expresses bizarre thoughts"
"他表达了奇怪的想法"

"his teachings sound foolish"
"他的教导听起来很愚蠢"

"the exalted one's pure teachings sound very different"
"世尊的清净教诲听起来很不一样"

"those teachings are clearer, purer, more comprehensible"
"这些教义更清晰、更纯粹、更易理解"

"there is nothing strange, foolish, or silly in those teachings"
"这些教义并没有什么奇怪、愚蠢或可笑的地方"

"But Siddhartha's hands seemed different from his thoughts"
"但悉达多的手似乎与他的想法不同"

"his feet, his eyes, his forehead, his breath"
"他的脚、他的眼睛、他的额头、他的呼吸"

"his smile, his greeting, his walk"
"他的微笑,他的问候,他的步态"

"I haven't met another man like him since Gotama became one with the Nirvana"
"自从乔达摩涅槃以来,我再也没有见过像他这样的人。"

"since then I haven't felt the presence of a holy man"
"从那时起我就再也没有感受到圣人的存在"

"I have only found Siddhartha, who is like this"
"我只找到悉达多,他就是这样的人"

"his teachings may be strange and his words may sound foolish"
"他的教导可能很奇怪,他的话可能听起来很愚蠢"

"but purity shines out of his gaze and hand"
"但他的目光和手中却闪耀着纯洁的光芒"

"his skin and his hair radiates purity"
"他的皮肤和头发散发着纯洁"

"purity shines out of every part of him"
"他身上处处散发着纯洁的光芒"

"a calmness, cheerfulness, mildness and holiness shines from him"
"他身上散发着一种平静、快乐、温和、圣洁的气质"

"something which I have seen in no other person"
"我从未在别人身上看到过这种东西"

"I have not seen it since the final death of our exalted teacher"
"自从我们尊贵的老师去世后，我就没再见过它了"

While Govinda thought like this, there was a conflict in his heart
戈文达这么想着，心里却在挣扎

he once again bowed to Siddhartha
他再次向悉达多鞠躬

he felt he was drawn forward by love
他感到自己被爱所吸引

he bowed deeply to him who was calmly sitting
他向那位平静地坐着的人深深鞠躬

"Siddhartha," he spoke, "we have become old men"
"悉达多，"他说，"我们已经老了。"

"It is unlikely for one of us to see the other again in this incarnation"
"我们中的一个人不太可能在这一世再见到另一个人"

"I see, beloved, that you have found peace"
"我看，亲爱的，你已经找到了平静"

"I confess that I haven't found it"
"我承认我还没找到"

"Tell me, oh honourable one, one more word"
"请告诉我，尊贵的先生，再说一句话"

"give me something on my way which I can grasp"
"给我一些我能掌握的东西"

"give me something which I can understand!"
"给我一些我能理解的东西!"

"give me something I can take with me on my path"
"给我一些我可以随身携带的东西"

"my path is often hard and dark, Siddhartha"
"我的道路常常是艰难而黑暗的,悉达多"

Siddhartha said nothing and looked at him
悉达多什么也没说,看着他。

he looked at him with his ever unchanged, quiet smile
他用一如既往的平静微笑看着他

Govinda stared at his face with fear
戈文达惊恐地看着他的脸

there was yearning and suffering in his eyes
他的眼里充满了渴望和痛苦

the eternal search was visible in his look
他的目光中流露出永恒的探索

you could see his eternal inability to find
你可以看到他永远无法找到

Siddhartha saw it and smiled
悉达多看见了,笑了

"Bend down to me!" he whispered quietly in Govinda's ear
"弯下腰来!"他轻声在戈文达耳边低声说。

"Like this, and come even closer!"
"这样,再靠近点!"

"Kiss my forehead, Govinda!"
"亲吻我的额头吧,戈文达!"

Govinda was astonished, but drawn on by great love and expectation
戈文达很惊讶,但被巨大的爱和期望所吸引

he obeyed his words and bent down closely to him
他听从了他的话,弯下腰,紧紧地贴在他身上

and he touched his forehead with his lips
他用嘴唇碰了碰额头

when he did this, something miraculous happened to him

当他这样做的时候,奇迹发生了
his thoughts were still dwelling on Siddhartha's wondrous words
他仍然在想悉达多的奇妙话语
he was still reluctantly struggling to think away time
他仍然不情愿地挣扎着想着时间
he was still trying to imagine Nirvana and Sansara as one
他仍然试图把涅槃和轮回想象成一体
there was still a certain contempt for the words of his friend
对他朋友的话仍然有某种蔑视
those words were still fighting in him
这些话仍然在他心里激荡
those words were still fighting against an immense love and veneration
这些话仍然在与巨大的爱和崇敬作斗争
and during all these thoughts, something else happened to him
在他思考这些事情的时候,他又发生了另外一件事
He no longer saw the face of his friend Siddhartha
他再也见不到朋友悉达多的面容
instead of Siddhartha's face, he saw other faces
他看到的不是悉达多的脸,而是其他人的脸
he saw a long sequence of faces
他看见一长串的面孔
he saw a flowing river of faces
他看见了一条人流如河的街道
hundreds and thousands of faces, which all came and disappeared
成百上千的面孔,来了又去
and yet they all seemed to be there simultaneously
但它们似乎同时都在那里
they constantly changed and renewed themselves
他们不断改变和更新自己

they were themselves and they were still all Siddhartha's face
他们还是他们自己,他们还是悉达多的脸

he saw the face of a fish with an infinitely painfully opened mouth
他看见了一张鱼的脸,嘴巴无限痛苦地张开

the face of a dying fish, with fading eyes
垂死的鱼的脸,眼睛渐渐暗淡

he saw the face of a new-born child, red and full of wrinkles
他看到一张新生儿的脸,红红的,满是皱纹

it was distorted from crying
它因哭泣而变形

he saw the face of a murderer
他看到了凶手的脸

he saw him plunging a knife into the body of another person
他看到他把刀刺进了另一个人的身体

he saw, in the same moment, this criminal in bondage
在同一时刻,他看到这个被束缚的罪犯

he saw him kneeling before a crowd
他看见他跪在人群面前

and he saw his head being chopped off by the executioner
他亲眼看到自己的头被刽子手砍掉

he saw the bodies of men and women
他看到了男人和女人的尸体

they were naked in positions and cramps of frenzied love
他们赤身裸体,疯狂地做着爱的姿势和痉挛

he saw corpses stretched out, motionless, cold, void
他看到尸体四肢伸展,一动不动,冰冷,空虚

he saw the heads of animals
他看到了动物的头

heads of boars, of crocodiles, and of elephants
野猪头、鳄鱼头、大象头

he saw the heads of bulls and of birds

他看到了牛头和鸟头
he saw gods; Krishna and Agni
他看到了神：克里希纳和阿格尼
he saw all of these figures and faces in a thousand relationships with one another
他看到了这些身影和面孔之间的千丝万缕的关系
each figure was helping the other
每个人都在帮助别人
each figure was loving their relationship
每个人都热爱他们的关系
each figure was hating their relationship, destroying it
每个人都憎恨他们的关系，并破坏它
and each figure was giving re-birth to their relationship
每一个人物都在重生他们的关系
each figure was a will to die
每一个身影都代表着一种死亡的意志
they were passionately painful confessions of transitoriness
它们是对短暂性的痛苦而又充满激情的告白
and yet none of them died, each one only transformed
然而他们都没有死，每个人只是变了样
they were always reborn and received more and more new faces
它们总是重生，不断迎来新的面孔
no time passed between the one face and the other
两张脸之间没有时间流逝
all of these figures and faces rested
所有这些身影和面孔都休息了
they flowed and generated themselves
它们流动并自我生成
they floated along and merged with each other
它们漂浮着，相互融合
and they were all constantly covered by something thin
它们总是被某种薄薄的东西覆盖着
they had no individuality of their own

他们没有自己的个性
but yet they were existing
但它们确实存在
they were like a thin glass or ice
它们就像薄玻璃或冰
they were like a transparent skin
它们就像透明的皮肤
they were like a shell or mould or mask of water
它们就像水的壳、模具或面具
and this mask was smiling
这个面具在微笑
and this mask was Siddhartha's smiling face
这个面具就是悉达多的笑脸
the mask which Govinda was touching with his lips
戈文达用嘴唇触摸的面具
And, Govinda saw it like this
戈文达是这样认为的
the smile of the mask
面具的微笑
the smile of oneness above the flowing forms
流动形态之上合一的微笑
the smile of simultaneousness above the thousand births and deaths
千千万万个生死之上同时的微笑
the smile of Siddhartha's was precisely the same
悉达多的微笑也一模一样
Siddhartha's smile was the same as the quiet smile of Gotama, the Buddha
悉达多的微笑与佛陀乔达摩的平静微笑相同
it was delicate and impenetrable smile
那是精致而难以捉摸的微笑
perhaps it was benevolent and mocking, and wise
也许它是仁慈的、嘲讽的、明智的
the thousand-fold smile of Gotama, the Buddha

佛陀乔达摩的千重微笑

as he had seen it himself with great respect a hundred times
因为他曾亲眼见过无数次,并且对此充满敬意。

Like this, Govinda knew, the perfected ones are smiling
戈文达知道,完美者正微笑着

he did not know anymore whether time existed
他不再知道时间是否存在

he did not know whether the vision had lasted a second or a hundred years
他不知道这幻象持续了一秒钟还是一百年

he did not know whether a Siddhartha or a Gotama existed
他不知道是否存在悉达多或乔达摩

he did not know if a me or a you existed
他不知道是否存在一个"我"或"你"

he felt in his as if he had been wounded by a divine arrow
他感觉自己好像被神箭射伤了

the arrow pierced his innermost self
箭刺穿了他的内心

the injury of the divine arrow tasted sweet
神箭的伤害尝起来很甜蜜

Govinda was enchanted and dissolved in his innermost self
戈文达被迷住了,他的内心深处也融化了

he stood still for a little while
他静静地站了一会儿

he bent over Siddhartha's quiet face, which he had just kissed
他俯下身子,看着席特哈尔塔平静的脸庞,他刚刚吻过那张脸。

the face in which he had just seen the scene of all manifestations
他刚刚看到的那张脸,

the face of all transformations and all existence
一切转变和一切存在的面貌

the face he was looking at was unchanged

他看到的脸没有变化

under its surface, the depth of the thousand folds had closed up again
在它的表面之下,千层褶皱的深度又闭合了

he smiled silently, quietly, and softly
他默默地、安静地、温柔地微笑着

perhaps he smiled very benevolently and mockingly
也许他笑得很仁慈,也很嘲讽

precisely this was how the exalted one smiled
世尊正是这样笑的

Deeply, Govinda bowed to Siddhartha
戈文达向悉达多深深鞠躬

tears he knew nothing of ran down his old face
不知为何,泪水顺着他苍老的脸庞流下。

his tears burned like a fire of the most intimate love
他的眼泪像最亲密的爱之火一样燃烧

he felt the humblest veneration in his heart
他心里感到最谦卑的崇敬

Deeply, he bowed, touching the ground
他深深鞠躬,触地

he bowed before him who was sitting motionlessly
他向一动不动地坐着的人鞠躬

his smile reminded him of everything he had ever loved in his life
他的微笑让他想起了他一生中爱过的一切

his smile reminded him of everything in his life that he found valuable and holy
他的微笑让他想起了生命中所有他认为珍贵而神圣的东西

www.tranzlaty.com

www.ingramcontent.com/pod-product-compliance
Lightning Source LLC
Chambersburg PA
CBHW010020130526
44590CB00048B/3832